ESCAPE FROM PRETORIA

ESCAPE FROM PRETORIA

Tim Jenkin

KLIPTOWN BOOKS

LONDON

First published in 1987 by Kliptown Books Ltd, Canon Collins House, 64 Essex Road, London N1 8LR.

ISBN No. 0 904759 77 6 (Paperback), 0 904759 78 4 (Hardback)

Phototypeset in 9½pt Melior and printed in England by A.G. Bishop & Sons Ltd, Orpington, Kent.

Contents

DIAGRAMS

Diagrams are numbered according to the order in which they are referred to in the text.

Breakout!

We stood staring at the last obstacle between us and freedom. How was it possible that this miserable little door would not yield to our persuasions? With minimal effort we'd opened 14 other doors to get to it, most of them the giant prison steel doors and grilles, yet this last one, an ordinary wooden door with an ordinary house lock, had decided to put a halt to 18 months' worth of planning and preparation. We would have none of it! If it would not give in to our gentler persuasions there was only one other option – force!

Alex asked for the chisel. He was going to dig out the wood from behind the locking plate on the doorframe and then when he'd removed enough he would be able to bend it back so that the bolt would clear it when he pulled the door open. I was thinking that maybe we should make our way back to our cells and try again another day. If we did not get the door open before the sentry came on duty in the street outside it would be the end of the road for us. We would not be able to try again as the damaged doorpost would be evidence that there had been an escape attempt and they would strengthen the prison's existing security to make it impossible to get out. But the others insisted there was only one direction we would be going – out!

I flinched as Alex dug the point of the chisel into the well-varnished wooden frame and a giant chip of wood fell onto the doormat. Now the prison authorities would know which way we had got out; our dream of having pulled off the perfect escape was no more. We had hoped to leave our captors completely confounded as to how three long-term 'terrorists' had spirited themselves out of their cells and out of one of South Africa's reputedly most secure prisons.

Alex furiously carried on chiselling as we watched in terror. We knew that the sentry normally came on duty at six and it was now approaching that time: it was more than an hour since lock-up at four thirty. The pile of chippings on the floor looked greater than the hole out of which they came but the locking plate could still not be bent back far enough to allow the bolt to pass. Several times Alex tried to force it back with the large screwdriver we'd brought along from the workshop but each time it just slipped and made a frightening noise. Each time it happened we were sure the night-warder, who was sitting less than 20 metres away and the guard on the catwalk just 5 metres above, had heard it. But nothing happened.

We prepared ourselves for departure. We pulled off our gloves and face masks and put on our running shoes: once we were out we'd have to get off the prison terrain, out of Pretoria and out of the country as quickly as possible. We knew they'd treat us as hunted fugitives and that there would be a nationwide search; we knew that if we got caught our already long sentences would be infinitely extended.

Eventually Alex had removed sufficient wood to allow him to bend the locking plate back far enough. He grasped the doorhandle and gave it a sharp yank. With a loud grating sound the bolt scraped past the plate and the door swung open. The sweet air of freedom wafted in.

Alex cautiously looked up toward the end of the catwalk above the door to see if the guard was in view. There was nobody – the guard had conveniently taken a walk down to the far end. Alex boldly stepped outside and signalled to us to follow him. I was the next out and then Stephen, who pulled the door closed behind him. It did not close properly on account of the still protruding bolt, but it did not matter at that moment – we were out.

After making sure the coast was clear, we walked down the few steps leading from the door out of which we had just emerged and stepped into the warm summer's sun in the street. We were free. Hours, days, months, years of boredom, frustration and isolation lay behind us. And ahead, freedom. . .

1

Recruitment

The question is frequently asked how white South Africans can abandon all the privileges which are theirs for the taking and choose instead to become revolutionaries and side with the oppressed. Outsiders see it as an impossibility: for most white people South Africa is the land of milk and honey where they can expect a standard of living probably unmatched by any other country in the world. A beautiful country with such wealth that it literally oozes out of the ground, and such an abundance of cheap labour that virtually every white family can afford a servant. A life of luxury, pleasure, holidays, travel, sunshine and sport. Good jobs, good salaries, little prospect of unemployment, good homes, good education . . . you name it. Why would anyone reject all this and choose instead a life of persecution: detention, prison, banning, ostracism, exile?

Hatred of the system under which they live and rebellion against it are not natural responses for white South Africans as they are for blacks. They are responses that have to be learned: from others, from unique personal experiences or from books.

For most whites, breaking free of the web of privilege and racism and finding the route toward enlightenment is not easy. The apartheid system, through the rewards it bestows on those who accept it and through its insidious propaganda, does not breed white dissidents. But despite all the forces ranged against them, some white South Africans do manage to break loose and find their way into the camp of those who believe in a non-racial democratic South Africa.

Some are fortunate to have enlightened parents and so never become deeply ensnared in the barbs of racism; they break free easily. Others may meet someone who influences their lives or have personal experiences which help them to break loose. Most whites who do manage to see the light, however, reach that position by the intellectual route. It cannot really be any other way, for whites are not usually at the receiving end of apartheid and hardly ever learn what it means in any practical sense. For all who do find the way, however, the route is uphill and slippery.

I was born and bred in South Africa and grew up a 'normal' complacent white South African. I unthinkingly accepted the system and for 21 years never questioned it. Why should I have done so? I knew nothing else and no one had ever told me anything else. I had never had any black friends, never spoken to any black person outside the master-servant relationship, never been in a black

1

township, into the home of a black person or worked with any black people. South Africans were white people – Europeans. Blacks just existed in the background, there to do the work and then disappear when we needed them no longer.

I absorbed the normal white prejudices against blacks and bore a 'healthy' hatred of them. The world view I had imbibed put everything in its place: blacks could not rule as they were uncivilised and would fight among themselves if granted power. They had to be kept separated from us as they had a different standard of living, a different – inferior – culture and a different set of moral values. Blacks were essentially lazy and dirty. All they wanted to do was steal the things we had acquired through our hard efforts. We lived here, they lived there in their dirty slums. We had our buses and train compartments, our beaches, our restaurants, our cinemas, and they had theirs. It was all quite fair, all quite just. What other way could things be ordered?

Occasionally the blacks would riot and some of them would get shot in the places where they lived. They would burn down the schools and bars which we whites had provided for them out of our taxes. How could they be so ungrateful for what we'd given them? But what could you expect from people who were drunk most of the time and inherently violent?

They would never be allowed to come and make trouble in our areas so it was OK if they got themselves shot, or killed themselves in their own areas. We whites would show them that we didn't need them. They could go on strike or go away for good. We'd manage. They needed us more than we needed them so they'd be the ones to suffer most.

I matriculated at the age of 17, leaving school totally ignorant of the world in which I lived. Not a single political thought ever arose in my head. Today I marvel at the advanced level of political understanding of young black scholars, even at the primary level. But then black people grow up in a totally different environment. Their whole lives are a battle to survive, a battle against the system from the day they are born. The politics of struggle is infused into their blood at an early age. Whites on the other hand learn only the politics of preservation. The world is theirs and no one is going to take it from them.

I was fortunate in not having to go to the army after leaving school. At that time not every white male had to go. There was a ballot system and I was one of the lucky few not selected. If I had gone my life would perhaps have followed an entirely different course: the army tends to amplify the worst racist tendencies instilled in young white South Africans in their education and upbringing. Instead I went out to work and within two years had been through a number of jobs. I wasn't much interested in working, nor was I interested in studying – I didn't quite know what I wanted to do. All I was really interested in

2

were my motorcycles and motorcycle racing. Jobs were easy to come by and the pay was good. Work a while, save a bit and then muck about for a few months. All quite normal; all part of growing up.

Wealthy parents kept me and my crazy hobby going. After three years I'd reached the top of the league in the local bike-racing scene and wanted to go further. Lack of money prevented me doing so and the only way I could see of making enough was to set up my own business. I had some experience in glass-fibre work and to gain more experience in this field I decided to go overseas—which means to Britain for white English-speaking South Africans. I was also keen to acquire experience on the far more sophisticated British bike-racing scene.

In April 1970 I took a boat to Britain. At first I was a model emissary for white South Africa. I would tolerate no criticism of my country and defended it with naive pride. South Africa was 'not half as bad as shown in all those outrageous propaganda films on telly', I often responded. I could not understand why people said such harsh things about my country. Nobody at home complained, and they were there. Why should these people who had never been to South Africa be so critical? Why couldn't they wash their own dirty dishes first?

I soon learned that I was totally ignorant of the reality of my own country and that most people in Britain knew more about it than I did. They asked questions and made assertions I could not answer— they told me about my country. From 10,000 kilometres away I had, within the space of a few months, learned more about South Africa than I had in all the time I had lived there.

After spending a few weeks with relatives in London I managed to get a job in a glass-fibre factory in Kent. It was on the shop floor and at first I was a bit reluctant to accept it, as I had always considered factory work beneath my dignity. In South Africa only blacks worked in factories. I only accepted the job because I wanted to gain experience and there was no better way than to actually do the dirty work.

I could not believe the conditions under which we were required to work. The itching glass-fibre dust in that factory hung like a mist from the ceiling and the air was infused with the pungent smell of resin. The management had filtered air conditioners in their offices while the people who did the actual work had to breathe in that vicious dust and the poisonous vapours. The resin stuck to your clothes like blobs of oil paint to a canvas, your hands got lacerated on hardened spikes of glass fibre and dried and wrinkled from washing them in acetone.

The management would periodically venture out of their comfortable offices with white coats and clipboards to inspect your work. They'd poke their fingers into your lay-ups looking for bubbles and berate you for wasting so much resin. Why couldn't they do the work if they were so good? At the end of the week you'd take home £13, or £20 if you'd worked overtime, yet what you'd produced in that time could be sold for hundreds of pounds. It was obvious that the lazy sods who sat in their dust-free offices and drank coffee all day were creaming off the profits we'd made: they all had smart new Jaguars and we had to catch buses.

The unjustness of this set-up as well as the sheer nastiness of factory work forced me for the first time in my life to sit up and consider the manner in which the world worked. How was it that the workers who created such wealth got paid so little? How was it that the management cared so little about the conditions under which we had to work?

In an attempt to find answers to these sorts of questions and others I began to read books. I didn't know where to start so began by reading books about self-improvement and human relationships. This led to an interest in sociology and psychology and ultimately politics. Before this I didn't even know what sociology was or the distinction between it and other social studies. Nor did I know the names of any sociological or political theorists – let alone Karl Marx.

I began to devour books by the ton and inevitably read some that I knew would not be allowed in South Africa. The fact that these were banned at home lent them a certain fascination. After a while I made a point of seeking out these books, not because I agreed more with the viewpoints expressed in them but because I felt that I had to broaden my horizons as much as possible while I had the opportunity. From them, however – especially the ones about South Africa – I learnt that there was another way of looking at my country and that the policies of its government were not altogether defensible.

My sudden awakening to the world led to a slight but shortlived religious spell. As I became aware of the complexities of the world and of the terrible things going on in it, I wanted to find immediate solutions to them. Not understanding the forces behind events and not knowing what I could do to change them, praying to God seemed to be the only answer.

While recognising that religion has motivated some of the most progressive opponents of apartheid and is often the starting point for many people in the development of a social consciousness, for me it served only as a barrier to further development.

At first the turn to religion, coming with my growing awareness, made me feel fresh, a new person – 'born again' so to speak. In my reading I had learnt that 'Marxists' were opposed to religion and I therefore became intensely anti-communist, in the most subjective sense. This was nothing more than the coming to the surface of the indoctrination to which I'd been subjected all my life. As I understood it, communists were the devil incarnate. The sole purpose of their existence was to make trouble and take away our freedom. Communists were always associated with evil and war;

Christians with goodness and peace. I did not understand that our rulers used the word 'communist' to label everybody they did not like, everybody who did not agree with them. By calling themselves Christians they made us believe that they were acting in the name of God and that their motives were honest and sincere. Consequently, I found myself in the curious position of wanting to see change but of harbouring negative views about all those who advocated change.

At the end of 1970, still in Britain, I decided to continue in a formal way what I had been learning through the casual reading of books: I enrolled at the University of Cape Town to do a course in sociology. This is how it is if you're white and relatively well off – go overseas, expand your consciousness and then decide you'd like to further your education. For the vast majority of South Africans this style of living is unthinkable.

University changed everything. It taught me how to be rational and critical; to question everything. Religion was the first casualty. It could not stand up to the questioning and it soon seemed to me no more than a set of superstitious answers to difficult questions. Science taught that things should only be believed on the basis of the evidence that supports them; religion required that I just believe things without any evidence at all, that is – by faith.

In the sociology class I met Stephen Lee. He, like me, preferred to sit in the back row of the class where you could talk and swap notes and books with fellow students. He had been at university for a year already, changing his course from business science to sociology. He found out in his first year that he did not want to become a 'capitalist' and had developed, as a reaction to what he'd been taught in the business classes, an interest in the Marxist conception of society. He had also involved himself in student politics and this had contributed towards the leftward direction of his political development.

On one occasion I agreed to swap one of the banned books I had brought back to South Africa for an interesting book he was showing off. This led to regular exchanges of books and to combined search operations for progressive articles and books in the university's exceptionally large library. There was not much literature of this kind as most books and magazines in that category had been banned, or 'appropriated' by the students. However, between the two of us we managed to ferret out a number of interesting titles, mostly Marxist-inclined, in the most unlikely locations. These we photocopied from cover to cover, bound and swapped with other students who were also searching for similar literature. Once we got into the right circles we were amazed at the large amount of banned literature in circulation. In a short while we possessed trunk-loads of banned books and articles that we'd photocopied. People would go to extreme lengths to obtain the books that were supposed to be bad for them. We were thankful to the apartheid censors for the valuable service they performed in publishing their lists of prohibited publications – we knew those were the ones worth reading!

The sociology course was a great disappointment. Economics, my second subject, was even more demoralising. Our textbooks were all tomes from the United States which claimed to teach their subjects 'scientifically' by looking at reality 'as it is' and not 'how it ought to be'. It soon became obvious to us that we were surreptitiously being given a conservative world view disguised as sociology and economics. The world, we were taught, was an essentially static and harmonious entity and all social structures, such as classes, served equally important functions by holding society together. Human societies were characterised by consensus and harmony and everything that happened was the result of conscious decisions by people to make things happen, not the result of the working-out of intangible 'social forces'. Change in society involved the authorities making small adjustments to relieve pressure points. There were no inherent antagonisms which could lead to conflict and, God forbid, revolution. Conflict was brought by outside forces impinging on this otherwise stable organism.

You didn't have to be a genius to see that this was just so much nonsense. It was particularly insulting to be taught this in a country like South Africa where social antagonisms were so blatant. By implication our lecturers were telling us that the reactionary politics of the apartheid rulers was science. They, the white politicians, were saying essentially the same thing as the sociologists every day: everyone in their station served a function; the whites had to rule as they had the skills and the tradition of ruling; the blacks provided the labour which society needed; South Africa's black citizens were happy with their lot and had no real grievances; all strains where they occurred would be relieved by slowly introducing reforms; conflict was brought from the outside by communists who incited and intimidated people to rebel against the government for the political ends of foreign interests.

The claptrap that we were being taught contrasted sharply with the Marxist perspective on things we were learning through books read on the side. These seemed to give a much more accurate portrayal of the society in which we lived, a society riven by antagonism and conflict. Blacks did not need any 'communists' to tell them that the society they lived in was oppressive and unjust or that the way to overcome it was to rebel against it. Apartheid meant conflict.

Marxism was also the best antidote for racism. It taught us that racial antagonism and conflict, far from being 'natural' and 'inevitable', were the products of colonialism and imperialism. Racism in South Africa began with colonial occupation and expansion and was fostered as part of the strategy of the settlers to win and maintain control over the local population. The racist policies of the apartheid regime were just the latter day manifestation of continued colonial domination – the particular form of colonialism where the colonisers and colonised inhabited the same country.

My friendship with Stephen grew and after several months he invited me to join him and others who were planning to build a seaside shanty on a small, remote, rocky outcrop named Oudeschip, about 15 kilometres down the coast from Cape Town. The hut was to be built out of driftwood and packing-case wood. The packing-case wood would have to be carted there some distance along a mountain track. We set to but the others dropped out after a short while when they realised how much work was involved. The hut was completed within six months and served as the perfect retreat for studying and discussing our changing world outlook.

It was not long before we began to treat our university courses with cynicism, learning only as much as was necessary to satisfy supervisors and pass exams. We regularly skipped lectures and spent the time at Oudeschip instead. There we could read more interesting and worthwhile things. This reading did not remain within the ambit of the few subjects we were studying: our interests broadened to studying the actual society we lived in, to history, to politics and to the struggle of the oppressed against racist domination.

The three years at university overturned all our beliefs, attitudes, prejudices and fears. The process was erratic, slow and traumatic. Deeply ingrained prejudices which we'd not considered as such had to be rooted out. Beliefs we'd thought our own turned out to be the product of years of racist and fascist indoctrination – notions of white superiority were the most persistent.

The great white myths had to be debunked. The first of these was the historical myth that white South Africans had a moral claim to the major portion of the country since most of the land was unoccupied when they moved into the interior. Those areas now called the 'homelands' by the government were the only parts occupied by Africans and that was why they were being granted 'independence'. It came as a shock to find out that in fact all of the country had been occupied by Africans for hundreds if not thousands of years prior to the arrival of the Europeans and that the history of the settlers was a history of plunder and death, a process continuing to this day.

The second myth, which flowed from the first, was that there were no majorities in South Africa – only a number of minorities. There were the Whites, Coloureds, Indians, Zulus, Xhosas, Sothos, Tswanas – 13 'ethnic groups' in all. Each of the African 'tribes' was different from the next and all antagonistic to the others. No group could claim a right to South Africa – it was a 'multi-national' country.

Once the colonial principle of divide and rule was understood, this myth fell flat on its face. Why did Africans have to be sub-divided into numerous linguistic-cultural groups while the whites were one homogeneous entity despite the fact that they were also divided linguistically and culturally?

The next was the myth that South Africa's blacks were the most well-off blacks on the continent and that the government was doing more for them than any black government in Africa was doing for its citizens. The total meaninglessness and irrelevance of this claim, which was brought up every time apartheid was criticised, was exposed when it was realised that this was no more than a ruse to deflect attention from apartheid onto some allegedly worse case elsewhere. Besides being untrue it was also an excuse for white privilege. The true injustice of apartheid was manifested when the comparison was made between the living conditions of white and black South Africans. Besides, were blacks supposed, after being told that it was worse elsewhere, to be grateful that they were living under apartheid and satisfied with their lot?

Overcoming belief in the political myth that South Africa was a democratic multi-party state gave a sharp boost to my political transformation. Realising that only 15 per cent of the population had the vote and that that vote was deliberately exercised to perpetuate a dictatorship of white rule over the black majority made the 'government' as bad as any military dictatorship where no one had the vote at all.

The apartheid regime was a product of the illegal colonial creation which Britain set up when it brought together the four colonies of Natal, the Orange Free State, Transvaal and Cape in 1910 to form the Union of South Africa. The wishes of the indigenous inhabitants of the country were ignored and only the white settler minority was consulted. Not once since then has a South African government been democratically elected – by *all* the people, that is – and the regimes in power have only been 'governments' in the sense that they have maintained control over the affairs of the area by force of arms.

The myth propagated with the most vigour was the one which claimed the omnipotence and invincibility of the regime. This had two sides: that white rule was complete and that the regime's 'security forces' could meet any challenge; and that black opposition was insignificant and would never be powerful enough to overcome white rule.

Any undemocratic regime which has no popular support needs to perpetuate the myth that resistance is futile, since this achieved is half the battle won. Understanding this liberated us from the intimidating effect that the regime's *kragdadigheid* (show of force and toughness) had on those who wished to do something to undermine apartheid.

There were many other myths to be shaken off – so many that it is

8

not possible to list them all. Life under apartheid is a life of lies. The system is so morally unjustifiable and indefensible that the only way most white people can live under it without suffering from debilitating guilt is by cloaking themselves in its lies and propaganda. As each lie is peeled off so the truth – and horror – of apartheid begins to be seen.

Now the naked reality of apartheid stood before us: what had looked 'normal' was a perversion; what we had always accepted, was unacceptable. When you are faced with something that turns out suddenly to be the opposite of what you have always believed, your attitude towards it changes rapidly: a friend who deceives you can no longer be your friend. We were angry at having been deceived for so long. The system which had bestowed so many privileges on us had done so at the expense of others – at the expense of black people. It could no longer be defended, only challenged.

As everything grew clearer we became fired with a burning desire to see the end of this monstrosity. Our desire was not motivated so much by guilt – a negative drive – as by the positive wish to see a new, more just and democratic society. To wish for the end of the society we'd grown up in and which had given us so much meant challenging everything. This was not easy for us as we'd always been taught to respect authority, to believe in the benevolence and justness of the government, and to believe that all change came out of the deliberations of politicians in parliament. Parliament was the ultimate political reality; everything outside that was the dark world of 'treason' and 'terrorism'.

But how could a regime that enforced segregation, legitimised exploitation, tolerated abysmal poverty alongside great wealth, turned the majority of its people into semi-slaves, deliberately stunted their education, prevented their free movement, forcibly removed them from one part of the country and corralled them in reserves which it called their 'homelands', jailed and tortured those who raised their voices in protest – how could a regime that did all this, and more, expect loyalty and respect? It could only expect from the majority of its citizens 'treasonable' behaviour. Only a truly democratic government which showed respect for its people, which responded fairly to its peoples' demands instead of eliminating those making them, could expect loyalty and respect.

As our perceptions changed, so we were faced with the inevitable moral dilemma that confronts whites when they begin to realise what apartheid is all about: what to do?

In contrast to the present period, in the early 1970s there was little committed opposition to apartheid among whites. The student movement on the English-speaking campuses, once a stronghold of opposition, was in something of an ebb as a result of repression. In

9

those days students like ourselves tended to follow several distinct routes, most of which ended in abandonment and a return to the apartheid fold. Some became so incensed by what they saw that they became instant super-revolutionaries demanding that everyone immediately come out on the streets with their pitchforks. These ultra-leftists, commonly found on university campuses, formed themselves into little cliques which splintered into various warring factions every few months over theoretical differences. The world in which they wished to make revolution was a purely theoretical one, having little connection with reality. After a few years they had burned themselves out and invariably turned into cynics or vehement opponents of their former views.

Then there were those who were revolutionaries for as long as parents paid the university fees. As soon as they had to fend for themselves or landed well-paying jobs there was no more time for playing revolution. They became taken up with their own lives; the pursuit of swimming pools became more important.

There were also those who pretended that apartheid did not exist. They preferred to be seen with black people, to spend most of their time in the black townships, and looked upon fellow whites as the enemy. Such behaviour was no more than a token protest and never led anywhere. The realities of life under apartheid soon 'corrected' this 'deviation'.

We were determined not to follow any of these paths but were not certain which way to go. We were treading new ground. There was no one to point the way and we had no examples to follow. It was easy to shout at apartheid from the comfort of our plush homes in the sanctity of our white suburbs, but to do something which was not patronising was another matter. Liberal-minded South Africans who reached this point found it difficult to take the next step.

The question of what to do was answered for me one day when a canvasser from the white opposition Progressive Party (now called the Progressive Federal Party) came to the door to sell the virtues of his party. When I expressed no interest he said that I should at least make up my mind about one thing. To make his point he held up a hand with outstretched fingers and said: 'There are five choices open to every white person'. Pointing with his other hand to his little finger he said: 'One, you can join the Nationalist Party'; to the next finger he said, 'Two, you can do nothing; Three, you can leave the country; Four, you can do something unconstitutional'; and finally to his thumb, 'You can join the Progressive Party'.

I thought about this and realised that he was absolutely right. The National Party, the party of apartheid, was obviously out of the question; doing nothing was the same as condoning the system even if you expressed rejection of it; emigrating was copping out; the Progressive Party, even if it claimed to be opposed to apartheid, seemed to me a totally irrelevant and ineffectual organisation which served no other purpose than to give credibility to the apartheid regime's claim that the 'government' was democratically elected and that the Nationalists were the legitimate ruling party.

That left only the 'unconstitutional' choice. From my re-reading of South African history I had learnt that constitutional opposition in South Africa meant not opposition at all: it meant acceptance of white minority rule. Real opposition, namely, opposition which sought to end exclusive white rule and put in its place the democracy of one-person-one-vote, was by definition unconstitutional.

The constitution in force had been designed by whites to preserve their political hegemony. It denied blacks any constitutional rights whatsoever – they were the subjects of what whites decided was best for them. Denied constitutional avenues for bringing about meaningful change, what were the victims of apartheid supposed to do? Unflinchingly accept whatever dispensations were foisted upon them? Sit back and wait on the magnanimity of the whites to take pity on them? By declaring that the African National Congress and the Pan-Africanist Congress were 'banned' in 1960, and the Communist Party before them in 1950, the regime had demonstrated that it would not tolerate any real opposition at all, constitutional or otherwise.

One could therefore not be afraid of this word 'unconstitutional'. It had none of the connotations that were associated with it in other parts of the world. What right in any case had an illegitimate regime to declare the bounds of constitutionality?

In the same way that it was more honourable to disobey the unjust laws created by an illegitimate parliament than obey them, it was more honourable to act outside the illegitimate constitution than inside it. Having accepted this, it was only natural that we should have sought a home for our views. All the white legal political organisations or parties were part of the system in one way or another. In them all you could do was raise your voice in protest at the prevailing political set-up – a waste of time in a situation where the repressive forces had been given such draconian powers that they could physically remove or eliminate anyone who raised theirs too loud. It seemed obvious to us that the only effective way of opposing this vicious regime was to confront it directly, but secretly and outside its framework of rules.

The only effective organisation which appeared to be doing this was one which had been declared 'banned' by the regime – the African National Congress. It was the one organisation that stood for the complete eradication of apartheid and for the creation of a democratic South Africa not based on any racial premises. It was also the one organisation that made no distinction as to 'race' when it came to membership.

The Freedom Charter to which the ANC subscribed was a particularly impressive document of intention. Its preamble started:

'We the people of South Africa, declare for all our country and the world to know: that South Africa belongs to all who live in it, black and white, and that no government can justly claim authority unless it is based on the will of all our people'. Its ten clauses began: 'The People Shall Govern! All National Groups Shall Have Equal Rights! The People Shall Share In the Country's Wealth! The Land Shall Be Shared Among Those Who Work It! All Shall Be Equal Before the Law! All Shall Enjoy Equal Human Rights! There Shall Be Work and Security! The Doors of Learning and Culture Shall Be Opened! There Shall Be Houses, Security, and Comfort! There Shall Be Peace and Friendship!' If belief in such principles amounted to 'terrorism' and 'treason' then so be it — we would be 'terrorists' and 'traitors'. These ideals were worth fighting for and worth any risk, even prison.

From this perspective our attitude towards the struggle against apartheid changed drastically. The ANC had been forced by the regime to adopt a strategy of resistance which included armed struggle and this meant coming to terms with the question of the use of violence to achieve political ends.

The ANC's adoption of armed struggle was not a question of the ends justifying the means. The history of South Africa quite clearly demonstrated to us the complete futility of opposing white minority rule by peaceful means alone. The ANC had for nearly fifty years striven by peaceful means to resist white domination yet every manifestation of peaceful resistance, whether it took the form of protests, demonstrations, boycotts or strikes, whether it was passive or defiant, was put down by the authorities with the utmost brutality and bloodshed. Thousands had died in the attempt to advance their rights or protect the few they had. Each campaign of action against the white rulers had been answered with new and increasingly harsh 'security laws', detentions, torture, imprisonment, bannings, banishments and death. How much more violent would the regime get when it saw that the demands of the oppressed went beyond demands for human rights and for the complete eradication of the system of white minority rule — for state power?

Peaceful resistance had led nowhere. Instead of halting or slowing down the implementation of the regime's apartheid laws, the apartheid rulers had enforced them with increasing vigour and barbarity. The laws were inherently violent in themselves: millions had been forcibly removed from their homes and dumped in the impoverished bantustans where they died of starvation and disease; urban black populations had been herded into insanitary townships on the outskirts of the white cities; millions had been arrested and imprisoned under the pass laws; families had been split up in the interests of 'racial purity'; the black population had been denied proper education; patriots had been tortured and imprisoned or driven into exile...

The ANC with its tradition of peaceful struggle had not taken to

12

armed struggle lightly or easily. Nor was the turn to arms an act of revenge or self-defence. A point had been reached where the only choice was to surrender to white minority rule or to fight on with whatever means were available. All peaceful and constitutional channels had been closed; the only alternative was to organise a people's army, *Umkhonto we Sizwe*—The Spear of the Nation—to defend the oppressed and fight for the kind of South Africa that the majority of people wanted.

We had little difficulty in accepting that the ANC's turn to arms was justifiable and that the armed struggle against apartheid was a just and legitimate form of struggle.

Many people argued that there still remained peaceful avenues of bringing about change and that therefore all activity should be concentrated in this direction; that violent struggle should only be resorted to when there was absolutely no other choice. But we believed that such a point had long been reached and that peaceful methods alone would never be sufficient to wrest political power from the hands of the racists. Were the oppressed just supposed to stand and take bullets in the back and not return the fire? Were they to deny themselves a form of struggle simply because some people found it difficult to justify it morally?

Whites who pleaded that there were never moral grounds for resorting to violence to achieve political ends were usually people who knew nothing of the violence of apartheid or of the history of the people's struggles against white tyranny. Such people seldom made moral denunciations of the unceasing violence used by the regime to preserve and perpetuate white privilege and rule.

In our final year at university both of us, naturally, began to think about our future after we'd completed our courses. Our political development had led us to a position where we could no longer live comfortably under apartheid. Our consciences would not allow us to find work and 'settle down': if we identified with the oppressed we could not live like the oppressor. The only way we could justify living in South Africa was if we were fighting the system. But if we were going to give ourselves to the struggle against apartheid it had to be through the medium of some organisation and the only organisation we could consider joining—the ANC—we did not know how to contact inside South Africa. We knew that the ANC had missions in various African countries, but our South African passports prevented us from visiting them. The only alternative was to go to Europe to make contact with the organisation there.

And that's what we did.

In February 1974 we set off for Europe by ship—the cheapest way. From Barcelona where we disembarked we made our way directly to Holland to spend a few weeks seeing as much of the country as possible before we went on to contact the ANC. Soon after our arrival, newspaper billboards greeted us with the announcement: 'Salazar overthrown in Portuguese coup'. Immediately we realised the profound consequences this would have for apartheid South Africa. All the buffer zones it had relied on for so long would soon disappear and the armed struggle would rapidly be brought to its borders. The coincidence of this news and our plan to go to the ANC somehow seemed auspicious. We were entering a new era, both personally and politically speaking.

Our stay in Europe lasted more than a year. Our incorporation into the ANC took longer than we had expected. During some of the time which we spent waiting we worked to provide ourselves with funds, Stephen in Holland, and I in Britain. It was while working in Britain that I met Robin, to whom later, for a while, I was to be married. She and a friend had left South Africa on an impulse because they were fed up with life as typists in the offices of Johannesburg. Arriving penniless, Robin was forced to take up a job as a typist in the offices of London.

For obvious security reasons it is not possible to give much detail of the training that was given to us. Nevertheless it can be said that it was designed to provide us with the practical and survival skills we would need to operate as a propaganda cell in underground conditions in South Africa. It was also to prepare us mentally for what could happen to us if we got caught.

The plan was that we would go back to South Africa as soon as possible after completing the training course and then lie low for a few months to ensure that we were not being watched. During those first months we were to find ourselves jobs, settle down and become 'respectable' citizens. Most importantly, we were in no way to expose our real political views but create the impression, especially among family and friends, that our trip overseas had 'matured' us and that our former radical views had mellowed. Over the period of our training we were required to read a vast number of books, mostly about the detention and prison experiences of people who had been captured during the second world war or in South Africa and other fascist countries. Although reading these was somehow romantic at the time, they did serve to prepare us for what was later to be our fate.

Since our major activity, at least for the first period of our operations in South Africa, was to be the production and distribution of propaganda material for and in the name of the liberation movement, the training concentrated on preparing us for this sort of activity. We were instructed in the art of writing political propaganda and how to reproduce it using simple methods such as stencil duplicating machines. Instruction was given on the use of the postal system for mass distribution and a number of mechanical methods of distributing agitational literature were demonstrated.

One of these methods was the 'leaflet bomb'. These were hardly 'bombs' in the real sense of the word but simple timed explosive devices for throwing bundles of leaflets high into the air in order to spread them over a large area where a target crowd of people were gathered. They had been used with spectacular effect many times before in South Africa and had become one of the hallmarks of the liberation movement's internal propaganda activities. Peculiarly, there was little evidence that this method of propaganda distribution had been used in other situations throughout the world where there was severe suppression of revolutionary viewpoints.

The last part of our training involved setting up communication structures and working out financial arrangements. We swopped false names and safe addresses and adopted a set of code words for open communications. These included a set of signals that we could relay to each other if we suspected the enemy was on to us.

This done, our instructors gave us a pep talk about the value of the work we were about to undertake: we would be letting the people and the enemy know that the ANC was alive and working for liberation; we would be participating in the historic task of removing from the face of the earth one of the most abominable scourges to be visited upon humankind. Finally, they wished us luck and said, jokingly, that they would write to us in prison. They never kept their word!

2
Underground

The two 'trained terrorists' arrived back in South Africa in July 1975. For me returning was not easy as I was leaving Robin behind. At first I repeatedly had to remind myself that the job we'd been entrusted to do was more important than any personal suffering I would have to put up with. Apartheid caused mass suffering on such a scale that feeling sorry for myself was pathetic and selfish. But private sorrows were closer to the bone and no amount of virtuous thought was able to stop the pain and loneliness of separation; only time would lessen it.

Robin and I had exchanged false names and safe addresses so that we could keep in contact, but neither of us knew when or if we'd ever see each other again. We had agreed that we could not maintain a proper relationship from such a distance and in any case I had been instructed to lead as 'normal' a life as possible.

Everything looked different when we got back; it also looked so much the same. While we had been away changing our lives so that we could help bring an end to apartheid, people we had known were carrying on with their lives in much the same way as before. They were doing the same old things in the same old places and bore the same old attitudes — they had kept their heads firmly buried in the ground. People who had been close to us, our relatives and friends, were now the enemy, and we found ourselves living in their midst as 'traitors'. Our own parents, sisters, brothers were on the side which stood against everything we were fighting for and for everything we were fighting against.

The full horror of apartheid was clearer than ever. It angered us intensely and made us more determined to do something about it than before. But no longer was there any question of feeling guilty about having to live the lives of white South Africans in apartheid South Africa — we would be doing so in order to end doing so.

Our first task was to sort out our mundane above-ground affairs, such as finding ourselves jobs and places to live. Within a few weeks I found work at the segregated University of the Western Cape, for those whom the regime had classified as 'Coloured'. The job was in a sociological research institute attached to the University, with the pretentious name of the Institute for Social Development (ISD). My job was to enquire into various matters affecting the 'Coloured' community — with what purpose I never really found out.

The job proved to be an ideal cover, for any whites who worked at such places – known as 'bush colleges' or 'tribal colleges' – were usually regarded as supporters of the regime. The facilities at ISD were immensely useful for our purposes. It received and kept vast quantities of information on all subjects, including a newspaper clippings library. After a while it became my responsibility to organise the marking, cutting, pasting and filing of the clippings and it does not require too much imagination to guess how the library was adapted to provide us with the information we needed for our ANC work.

Not only were the facilities useful but the research took me right into the townships and into black people's homes where I was able to feel their mood and begin to understand what it meant to live under apartheid. I got to know every township in the Cape Town area inside out. This was important as I was still living the life of a white person and the whole exercise could have become academic if I had been confined to my secure little white suburb.

There were no strict hours of work at ISD and you could even 'work at home' if you wished – they were only interested in results. The freedom to come and go as I pleased was the most valuable aspect of the job, without which participating in an underground cell would have been much more difficult.

Stephen was not so lucky in finding work but as ISD had just been set up and was looking for more staff I suggested he apply for a job there as well. He was given employment but could not see eye to eye with the boss and resigned after a few months. This was a great pity as he was not able to find another job after that and eventually had to leave Cape Town to earn a living.

At ISD I met Daphne, who was also working as a researcher. Correctly I shouldn't have developed a relationship with her as she was 'Coloured' and therefore unsuitable as a girl-friend for someone who was meant to be working underground and attempting to appear 'normal' while doing so. But what could I do? I felt attracted to her. Was I supposed to reject friendships with people with whom I worked every day because of their colour? In that university environment it would have appeared even less 'normal'.

Daphne and I got on well but she couldn't help thinking that I was a very secretive person. I'm certain she believed I was having an affair with another woman because I kept disappearing for long periods with only feeble explanations. Whenever our conversations led onto political matters I would attempt to steer them away from the subject, leading her to think that I was totally apathetic and cynical. At times my lack of conviction about the awkward situations our 'mixed' relationship led us into drove her to desperation and she would walk out on me. I found it extremely difficult to maintain a close

17

relationship without being able to talk about the most important things in my life.

After a couple of months Stephen and I began to grow restless. There had been no signs of police surveillance and any further delay in getting on with the job of setting up our cell seemed to be overcaution. Both of us began to collect newspaper clippings of current events and carefully pasted these into scrap books for use when we got going. I went to a number of estate agents to see what sorts of premises we could hire to set up 'shop'. There were three possibilities: small flats, offices and garages. Most agents advertised all three but only garages were within our meagre budget at that time. I noted the addresses of a few and went to see if they would be suitable. Most weren't as they were just fenced off parking bays at the bottom of blocks of flats, but some looked OK.

Towards the end of the year we found a garage in a large block of flats in Green Point, a suburb of Cape Town, and took out a lease for six months. The garage appeared to be suitable as it had thick walls and a strong door to contain the sounds of printing. Its position allowed us to reach it in such a way that we could tell if we were being followed.

We bought a second-hand typewriter and duplicator, as well as the stationery needed to print and post pamphlets. Our first purchases were made with obsessive attention to the rules of conspiracy that we'd been taught: only small quantities bought at a time so as not to attract attention, no names given and appearances changed so that sales staff would not remember us.

We produced the first pamphlet for the ANC in early December 1975 – about the South African invasion of Angola. The garage proved to be absolutely unsuitable for the job. It had no light and ventilation when the door was shut. To provide light we had to use a gas lamp, but coupled with the mid-summer heat it became unbearably hot. Lack of familiarity with the duplicator meant that there were more dud than good copies and there was nowhere to dispose of the bad ones. There was also nowhere to wash our hands which got covered in ink. The surplus leaflets we later took up the side of the mountain and burnt in a sacrificial bonfire, but the wind, of course, blew bits of charred leaflet all over the place. We were learning.

That one experience convinced us that we would have to find a more suitable place from which to operate, so it was back to the estate agents. A few weeks later I found a small room in an annexe to a block of flats in the Gardens area of Cape Town. It was not ideal but all we could afford and far better than the garage. It was a small, sparsely-furnished room but with a window for ventilation, a light for working at night and a hand-basin for washing ink off our hands. There was also a bathroom and toilet down the passage which were shared with the other tenants in the block. The only drawback to the place was the presence of other inhabitants: they were too friendly and kept knocking on the door for a chat or to invite us around to their rooms for a drink. They must have found us very unfriendly and thought it strange that we were hardly ever there.

Stephen was still without work and getting desperate. The two of us were sharing a flat with his sister in the respectable suburb of Rondebosch and this was costing a lot of money. He was beginning to think of going to Johannesburg to look for work.

In February we produced a second pamphlet, the first in the new place. Like the first pamphlet it was about the South African invasion of Angola, but we produced it in far greater numbers. As we had no addressing machine at that stage we had to laboriously type the addresses onto the envelopes.

The room proved to be much more suitable than the garage. We could type the stencils and envelopes in it rather than at home and do the printing at leisure with genuine tea breaks. The spoilt copies, of which there were far fewer, we disposed of down the toilet after first soaking them in water and tearing them into shreds. Best of all we could wash ourselves and emerge from the room with clean hands.

There was one problem we had not considered before: how to post 6 or 7 hundred envelopes without exposing ourselves. The dilemma was whether to post them all at once or over a period of time, a problem we were never to resolve satisfactorily. If we posted them all at once the post-collectors or sorters would notice the sudden flood of letters in the post and intercept them for inspection. If we posted them over time in small batches the post-collectors and sorters would not notice anything unusual but we would increase our chances of being seen posting the envelopes, especially if the police were watching post-boxes after intercepting some. Obviously, whichever method we chose, it was important to vary the appearance of the items as much as possible by using different sorts of envelopes, addressing systems and stamps. Uniformity was what the cops looked for.

In March Stephen decided to go to Johannesburg to look for work. Conveniently the ANC had sent us a draft for a leaflet that they wanted dispersed by leaflet bomb in Johannesburg on or around the 21st of March—the anniversary of the Sharpeville massacre in 1960. So we decided to kill two birds with one stone by combining his search for work with our first leaflet-bomb mission.

Stephen left for Johannesburg a few days before I did and booked himself into a hotel. He went to a few places to look for work, and while doing so sought out the best locations to place the bombs, such as railway and bus stations around the centre of Johannesburg. I took a plane to Johannesburg the day before we were due to place the devices, having left word at work that I would be 'working at home' for the next two days.

Stephen had taken three leaflet bombs with him and I brought another three. He met me at the airport bus terminus and took me to his hotel. Fortunately he had been given a double room so there was a bed for me too and I was able to stay without having to put my name in the hotel register.

Both of us were absolutely terrified at having to carry out the mission. We'd never done anything like it before and were only too aware of the consequences of being caught. Neither of us slept a wink that night, lying awake wondering where we'd get the courage to do it.

The next morning Stephen took me on a tour of the centre of Johannesburg to point out the places he'd chosen for the bombs: the black entrance to the main Johannesburg railway station, a bus station, a narrow market street, the *Rand Daily Mail* newspaper office and Faraday Station – a station from where many blacks caught trains back to Soweto.

I booked into another hotel and then we divided the targets between ourselves, planned routes to get to them and worked out a plan of action. We would each first take one bomb from our respective hotels, set them off, and then return for the other two if the first ones had been a success. The time chosen was the afternoon rush hour.

At midday we bought a large bottle of wine in the hope that the alcohol would give us Dutch courage, but the stuff was totally ineffective against the torrents of adrenalin our hearts were pumping around. At about four we separated and went to our respective hotels to prepare the bombs. We had agreed to meet after it was all over on the observation floor at the top of the Carlton Tower – Johannesburg's tallest building.

I took one bomb out of my suitcase and placed it on the dresser to make sure everything was in order. The device consisted of a wooden base about the size of an average book. Mounted vertically on the base was a piece of aluminium tubing. Sitting on top of the tube and fixed to a plunger made from a piece of broomstick that fitted inside it was a platform the same size as the base. On this I placed five hundred of the leaflets we had brought with us. An ordinary kitchen timer gave the time delay and a battery fired the home-made detonator inside the tube. The whole device was placed in a topless cardboard box, put inside a plastic shopping bag and then covered with newspaper to disguise it.

I walked out of the hotel as nonchalantly as possible but couldn't help thinking that I was transparent and that the people sitting in the lobby knew what I was carrying. They were all laughing inside because I was about to be caught. 'Terrorists' had no chance!

I had been allocated the black entrance to the Johannesburg railway station. First I went into the station toilet – the 'whites-only' toilet of course – to prime the bomb. In a cubicle I removed the leaflets and lifted off the platform so that I could pour the ready-mixed explosive powder down the tube. Then I set the timer for twenty minutes, enough time, I thought, to get around to the other side of the station and away. My heart was pounding so violently that I was certain people could hear it. I felt faint, sick with fear.

With my shopping bag ticking away I emerged from that toilet feeling quite ridiculous. Surely everyone could hear the ticking? Surely they could all see the guilty look on my face? I just knew I would bump into some long-lost friend who would want to stop for a chat and then the bomb would go off in my hand.

I walked around to the rear-side of the station where the black entrance was located. For the life of me I could see no suitable place to deposit the bomb. Some distance from the entrance I spotted a rubbish bin – it would have to do. Fortunately it was nearly empty, so I dropped my bundle in it and made off as quickly as I could. There were hundreds of black people walking by, so even if it was not as close as it could have been it was a good place. I continued walking past the black entrance and disappeared into the bustling crowd of homeward-bound commuters heading for the station.

I rushed back to my hotel without waiting to hear if the bomb had gone off. Back in my room I primed the other two, set the timers for half an hour and placed them next to each other in a very large shopping bag. This time I was feeling more confident. Some of the fear had subsided and I was beginning to feel defiant instead of feeling that I was just doing my duty.

It took longer than I'd calculated to reach the bus terminus where I was to place my second bomb. As soon as I reached it I took one of the bombs out of the bag and deposited it next to some rubbish bags on the pavement. It was in its own bag so did not look out of place; I just hoped some curious person would not come and look in it.

There was less than ten minutes left to get to the next place, a narrow, busy shopping and market street. The ticking of the timer seemed to be in unison with my heart; both would explode simultaneously if I did not get to the place in time. With what I thought was about a minute to spare I reached the place, dropped the bag and ran. As I turned the corner I heard a loud bang – it had been less than a minute. I raced from that place as fast as I could without breaking into a sprint, and headed for the Carlton Centre, top floor.

Stephen was already there and looking through one of the telescopes at the flashing lights of police cars outside the offices of the *Rand Daily Mail* where he had placed one of his bombs. Multitudes of cops were milling about investigating the remains of the bomb and picking up the remaining leaflets that were still blowing about in the street. We turned the telescope to Faraday Station where he'd placed his other two. There we could see hundreds of leaflets in the street but no sign of cops or of the bombs. Someone must have scooped them up and made off with them.

We congratulated ourselves on our success and felt a sort of defiant pride in having pulled off the operation and brought out the police. We treated ourselves to a lavish meal in downtown Jo'burg that night to reward ourselves. The next day it was headlines in all the papers. That was the time when a small thing like a leaflet bomb made big news.

That first round of leaflet bombs was successful in that all went off and the message got spread. It also taught us a number of valuable lessons. The most important of these was that we needed some form of triggering mechanism so that we did not have to walk through the streets with the bombs ticking away in our hands. Anything could go wrong: you might not be able to deposit your bomb at a chosen place (a cop at the spot, perhaps), you might meet someone you knew, there might not be the anticipated crowd, there might not be a suitable dropping place, and so on. Altogether it was too risky to be walking around with a 'live' device.

The solution was very simple—a triggering pin to hold the timer at the desired timing. On location the pin could be pulled out to set the timer going. I used this mechanism two months later on Cape Town's Grand Parade, which becomes a market area on Saturdays. The triggering mechanism gave me such confidence that I was able to walk around with the bomb for a long time in search of the ideal dropping place. I didn't wait to see if it had gone off but reports in the papers later in the day confirmed that it had.

Stephen by this time had secured a job as a careers' adviser at the University of the Witwatersrand in Johannesburg—his period of job-seeking had given him a unique qualification.

Working on my own was the most thoroughly lonely experience in the world. Everything took twice as long to do and there was nobody to discuss things with. While friends were going camping, to movies, parties, and the beach I was buried in that dark little room like a hermit mole.

Many people have the impression that underground work is romantic and exciting. This is far from the truth. It is laborious, lonely, monotonous work with no immediately observable rewards. My average day, after work, consisted of reading through three or four newspapers in fine detail, dating the important articles, cutting out and pasting them, and then writing articles for the next pamphlet. I had to do these time-consuming tasks out of sight of friends and on top of all the other daily tasks, such as making small purchases of stamps and stationery. Weekends I would invariably spend at the room preparing leaflet bombs, typing stencils, duplicating leaflets, shoving them into envelopes and licking stamps. Postings usually took me a whole night as I had to drive at least 200 kilometres to spread the load as thinly as possible in the post-boxes of Cape Town and its environs.

There was so much to do and it had to be done with such meticulous care that the distinction between underground life and normal life became increasingly blurred. Yet life had to be lived and people convinced that I was not involved in anything suspicious. Living became a complete lie – a double-sided existence in which I was often unsure which side I was living on. Such a schizophrenic existence was hard to maintain; at times I thought I was going mad. What normal person spent hours cutting up newspapers, rushed about buying fifty stamps here, a packet of envelopes there, or hid themselves in secret rooms on sunny weekends to duplicate leaflets? What normal person had to tell lies constantly to explain periods of disappearance from the real world?

At the end of July, four ANC operatives were arrested in Cape Town for engaging in more or less the same kind of work that Steve and I had been doing. Their names were David and Sue Rabkin, Jeremy Cronin and Anthony Holiday. Steve and I were not to know it then but we were to meet Dave, Jeremy and Tony in prison two years later.

At the end of 1976 I abandoned the secret room for a new place. I had found the perfect premises: a small flat in a quiet area of Cape Town on the side of Table Mountain. The flat was around the back of a block of flats and had originally been used for housing a caretaker, but for some reason was no longer used as such. It was separate from the other flats in the block and did not use the same entrance. It had a bedroom, kitchen and small bathroom. Our finances had improved somewhat so I fitted it out to look like a normal habitation. I brought in furniture, a small cooker, a fridge and other paraphenalia of living. While most of these luxuries were superfluous to the job in hand, they made the work more bearable as I could carry on late into the night, fix myself meals, have a shower, stay overnight and then go to work the next morning.

Not only did I change our premises but I changed our equipment too. I bought an addressing machine and a new typewriter, and buried the old one in a deep hole in the dense bush of the Cape Flats. We had been taught that it was essential to make regular changes of equipment – typewriters especially – as the police could only prove that you had produced a particular pamphlet or leaflet if they could link it to specific items of equipment in your possession.

Changing premises, purchasing equipment and just doing what we were doing made us realise what an advantage it was to have a white skin while running an underground cell. No one suspected a white person of being engaged in subversive activities against the state – whites were never 'terrorists'. A white skin was a passport to places where blacks would automatically be under suspicion. A black person could not, for instance, walk into a shop and buy a duplicator without questions being asked; go to an estate agent and rent a flat to set up a printing factory or to hide arms. In the overcrowded housing in the townships where could a black person hide to produce revolutionary literature or make weapons for the armed struggle?

It struck us as a great pity that so few whites were prepared to participate in the struggle for a free and democratic South Africa.

In January 1977 I carried out the first major job in our new role. It was to reproduce and distribute *Vukani!–Awake!*, the underground journal of the 'ANC Support Group'. Pamphlets under this title had been produced and distributed by several groups before us – Dave Rabkin's and Jeremy Cronin's being the last. Our mailing list had grown very long by this stage so the job took me many days to complete. How I wished Stephen were there to help me.

In early June Stephen rang to tell me that some right-wing outfit at his university was organising a sociological conference at the university and were so desperate for delegates that they were dishing out free air tickets. I understood him to mean that I should take advantage of the offer to bring him some leaflet bombs to be set off on the anniversary of the start of the Soweto uprising on 16th June. I felt no compunction in doing so as the organisation in question had clearly demonstrated its antipathy towards the liberation struggle, and the ANC had said that we should try to set off some leaflet bombs around that date.

So off I flew to Johannesburg, free of charge, with a suitcase full of bombs for Stephen. I attended one token session of the conference and then returned to Cape Town. Stephen did a marvellous job with the bombs on the 15th and 16th of June, the incidents receiving wide coverage in the press.

Leaflet 'bombings' had become our stock in trade and we no longer regarded placing them as any big deal. In fact we looked at them as routine operations and enjoyed watching their effects. From the half hour to which we'd set the timers on the first occasion we had reduced the timing to three minutes. That gave us plenty of time to get out of the immediate vicinity of the blast and to a suitable vantage point. The packaging of the bombs was such that they never aroused suspicion and no one ever took any notice if you dumped one next to a pile of rubbish or in a bin. We could not help thinking how easy it would have been to carry out acts of sabotage in the same way, for the leaflet bombs were, technically speaking, the same as real bombs. This, probably, was why the cops took them so seriously.

To coincide with a visit by Stephen to Cape Town in September I made two leaflet bombs and a large banner to hang from a high building in the centre of Cape Town. The banner was huge: about 10 metres long by 1 metre wide with the words 'ANC LIVES' painted on it and at the bottom the black, green and gold colours of the ANC flag. It was rolled up with hundreds of leaflets inside and fitted with an exploding release-device set to go off after five minutes of being hung up. With a loud report it would unfurl and drop the leaflets into the street below.

At lunch-time on the chosen day I fixed the banner to a railing on the top floor of the outside of a parking garage in the centre of Cape Town by means of a steel chain and a huge padlock. To prevent the cops simply cutting the chain to remove it I'd threaded electrical wire through the chain to make it appear as if the device was booby-trapped. And on the box containing the timer and battery I stuck a label with the words: *'Danger!/Gevaar!* Do not remove. Explosives inside'. The timer controlling the explosive release-device was started in the same way as the leaflet bombs by pulling out a triggering pin.

At the same time as I fixed the banner, Stephen placed the two leaflet bombs in the street below. All went off more or less simultaneously, creating a tremendous effect with leaflets cascading to the ground from the banner above and rising to the sky from the blasts below. Leaflets were blowing around in the air for a long time afterwards.

We stood around to watch the effects. People ran from all directions to snatch up the leaflets, others in the opposite direction to escape the scene. Some civic-minded citizens (white of course) gathered up as many leaflets as they could to hand to the police. But there were so many leaflets in the street that there were enough for all. People stood in bewilderment at the spectacle. One pedestrian even asked Stephen what was going on: 'Some bloody terrorists have put a bomb in the street', he replied agitatedly.

In no time police vehicles with sirens blaring and lights flashing arrived on the scene. Even an ambulance arrived – to create an effect no doubt. The banner remained in position for at least half an hour as the police struggled to remove the lock. Clearly the fake wires had acted as the deterrent they were intended to be. A cop told us after our detention six months later that they went through half a dozen hacksaw blades trying to cut the hardened steel hasp of the padlock.

While Stephen was in Cape Town he indicated that he could tolerate Johannesburg no longer and that he was thinking of chucking in his job at the university and returning to Cape Town. He realised that he would be out of work but had decided that unemployment was preferable to doing no ANC work. To survive he could get a grant to do a master's degree in sociology at the University of Cape Town. This would have to be paid back at a later date but the imperatives of our underground work were more important than any future financial problems he'd have to face. He could only return to Cape Town at the end of the university term in December, however.

After the banner a *Vukani!-Awake!* was produced every month until February 1978. Producing the pamphlets – you could call them newspapers – was a mammoth task as each consisted of about six typed foolscap-size pages. The articles were thoroughly researched and carefully written and covered a range of topical subjects. Vast quantities of paper, envelopes and stamps had to be bought; our mailing list had become as long as we could handle.

Several frightening incidents happened while out posting the *Vukani's*, which in retrospect seem to have a light side to them. On one occasion when I got out of my car to post a bundle of letters across the road, the door slammed shut and I was locked out with the engine still running. I had no choice but to smash a fanlight window. The street was busy and I'm sure a passing pedestrian took my number. On another occasion I was stopped for speeding. On the back seat were two suitcases full of unposted *Vukani's*. When the cop jumped out into the road to flag me down I did not know it was for speeding and thought it was a roadblock. When he did not search my car or arrest me for subversion and only presented me with a speeding ticket I actually thanked him gratefully. He thought I was weird.

The most frightening incident happened, of all places, about 100 metres from the headquarters of the security police in Cape Town. As I pulled away from a set of traffic lights I smelt burning. Suddenly a cloud of smoke poured through the dashboard. The car was on fire and on the back seat were thousands of leaflets in suitcases. I quickly stopped at the side of the road, opened the bonnet and saw that the battery lead was shorting against the bodywork – the sparks had set alight the oily gunge on the side of the engine compartment. Fortunately I had some old rags in the boot and was able to smother the flames. If the car had burned out at that spot I would undoubtedly have been in hiding that night.

At the end of the year Stephen handed in his resignation and moved back to Cape Town. As my two flatmates, Heri Hirt and Klaus Hartmuth, German students at the University of Cape Town, were away on holiday, Stephen temporarily came to stay with me. When he started his course he would move to his parents'.

It was good to have comradeship again: to be able to work together and plan our operations collectively. On my own I had tended to become a bit anarchic. There was no one to observe whether I stuck to my programmes or even if I had any. Hardest of all was maintaining discipline. I tended to work too much as there was more certainty in my underground life than in my above-ground one. This resulted in endless personal problems and family complications. Daphne broke up with me a number of times but I could never tell her the reasons for the tensions in our relationship; my family thought I was the most uncommunicative person in the world.

Our first action as a reconstituted cell was also our last leaflet bomb action. We planned it for the 16th of December, Heroes' Day, again. But acting on a premonition we decided at the last moment to postpone it for a week. Since we'd carried out most of our actions around commemorative days we reckoned it would be safer to avoid them for a while. And we can thank our lucky stars that we did, for the security police, as we later found out, had sent one of their big-shots to Cape Town to witness the expected 'bombings'. This particular cop later told us that he was 'damned annoyed' that he had to come all the way to Cape Town for nothing and then as soon as he got back to Pretoria he saw on his television that a spate of leaflet bombs had gone off in Cape Town.

Over a period of two days we set off ten leaflet bombs targetted at crowds of Christmas shoppers in the centre of Cape Town and other suburban shopping areas. So that we could watch the fireworks, we set the timers for a mere two and a half minutes. They certainly were spectacular. The leaflets would spray into the air about 15 metres high but if there was any wind they would be lifted much higher. A cop later told us that they found leaflets on the tops of buildings 75 metres high and up to half a kilometre away.

During January and February 1978 a number of strange happenings took place which worried us greatly. Every few days there would be odd phonecalls. Someone would ask for 'John' and we would reply that there was no 'John' living at the number. It would always be the same voice. After a while we started to keep a diary of the phonecalls. Then one day there was a suspicious-looking character sitting on the balcony railing directly outside our front door. Another day there was someone standing on the pavement directly opposite our flat. The person looked like the stereotypical security cop: short hair, obligatory moustache, clashing outfit, mean appearance.

From all this it might seem obvious that we were being watched. But after you've being working underground for two and a half years you begin to think everybody is watching you—paranoia easily gets the better of you. The trouble is that you're never quite sure. You can't flee the country every time someone appears to be staring at you or every time you receive a wrong-number call. In the end, when you do see someone who appears to be watching you, you tell yourself that you're just getting paranoid and that you shouldn't worry yourself about it.

But, as it so happened, these were real cops doing real surveillance and not our imagination playing games with us. The police told us after our arrest of some of the things we'd done while they had us under observation, which indicated to us how long we'd been watched. On one occasion we had lost them by driving down a one-way street. On another they had placed someone disguised as a drunkard in the graveyard opposite our flat who was able to relate how I had removed and replaced my diving equipment from the built-in wardrobe in my bedroom.

How the cops got on to us we will probably never know. I doubt whether it was the result of one particular mistake on our part; more likely the result of careful police work over a long period of time. The security police were meticulous in their investigations and followed up the minutest details. For instance, the wood I had used for the bases of the leaflet bombs I had always bought from a certain hardware dealer who sold it as off-cuts. The cops measured the wood and found it to be a non-standard gauge, left-overs from a commercial job. They were able to trace the manufacturer of the wood, who had used it and ultimately where the off-cuts ended up – the hardware store from which I bought them.

Naturally we did make mistakes – that was inevitable. But I don't believe any of them were major; mostly just the result of not being thorough enough. It was easy to take short cuts, to not take enough care; you never knew how careful you needed to be. For example, to spread the word about ANC Radio Freedom broadcasts I made up a rubber stamp giving the frequencies and times it could be received. I used it to stamp the details in telephone directories and on railway timetables but was not careful enough to do this far enough away from where we lived. It would thus have been reasonable for the police to conclude that the mystery stamper lived in the vicinity of the stampings. If the cops had investigated where most of our envelopes had been posted they would have found the heaviest concentrations nearest to where we lived.

Piecing together hundreds of unrelated scraps of evidence the cops were probably able to narrow down their suspicions to a very small number of people. Without doubt they had files on us from long before we began our work for the ANC. At university neither of us had been very circumspect in hiding our political leanings. From that starting point they would at a certain stage have been able to direct some of the evidence at us. Then it was only a matter of time if they had decided to watch either of us.

Our own manner of operation and living was not beyond criticism. After a while it is easy to become *blasé* and let your guard slip: you stop taking the necessary precautionary measures; you stop looking over your shoulder and in your rear-view mirror; you stop being disciplined in the way you were taught. I was going out with Daphne, a 'Coloured', and Stephen was going out with an Indian woman, Feroza. This open contempt for racist laws was bound to attract attention. While in Johannesburg Stephen had made friends with 'banned' people, some of whom regularly flouted their banning orders and visited him at his flat. Many of his other friends were politically involved types. Through my job I too had made a number of 'undesirable' friends – i.e. blacks – who invited me to their homes in the townships, some of which places were out of bounds for white people.

Our last act was one over which the cops must have gloated and which they used to time the moment of our arrest. We had decided to move our operating premises again and at the end of February foolishly brought all our equipment together for the move. We did this because the new place was due to become available a week after the old one had to be vacated. To span the gap we hired a garage near our (residential) flat and moved everything from the old premises into it. We also moved to it several trunks of equipment and banned books that we had hidden in other places, so that they too could be moved to new places.

The cops observed the move, which we carelessly made in broad daylight. From that moment a permanent watch was placed over us, which if we'd been alert enough we would undoubtedly have noticed. In fact we were so blind to what was happening that the cops started to play games with us. On the last Sunday before our arrest Steve and I, together with Heri, Klaus, Daphne, Feroza and several other friends, held a *braaivleis* (barbecue) at the side of the road running along the base of Table Mountain. While we were cooking our meat and swigging our wine the cops drove up in their car and started making their own *braaivleis* just 30 metres away. As we were a 'multi-racial' gathering someone from our group jokingly suggested that they were cops spying on us. To find out, Stephen in his drunken state went over and invited them to join us. Needless to say they declined the offer!

Probably thinking that the moving of the equipment signalled that we were about to cease production or scarper, they decided to close in. Convinced that we were unaware of their surveillance, the cops planned their moves carefully, choosing the worst possible moment for us.

In the early hours of the morning of Thursday the 2nd of March 1978 they moved in. Talk about being caught red handed!

3
Detention

They came at three in the morning. The bell rang in an aggressive way and there was a loud banging on the front door. Instinctively we knew who it was. Stephen said to Feroza, who was sleeping with him that night, that he thought it must be the police, but he was thinking of a different sort of police to the sort she was thinking of. She leapt out of bed and made herself a 'separate' bed of blankets on the floor – she was thinking that she was about to be arrested for breaking the law by sleeping with a white man.

I sombrely climbed out of bed and made for the front door. What about all those contingency plans you've made for the day they come? Leap out the window, barricade yourself in your room and shoot at the bastards through the door! It all seemed a bit unrealistic just then and I found myself moving lemming-like towards my doom. Stephen parted the curtains above his bed and peered out into the street. The place was surrounded with police and police cars.

I could see torches waving about through the glass-panelled front door. I loosened the latch and immediately the door was pushed open. A beam of light shone in my face and someone asked if I was Timothy Jenkin. I replied in the affirmative, thinking fleetingly that maybe I should have said 'No, he's out!' A crowd of nasty faces leered at me. One of them formally pronounced: 'We have reason to believe that you have been engaged in terrorist activities. We're coming in to search.' Whereupon six or seven brutes barged in and began to tear the place apart. Whatever happened to search warrants?

The one who had spoken to me was dressed in clothes which were covered in blood. If this was meant to intimidate us, it did. When I saw it I thought, Oh God! that must be the blood of some poor bastard he's been torturing. Soon mine'll be on there too. Later we found out that this blood-bespattered security policeman, who seemed to be heading the investigation, was the notorious 'Spyker' ('Nails') van Wyk. His name cropped up in practically every major political case and especially whenever allegations of torture were heard. A self-confessed admirer of Hitler, he sported a little moustache like the Fuehrer's but parted his dark, greasy hair down the centre. He was widely regarded by those who had the misfortune to find themselves in his company as a pathological sadist, the ideal interrogator for a totalitarian regime. The blood on his clothes could have come from a torture victim but it would not have surprised me if he had bought a pound of prime beef and squeezed the blood onto his trousers and shirt. His name must definitely go near the top of the list of apartheid criminals.

I sat cross-legged on top of my bed and watched dejectedly as two or three of them emptied my drawers and wardrobe. The bookrack was a source of considerable fascination and all 'suspect' books were put to one side. I had always been careful to have only the most innocuous books on the shelves but different people have different ideas of what is innocuous.

Two policewomen walked past my bedroom door accompanying Feroza. They took her outside, presumably to an awaiting car. Then Klaus was taken out, with a rather bewildered look on his face. Lucky thing that Heri moved out last week, I thought. He wouldn't have liked getting tangled up in something like this.

The chest at the end of my bed was locked so they demanded the key. I picked up from my bedside table the bunch of house and car keys which contained the key for the padlock on the chest and tossed it to the cop. The chest was opened and the bunch of keys pocketed. As he did so a vision still lingering on my retina made me look back at the bedside table. On it lay the bunch of keys for the secret flat, the garage where all our equipment was stored and for all the trunks and tool-boxes in it. It was a personal rule that those keys were never to be brought into the flat; they were always to be hidden in the springs under the front seat of my car. And never before had they been brought into the flat, except on that night. Life is cussed.

Inside the chest were about fifteen volumes of carefully pasted and bound newspaper clippings, the main source of our articles for *Vukani – Awake!* Between the volumes the cop retrieved what at that moment seemed like a big 'find'–my 9 mm Star pistol.

I had bought the pistol on the instructions of the ANC and with ANC money at the height of the Soweto uprisings in 1976. The day I went to the gunshop to buy it there were so many scared whites clamouring for firearms that there were three rows of people against the counter. When I finally made it to the front they presented the Star and said that it was all they had left. It looked suitable to my untrained eye so I paid three hundred rand for it and forced my way out of the shop.

I had been instructed to take a gun on leaflet-bomb missions and to use it on such occasions if threatened with arrest. I took it along once–at the time we did the banner–but never again because it was so bulky under my jacket it would have prevented me making a quick get-away. I probably couldn't have fired it in defence anyway–not for a leaflet bomb.

The cop who found the gun asked what I intended to use it for, but wasn't interested enough to wait for a reply. They must have known that I had a licence because no issue was made of it, and the gun was even handed back to my parents after our trial. The clippings seemed to be of more interest. The volumes were tied together and carted away, most of them never to be seen again.

After about half an hour I was told to get dressed and was then accompanied outside to an awaiting car in which Stephen was already sitting. In a convoy we headed for Caledon Square Police Station, the head office of the Security Branch in Cape Town.

Up till then nothing too bad had happened but when we arrived at Caledon Square the weight of what was happening suddenly descended upon me: I was in the hands of South Africa's security police, a gang of thugs with not a happy reputation. What we had always thought about was now really happening and the reality of it was far more frightening than I'd ever imagined.

Events began to connect: all those strange phonecalls; the dark characters lurking about outside the flat. Why the hell didn't we trust our suspicions? If they've arrested us now they must have been watching us for the past several days or weeks. They must have seen us moving all the equipment, seen where our secret flat was. They must know everything!

At Caledon Square Stephen and I were separated. I was taken into a room which was bare, save for a couple of tables and chairs. My right arm was handcuffed to the backrest of one of the chairs and I was told to sit. The cops vacated the room except for a tall, lanky and thick-looking one. He sat himself on the other chair and began to read his newspaper, as if what was happening was a quite normal part of his day's work. Stephen was being processed in another room.

I was left in the room like this for about half an hour before they came back. Some of them I recognised from the party that had invaded our flat; the others were new. One of them seated himself next to me while the others crowded around behind. Without saying anything the sitting cop dropped the offending bunch of keys (the ones I'd forgotten to hide) on the table in front of me. The clever bastards! How are you going to get out of this one? In front of me lay not just a bunch of keys for doors and padlocks, but the keys to unlock us—the keys to our entire case.

I sat staring at the keys for a long time not believing my rotten luck. I admonished myself: If only you'd been more disciplined and made sure the keys were put in their place under the front seat of your car. But you've always put them there. How did they know to come on the one night you forgot?

Eventually the sitting cop asked what the keys were for. To make sure I gave the right answer he whisked my bunch of flat and car keys out of his coat pocket, jingled them in front of my nose and said that the keys on the table were neither for my flat nor my car—they had been tested. I looked at his mean face and swallowed, but said nothing. I stared at the keys again. The silence was terrible. I wanted to speak, just to hear a friendly voice, but couldn't. Everything I'd read and been told about interrogation suddenly came back to me:

Hold out as long as you can so that your comrades can get away. But there are no comrades to get away; we've both been captured. Be strong, never admit a thing and deny everything. But it's obvious they know what the keys are for, otherwise why would they use them for their opening move? Well just for your own self-respect don't speak to the fascist bastards.

I sat staring at the keys for what must have been the best part of half an hour. They seemed to be in no immediate hurry. The interrogator did not become vicious, and remained remarkably patient. He pointed to a particular key on the bunch and asked what it was used for. 'What about this one? And these ones here?' I refused to respond.

Some of the spectators could not contain their curiosity and began to egg on the interrogator. 'Perhaps his tongue needs a little loosening? Should we bring some oil? We'll make your tongue start wagging. Soon you won't be able to stop talking.' In response the interrogator appeared to become a bit impatient and started to raise his voice, which cut at the nerves in my stomach. The others joined in, in chorus. Then the name-calling and racist taunts started – the usual fare of South African interrogation sessions. 'This little kaffir-lover must speak to us now. He's been *naai*-ing Coloured girls again' (from the Afrikaans to 'sew', but meaning to have sex with). 'Can't find a white *meisie* (girl) so he's got to screw kaffir *meide* (maids). This one likes to *naai* with the dame on top. The other one likes to do it standing. You piece of communist filth, you shouldn't be allowed to live. You're just wasting air. Let's muck him up.'

They didn't muck me up. The mob went away and I was left in peace again. It was obvious that their strategy, apart from trying to frighten the hell out of me, was to make me feel like a piece of worthless rubbish – a well known interrogation tactic. Make them hate themselves; make them lose their self-esteem.

A short while later the second shift came in. At the head of the team was the ubiquitous Spyker van Wyk. This time he was washed, shaved, combed and dressed in a fresh safari suit. No sign of any blood. A clean canvas, I thought. With him was a particularly nasty specimen of a security cop by the name of Van Aggenbach. Torturer's lines were deeply engrained into his prematurely wrinkled face and his drooping mouth uttered suitably vicious threats of actions he would soon be carrying out.

Spyker sat down beside me and grasped the bunch of keys. 'You're going to tell us what these keys are for. I don't care if you won't tell us now. We've got plenty of time. We've got ways of making you talk.' 'Ve haf our vays!' – so fascists really do say these things. I had thought they were only said in caricatures of evil nazi interrogators.

Spyker was the heavy. He was the nasty, course, rough interrogator who frightened the life out of you but to whom you were determined not to say anything. The previous one was the pleasant, civilised, friendly interrogator who pretended almost to be sympathetic with

33

you, in whom you almost felt you could confide after the rough one had done you over. This was the 'hot and cold treatment' we'd read about – another well known interrogation tactic.

Spyker wanted an answer – quickly. The threats increased. He alluded to the previous interrogator by saying that it didn't pay to have patience with the likes of us. Van Aggenbagh in particular wanted action. He wanted Spyker to hand me over to him; he would soon get me singing like a canary.

Their next moves were totally stereotyped: 'We know everything so you may as well speak. Your "comrade" has told us everything. He's not being stubborn like you. This will soon be over if you just co-operate.' Spyker then accompanied me to an adjacent room where piles of intercepted *Vukani's* were being sorted and processed by a team of typists. 'See how you've been wasting your time. We pick up every pamphlet you send. We've got them all, every one you've ever sent. We've been watching you since the day you put your foot back in South Africa. The ANC just used you people to do their dirty work. Those bastards in London are the ones we'd really like to get our hands on. They're the ones who cause all the trouble, from the comfort of their big mansions. The ANC has forgotten you now. You're all on your own. Nobody cares. . .'

Then up to the photographic department. For some unkown reason a balaclava was pulled over my head and a dozen pictures of different profiles taken with blinding floodlights shining in my eyes. 'That's him. We've got him now. He's the one whose been causing all the trouble. You're in for big shit my friend'.

After about two hours with Spyker and his team I was beginning to feel that there was no longer any reason for not saying what the keys were for. It was obvious that they knew, otherwise why would they be so interested in them. Spyker would not listen to answers that I didn't know what they were for or that they belonged to someone who had left them in my flat by mistake. I could sense that Van Aggenbagh was dying to get on with the tongue-loosening procedure and to prevent Spyker getting any more blood on his clothes I said I would take them to see.

This seemed to please them but it made me hate myself. I felt like a collaborator. But I had no stomach for the sort of violence that would surely have followed. A protected upbringing had not prepared me well for the interrogation room. I had always been one of the smallest at school and soon learned to avoid playground fights. Later I abhorred body sports such as rugby which were compulsory at high school.

They handcuffed me to another cop and marched me out to an awaiting car in the street. Without me giving them any directions they set off for Mowbray where the garage was located. When the car turned into the narrow cul-de-sac where the garage was situated, there was a grand reception waiting for us. There was Steve, Klaus and – oh no! – Heri too, all waiting with their escorts to whom they were handcuffed, plus a large contingent of police spectators. I felt like the star arriving at the gala opening of the opera.

Despite the reception ceremony directly in front of the suspect garage the charade was kept up. I was handed the bunch of keys and asked to open whatever it was I had brought them along to see. I unlocked the padlock on garage number 50 and swung up the door. There it all stood. All the evidence any prosecutor could ever want. I don't know what they had told Heri and Klaus but I'm sure the two of them were thinking that they'd got themselves tied up in a big-time robbery investigation. A garage full of furniture, metal trunks, toolboxes and household goods. What else could it be?

The detectives moved in. They opened the trunks but did not touch the contents until everything had been photographed. One trunk contained all the banned books we'd accumulated over the years. Goodbye to those. The other trunk contained all our addressing machine stencils – thousands of names – and bits and pieces of partly-made leaflet bombs. The toolboxes contained the specialised collection of tools we'd managed to build up. Goodbye to all that.

One of the cops dug out of the trunk with the books a Russian dictionary I'd bought seven years previously with the intention of learning the language one day. 'Aha!' he exclaimed in seriousness, 'I suppose you're working for the KGB too.'

Vaunting his investigative skills Spyker asked if we had not seen his 10-year-old son watching us the previous Sunday while we were offloading the equipment into the garage. Maybe we had but who would suspect a little kid of spying on you?

On the way back to Caledon Square I wondered what more they could possibly want from us. They already had enough evidence to put us away for life. In our carelessness we'd certainly made things easy for them. I felt embarrassed in a way. In one of our leaflets we'd advised activists how to run an underground cell: 'Don't keep all your equipment in one place; keep revolutionary literature and secret documents hidden...' We had broken all the most obvious and basic rules. We hoped our comrades would never find out.

Back in the office a pad and pen was thrown on the table in front of me and I was told to write: about everything, from the first day till the last.

So I started to write. I wrote four pages and handed it to them. Spyker took one look, smiled, and tore it up. He repeated threateningly that he wanted everything, not just the obvious. He wanted to know how we had got involved with the ANC, what sort of training we had received, what we had done in South Africa. Everything, and lots of names. He especially wanted names.

The next pad I filled completely. It was taken away for scrutiny and

35

I was presented with another and told that I'd be filling many, many such pads before I was finished. I felt as if I was writing an examination.

So I continued to write. I didn't mind writing. So long as I was writing I wasn't being beaten up. I reasoned that if there was going to be any violence it would surely be at this early stage soon after capture. If I was to write about things they obviously knew then it would be possible to write without giving anything away. The things they didn't know about needn't be given away provided I wrote within the realms of the possible. I invented many names, James Bond situations and fantastic 'terrorist' plans to satisfy their insatiable interrogators' appetites.

As soon as I completed each pad it was whisked away for examination and a new one was placed on the table. By the end of the day I had written so much that I was suffering from severe writer's cramp. What I'd written was based on the truth but was mostly lies: how we'd gone abroad to join the ANC, how the organisation had given us months of specialised training in secret hideouts deep in the countryside, how we had been 'indoctrinated' and taught to write 'subversive' literature, how we planned to set up nationwide underground networks and anything else I thought would excite them. I was able to avoid giving away any names by saying that the people who trained us had used *noms de guerre*.

By late afternoon the cops who had been up all night decided that they'd had enough. I was handed over to three fresher-looking specimens and driven to the Milnerton Police Station about 10 kilometres away to be stored for the night. In the charge office my spectacles, watch, belt and shoelaces were removed: they wanted no suicides on their hands.

Then to the cells.

I had never seen a cell before. First a heavy, solid steel door. Then a sort of cage with a barred gate. Through this and into what appeared to be an 'exercise yard': a small concrete rectangle with smooth, high walls and more bars across the top. No helicopter is going to lift you out of here, matey! Then into the cell proper: first another solid steel door, then another cage and grille, and then the cold concrete darkness of the cell itself.

The clang of the doors closing on me and the sound of the keys turning suddenly drove home the gravity of my situation. I stood for a long time staring disbelievingly at the back of the closed door. Was this really me in this situation? The cell was cold, dank and stark; the two windows so heavily barred and meshed that very little light penetrated from the outside and the cell's lamp so weak that it lit no more than an orange ring around itself.

I thought of those books we'd been made to read while receiving our training. Yes, they were accurate. I almost feel as if I've been here before. What did the prisoners in them do to overcome the nothingness of their situation? They paced up and down. But there's no space to walk in here. Two paces and I'll be up against the wall.

I wasn't going to be like them so I lay down on the bed and stared at the ceiling. Spider webs hung from the corners and the paint was grey and peeling. As I looked at it I saw the face of Spyker in the dust and flaking paint. Terror filled my body and I burst into tears.

At no stage of our detention were Stephen and I informed that we had been detained under Section Six of the notorious *Terrorism Act*. Although we guessed that this was the case, no mention was made of any 'rights' that we might have had, of the nature of our detention or even of why we were being detained. Both of us knew that under Section Six we had no rights at all. No outside people, not even lawyers, family or friends were allowed access to, or any information about, or from us. No court was allowed to 'pronounce upon the validity of any action taken under the section.' In other words we were held incommunicado and at the mercy of the security police in a totally closed system. What had happened to the rule of law?

Section Six was created explicitly for interrogation purposes. You were held indefinitely without charge until you had 'satisfactorily replied to all questions' or until 'no useful purpose (was) served by ... further detention.' 'No useful purpose' usually meant that no more statements could be forced out of you – or that you were dead. From June 1967 to July 1982, the period the Act was in force, no less than sixty people died in detention while being held under Section Six. Naturally, the police denied on all occasions being responsible for the deaths and always explained them away as 'suicides' or due to 'natural causes'. Even if this was the case, it was never explained why so many detainees found the need to commit suicide while being held under Section Six.

The Terrorism Act came under such intense criticism that it was replaced in July 1982 by the *Internal Security Act*. The new Act is a more refined piece of legislation but Section 29 of the Act, which is the equivalent of Section Six, differs very little from the latter as far as detainees are concerned. To mollify public opinion about mistreatment and torture, certain 'safeguards' were added to give the impression that detainees are held under the watchful eye of 'inspectors', doctors and magistrates and thus protected from harm. But in a totally closed system there is no one to check that the 'inspectors' have carried out their duty, and even if they have, no one can know what the outcome of the 'inspections' was or whether any action was taken if it was necessary. In theory there is a maximum detention period of six months built into the Section but this can be extended if the police provide reasons to the Minister of Law and Order (euphemism for Police) why the detainee should not be released. Many people have been held for well over the six month period and deaths in detention continue.

These so-called security laws are merely a disguise used by the regime to give a legal appearance to arbitrary actions it takes against its opponents. They are the direct antithesis of law, a cover for barbarism, a means to bypass the law altogether.

The interrogation continued the next day. While I was waiting for them to begin, Stephen was brought into the room. Spyker pointed to Stephen's knee which was swollen and told him to tell me how it had happened. He'd tried to escape! I felt very proud of him at that moment although the object of the demonstration was to try to show me how silly it was to try to get away. Although I was not allowed to know then, Stephen had very nearly broken free of their clutches. The previous day he had complained of a serious stomach-ache and was taken to a doctor who happened to have his rooms on the first floor of a building. In the doctor's surgery Stephen's minders had carelessly not placed themselves between him and the window, so Stephen, seeing his chance, leapt out of the window, onto a ledge outside and then onto a lower building next door. As he made the final leap his knee caved in and he crouched for a moment in agony. This gave the cops their chance. One of them ran to the window and pointed his pistol at Stephen and ordered him to freeze. The cop was so shocked at this brazen escape attempt that his hand was shaking violently, but Stephen reckoned it wisest not to take another chance and raised his hands in submission. He would have got clean away had he landed properly because the next leap to the ground was a short distance and the cops would have had to run from the first floor and a long way around the building to get to the place where he would have reached ground.

Stephen's fine example that first day set the tone for the future. He planted in our minds the seed which grew into an obsession to find ways of eluding our captors. I wasn't to see him again after that until much later. However I found out later that his interrogation followed much the same pattern as my own.

Meanwhile I was required to continue writing and each completed pad was followed by a question session. After a while they appeared to lose interest in what I was writing. I was making it too easy for them. They appeared also to lose 'respect' for me because I did not resist their demands sufficiently. I was accused of not being properly trained and the names of certain people, who had alleged torture while in detention, were mentioned as examples of people who had been 'well-trained'. Plainly I had denied them the opportunity to engage in some wholesome torturing and this had led to their declining interest in me.

What they were most interested in was in laying their hands on the different typewriters we had used in our work since 1975. Only if they could connect the different typewriters to us could they positively identify a particular leaflet or address label as being produced by our cell. If there was no typewriter they could not claim that we were responsible for producing a particular leaflet or for posting it, even if we had admitted it.

By studying the type-faces of the leaflets and addresses they had identified five different typewriters. One was already in their possession, found in the garage with all the other equipment. It could only be connected to the leaflets and pamphlets produced during the previous year – in other words, our current typewriter. They wanted to know where all the others were.

One I admitted belonged to my parents, so that was immediately fetched. Another was one at the university where I had worked, which had only been used to type some address labels. So into the cars and off in a convoy to the university. At the university the rector, Dr Richard van der Ross, received the delegation. He insisted that I be unhandcuffed and then proudly led the way to the outbuilding where I had worked. As we trooped down the corridor of the Institute, sympathetic (to me) heads peeked out of doorways, but no one said a word. The secretary was busy typing on the offending typewriter and was unceremoniously forced to end her task when the typewriter was unplugged and carried off.

The cops wanted the other two typewriters, one of which they knew had been used to type all our leaflets of 1975 and 1976. The one they had in mind was the one that I had buried, but I was damned if they were going to get it. The fifth one I wasn't sure about: it could have been one of many but probably another one at the university. Because of their eagerness to get the typewriters I told them that the one that we'd used for the leaflets (the buried one) I'd thrown into the sea and the other probably belonged to my brother who was then living in Johannesburg. Being so far away I thought they would just write that one off as it had been used very little. But no. Not only did they get the Johannesburg police to 'arrest' the suspect typewriter, they arrested my brother too.

The typewriter that I said I'd thrown into the sea they wanted too. Some quick thinking was needed. The Cape Peninsula consists of many kilometres of coastline, much of it sandy beaches. It was these parts that I knew best but I couldn't say I threw it into the waves on a flat beach. I had to think of a particular precipitous and rocky place where the water was deep. There was only one such spot that I knew well, a place where I had frequently been to poach crayfish, so I thought I'd try it on. The place was a rocky headland a few kilometres south of the coastal suburb of Camps Bay along the scenic coastal road to Llandudno. At that point the rocks rose steeply out of the sea to the road about 50 metres higher. A short distance down from the road was an ideal place from where it would have been possible to discard a typewriter. The pools below were deep and surrounded by rocks. Invariably the water was rough.

One afternoon they took me to point out the spot. It certainly was splendid to see the sun and waves again after the days and nights in the dark interrogation rooms and police cells. Having pointed out the supposed location and been photographed doing so I imagined that that was the end of the story. Not a chance. Two days later I was driven back to the same spot and there waiting for us was a team of reserve-police divers, all kitted out with wetsuits and aqualungs and raring to go.

The divers donned their equipment and each chose an area of the seabed to cover. The search went on for a good two hours, but I didn't mind: I was getting a nice tan and knew that I wouldn't be seeing that beautiful place for a long time. Eventually the divers emerged from the water, cold, tired and without a typewriter. The leader of the group wagged an angry finger at me and accused me of misleading them – the nerve. He demanded to know exactly where the machine had been dropped. I could be no more helpful. Maybe it had corroded away or some other divers had found it. This he would not accept, claiming that his team had found wedding rings in muddy dams. I was hurriedly taken away from the place by security policemen mumbling horrible retribution. I expected the worst but nothing more was said about the typewriter. I suppose they had enough evidence without it.

The next stage of the investigation involved our being taken out, separately and without the other knowing, to the places where we had placed leaflet bombs. These 'pointing-out' sessions are common in the investigation of political cases in South Africa: the accused are forced to point out the places where they were supposed to have committed their alleged crimes.

In our case they told us to direct them to the places where we had planted the leaflet bombs, even though they knew exactly where most of these were. At the places we were told to stand and point to the exact spot so that a photograph could be taken. While this gave the police evidence for their case against us, it also gave us evidence of how effective their efforts had been in tracing the places where we had placed leaflet bombs. On a number of occasions both of us pointed out spots about which the police knew nothing. This made them really mad because they thought we were having them on. As it turned out the police only knew of 26 of the leaflet bombs while we'd planted at least 10 more. Never had any failed to go off so technical failure could not be an explanation for this disparity. Excited witnesses of the explosions on the undiscovered occasions must have scooped up all the leaflets as well as the remains of the bombs.

Under ordinary law you would of course never allow yourself to be used by your legal opponent to assist in the collection of their evidence to be used against you. Lawyers would definitely advise against doing so, that is, if you were allowed to receive legal advice

40

while being held in detention. But what can you do when you are in the clutches of the security police and entirely cut off from the outside world? They keep you in detention for as long as it takes them to amass all the evidence they need—and sometimes longer. They are not much concerned about your defence or with the niceties of the law.

After pointing out the scenes of our 'crimes' in Cape Town we were taken (separately in two cars) to Johannesburg to point out the places where we'd placed bombs there. Arriving on a Friday evening they deposited us at the notorious John Vorster Square police cells to be lodged over the weekend, while they had a restful two days at a comfortable police residence.

At first the local cops, after issuing us with straw mats, ordered us to undress and hand in our clothes. But when we protested strongly at the prospect of being kept naked for two days, our security police mentors for some reason supported our pleas and we were allowed to remain dressed. Our cells were dreadful—large, dirty and barren. There was no water apart from what you could get from your toilet when you flushed it and they refused to supply any toilet paper. Since I could not bring myself to use my hand to clean myself I was compelled to rip out and use pages of the tatty bible they provided. Forgive me God for it was all I could do!

John Vorster Square is also a police station and the headquarters of the Johannesburg District and Witwatersrand Division of the South African Police. It contains one of the main offices of the security police and from it many floors up a number of detainees have been slung out of windows to meet their death on the pavement below. Both of us were taken up to these offices for further interrogation and, in Stephen's case, for an identification parade. In passing, the distance to the pavement below was pointed out to us.

Stephen's identification parade was a complete farce. The other members of the parade were all well-groomed and well-dressed security policemen while Stephen was haggard and unshaven after spending two days in the cells. It did not take the witness long to put her hand on his shoulder. It was alleged that the witness was a fruit-seller who had seen Stephen place a bomb near the black entrance of Johannesburg station nine months earlier.

After returning to Cape Town there were no more interrogation sessions—they'd got all the evidence they needed. I was dumped in the Milnerton police cells to rot while Stephen was kept in the less salubrious cells at Caledon Square. The only reading matter they allowed us was the bible. Stephen managed to read quite far into his but I found it so boring that I gave up after a few pages and preferred to lie against the wall with only my thoughts to comfort me. I dreamed of escaping—I was not going to allow these fascists the privilege of seeing me put away for years. I studied my cell and exercise yard looking for cracks. But without my glasses I couldn't find them. The time would come though. I could be patient.

Our interrogation had been relatively uneventful compared to what the average detainee had to go through. We were fully aware that it was our white skins that had saved us from the usual mistreatment and torture. It was not that the security police never tortured white detainees—they were just more reluctant to do so. Coming from 'respectable' backgrounds also helped us. My father was an eminent Cape Town anaesthetist and it would not have looked too good for the security police if it had come out in our trial that they had tortured the son of a well-known doctor.

Another factor which helped us, we found out later, was that the security police thought we were the last propaganda cell operating in the Cape. They knew what we had done and thought that there were no more cells to round up. David Rabkin and Jeremy Cronin before us had had a much rougher passage as the cops knew that there was at least one other group operating at the same time as theirs and wanted to know what they knew about the other group(s).

The period of detention ended abruptly on the morning of 31st March, four weeks after our arrest, when I was unexpectedly unlocked and told there was a surprise for me. I was taken into the charge office and there waiting for me were my sister and my mother, tearful and looking burdened by the month's traumas. They brought the news that Stephen and I were to appear later that day in the Cape Town Magistrates' Court to face charges and that an attorney had been appointed by my father to look after my affairs. My mother muttered something about whether it was true that I'd been held for planting bombs. As it was too complicated to explain there and then, I could only reply that it was the function of the court to find out.

By prevailing standards our period in detention was almost a record for shortness. We put this down to the same factors that applied to our length of interrogation, but also because we handed the police all the evidence they could want on a platter. The worst aspects of detention, apart from what could happen to you while being interrogated, are not knowing what is going to happen next and the solitary confinement. You always expect the worst but hope for the best. You wait for them to come in and tell you it's all been a terrible mistake, that they don't think what you've done is very serious and you can go home. It's the solitary that messes you up. Left with your disturbed thoughts you are unable to think things through rationally. When they lock you up after a day's interrogation you are happy to be left on your own but if they don't turn up the next day you wonder where they are, when they'll be coming and what they have in store for you.

Solitary is very disorienting, a torture in itself. A week without seeing anyone feels like an eternity but knowing that you might lie there for six months or longer is enough to weaken even the strongest.

Certainties give hope; indeterminacy breeds despair. It was a very unpleasant experience but our period was too short and uneventful for me to be able to comment on its long-term effects.

As I have mentioned, our detentions were not the only consequence of the police actions on the 2nd of March and after. Our girl-friends Daphne and Feroza, our flat-mate Klaus and ex-flat-mate Heri were detained under Section Six for between four and seven days. Klaus was the first to be released, after four day – probably because the German embassy kicked up a stink. Daphne and Feroza were released after six days and Heri after a week. All were held in solitary confinement in separate police cells around Cape Town. They were all throughly grilled for information on us but were unable to provide anything the police did not already know. Heri's room in the house he shared with several other students was turned over but was also found to be devoid of any clues about our activities.

My brother Michael was also detained for several days; his typewriter for longer. The reason he was held, apparently, was to find out what he knew of Stephen's acquaintances while Stephen had been living in Johannesburg. The two of them had shared a flat and knew many of the same people. He also provided the police with information about my personal life. I do not hold this against him as he is not a political person and probably did not know why we had been detained. Presumably he thought he was pleading in mitigation for me.

Meanwhile Robin in London had not taken our detentions sitting down. By this stage she was working full-time in the ANC office and so was in a good position to muster forces. Together with an uncle of Stephen's who was incensed by his nephew's predicament, friends who knew us while we were in London in 1974/75 and the Anti-Apartheid Movement, she organised a 'Stephen Lee and Tim Jenkin Defence Committee'. Hundreds of postcards protesting at our detentions were printed for sympathisers to send to Prime Minister B J Vorster. The Committee also, amongst other things, commissioned articles about our plight in trade-union, left-wing and Catholic newspapers – the latter through Stephen's uncle. A demonstration for the start of our trial was held, outside the South African Embassy in London calling for our release and the release of all South African political prisoners.

4
Awaiting trial

The court appearance on the 31st of March served no other purpose than to convert us from detainees into awaiting-trial prisoners. The security police had finished with us and were now placing us in the custody of the Prisons Service. Their preparations for indicting us were not complete but as the real trial was set for the 1st of June, two months away, they had plenty of time to complete their work.

In a sense the appearance in court was a relief. It meant the re-establishment of links with the world and an end to uncertainty. Although our period of detention had been short compared to the average time detainees were held, it had been wearing enough. In fact it was hard to imagine how people managed to put up with the strains of detention for six months or more.

The best part was being able to see some familiar and friendly faces again. In the courtroom were members of our respective families, friends from work and Heri, Klaus and Daphne. The appearance only took a few minutes. The Magistrate announced that we were to be charged under Article 2(1) of the Terrorism Act of 1967 and Article 11(e) of the Internal Security Act of 1950 (formerly called the Suppression of Communism Act). We were not asked to plead to the charges and a state-representative handed to the Magistrate an order from the Attorney-General stating that we were to be remanded in custody until we appeared for trial in the Cape Town Supreme Court. Bail is seldom granted in political trials, especially when the charges are considered to be 'serious'.

The security police delivered us personally to Pollsmoor Prison – Cape Town's main prison – not trusting the courts or Prisons Service to do the job. The new section of Pollsmoor to which we were taken had only been completed two years earlier and looked like a huge square fortress. Several floors of tiny slatted windows pock-marked the red exterior wall and at each of the four corners of the block was a tall guard-tower staffed by armed guards.

Spyker and Van Aggenbagh accompanied us into the reception room and then left without any human remark, not even a rude one. Hundreds of black prisoners were sitting in rows on the floor waiting for their turn to be fingerprinted and signed in. Those who had had their fingers done were hustled out of the room by impatient warders. There was much shouting and racist cursing, an ugly apartheid scene being repeated in one of the hundreds of prisons across the country.

We felt like queue jumpers when we were told to go to the head of the queue. But then we were white and no white person was to be made to stand in the same queue as blacks. Not only were we treated more speedily but a pair of subdued warders personally accompanied us through the reception process and the maze of corridors to our 'quarters'.

We had never seen the inside of a prison before. We had certain preconceived ideas about them from seeing American cop-movies, but this was something different: very long corridors stretching into the distance with highly polished floors and along both walls, every two metres or so, large flush-fitting steel doors looking like giant safes in some vast underground bullion vault. The clinical, almost sterile, atmosphere was frightening. It was impossible to imagine how human beings could live in such a place.

This was the awaiting-trial prisoner's section where unsentenced prisoners who had not been granted bail or who could not afford bail were held. At that time there were at least 20,000 such prisoners in custody in South Africa each day, most of them black.

Stephen and I were placed in two completely isolated cells in the section. They were extremely small, even smaller than the police cells we'd been held in while in detention: about 2 metres by 1.5 metres. The cells were bare save for a tiny stainless steel basin on the one wall, a toilet bowl, and a small metal locker fixed to the opposite wall. High in the outer wall was a sealed, vertically-slatted window with frosted glass, and looking into a short corridor was another, smaller, slatted window.

Two prisoners brought us thin rope mats – our beds they informed us – and our bedding. The same two later brought us a 'meal' and asked us why we had been placed in the 'bomb'. At first we thought this meant that we had been placed in special cells set aside for 'bombers' like us. They gave us our first lesson in prisonese: the 'bomb' was an isolation section consisting of three cells used for the punishment of prisoners who had infringed prison regulations. Through the door of the 'bomb' section we could hear the movements of other prisoners. They did not appear to be confined to their cells like us. So, our punishment was to start here, before we had been sentenced.

Although Steve and I could talk to each other through the locked, barred grilles (inner doors) of our cells (the outer steel panelled doors were left open during the day) both of us wondered how we were going to last two months being cooped up in those tiny cells with only half an hour's 'exercise' per day. Admittedly things were not as bad as detention as we were permitted visits from relatives, reading matter, food parcels and could write letters. On the other hand the food was worse and the cells more cramped. In fact the food was so awful that it made us vomit after two or three spoonsful. Everything was boiled in fat and it was as though all the various ingredients had been slung into a giant boiler and cooked for at least six hours. The only way you could distinguish chicken from pork, say, was by the shape of the pieces of bone on which you choked. There was no way of identifying which vegetables, if any, had been thrown into the slop. After eating this swill for a few days both of us refused to eat it any longer and persuaded our parents to bring us salad vegetables and tinned meats which we could turn into relatively respectable meals.

It was hard to believe that black prisoners were much worse off than us as far as food was concerned. There were at that time graded diets according to your 'racial group'. The Prisons Service now claims that such diets have been eliminated and that everyone receives the same diet which is 'prescribed by professional dieticians ... and based on modern requirements for the maintenance of health'. Africans received the worst and least food while 'Coloureds' and Indians received intermediary diets below the Grade I 'white man's diet' that we received. Later we were to see black prisoners being made to squat in the exercise yards while they ate their meals. Their diet appeared to consist mainly of *mielie pap* (maize-meal porridge) with sometimes what could have been a piece of meat floating on top.

At his first visit Stephen's father brought him, amongst other things, the book *Papillon* by Henri Charrière. This is the story of the multiple escapes by the author from the French prison colonies on Devil's Island and in Guyana. Although reputed to be a true story, much of it is too fantastic to be believed. Nonetheless, it is one of the most fascinating books I have ever read and without doubt one which profoundly affected our lives.

Both of us, naturally, had thought about escaping but only in the most reflexive way; *Papillon* set us on the course of seriously considering the prospect. It taught us a number of valuable lessons which guided our thinking and actions in the months ahead. The first and most important of these was that if you want to escape from prison you have to approach the task with single-minded determination. Every moment of every day has to be devoted to observing, planning and preparation. No escape will be successful if it is approached in a half-hearted manner or if you place it below other objectives.

The second lesson was that while lucky breaks do occur, you can't depend on them. You have to plan your way out with obsessive thoroughness, taking into account every conceivable factor. At every point where something may not go according to plan you have to have a contingency plan. While every plan has to take into account the minutest detail it should also be flexible enough to adapt to changes in routine or security that take place.

The third, and most practical lesson, was that an escape does not end once you are beyond the physical confines of your prison. This point boiled down to the fact that if you want to get away from the immediate vicinity of your prison quickly you must have money. Four days in the isolation cells were as much as we could stand.

When the officer-in-charge came around to hear our 'complaints and requests' we asked him why we were being kept apart from the other prisoners and subjected to the punishment of segregation before we had been sentenced. His reply surprised us as we had thought that our separate confinement was something that had been prescribed by the security police or because they feared that we would contaminate the other prisoners with our political ideas. He said that he had thought he was doing us a favour by keeping us apart from the 'scum' as he could see that we were 'decent' people. No, we assured him, we would rather be placed among the other prisoners because we did not wish to be treated differently. He shook his head and went away.

Within an hour we were moved out of the 'bomb' and relocated in cells alongside the 'scum', although next door to the warders' office in the section. Life was more bearable after that. Most of our fellow awaiting-trial prisoners were harmless down-and-outs who in most cases were in prison because they could not afford the bail that had been granted them. One poor fellow had been inside for four months because he could not muster the R2 bail. He'd stolen a blanket from a train.

Some of the other prisoners were out-and-out criminals but interesting to talk to. There was a bloke who had shot his wife with a crossbow, several drug smugglers – one of whom proudly went about displaying the hole between his nostrils caused by sniffing cocaine – some pimps and others who could not explain why they were in prison.

One talkative crook who tried to cultivate our company in order to get at our food told us of the many ingenious methods he had devised to smuggle money out of the country for rich businessmen. On one occasion he hollowed out a pair of cricket pads and re-stuffed them with rolled up banknotes. He flew out of the country with his cricket togs to the accompaniment of well-wishes from the passport controller. On another occasion he cut up the frame of a scrambler motor-cycle, stuffed the tubes with notes and then welded it together again. He crated the bike and had it lifted aboard the ship on which he was travelling to Britain. He explained to customs that he was a member of the team of motor cyclists who were 'going to show the Brits how to ride'. Again he was sent off with the blessings of the authorities. His philosophy was that if you were into smuggling you always had to have a reason for travelling which met with the approval of the authorities. That way there would be no problems.

He was also into fraud. He would hang about the lobbies of large blocks of flats where the post-boxes were situated. After the postman had been he would put his hand into the boxes and feel for credit cards. When he found one he would do a preplanned lightning tour of all the banks in the area where the card was valid and withdraw R50 from each. If he 'hit' 30 banks he could take home R1,500 in a day. He could also buy himself a new wardrobe of clothes and much else besides.

There were many other crooked types who were only too eager to boast about their misdemeanours. Most of them were sordid characters who were incapable of separating fact from fantasy. They could all sense that we not 'ordinary criminals' and at times we had them queueing up to clean our cells in return for favours of tobacco and food.

Visitors were permitted to see us twice a week for half an hour at a time. There was no physical contact and speech was through a telephone intercom. The panes through which prisoner and visitor viewed each other were of thick bullet-proof glass. To demonstrate the strength of the panes the warders were wont to point out the marks on one of the windows caused by a bullet fired at point-blank range.

Usually there was a warder in attendance on the visitors' side but as you sat in a sort of cubicle it was impossible for him to see all the prisoners at the same time. When he was not looking directly at you it was possible to quickly flash up a message written on the palm of your hand or a piece of paper for your visitor to see. This had to be done if you wanted to pass an important or confidential message because conversations through the telephones were recorded. We found this out after my father had read a letter to me during a session when no warder was in attendance. When he left the visiting-room he was severely reprimanded and told that he would be prohibited from visiting me if he did it again. All letters had to be censored first.

Daphne applied for permission to visit me but it was not granted on the grounds that she was a 'Coloured' and could not use the 'whites' visiting room. When I then asked to be able to see her in the 'Coloureds' visiting room I was told that that too was out of the question because white prisoners could not use the 'Coloureds' visiting room. They were not being vindictive – just following the rules.

Awaiting-trial prisoners were not only entitled to receive food, books, newspapers and magazines from outside but could send out their dirty clothes for washing and receive clean clothes in return. This twice-weekly exchange afforded an excellent opportunity to have sent in all manner of contraband and to send out screeds of uncensored written material.

Theoretically you were allowed to write and receive as many letters as you wished. In practice the censorship was so rigid that very few letters got through in either direction. When they did get through they were so cut to pieces or blanked out that alternative methods of communication were inevitably sought. Many of the other prisoners

48

sent out their letters with prisoners going to court but this had its dangers as some of them would report the 'felony' to a warder in order to ingratiate themselves. Stephen and I, after first using the official channel and finding it unsatisfactory, wrote our letters on sheets of toilet paper (*see picture*) and then folded and sewed these into the hems of our trousers to be sent out for washing. Our parents did likewise in the opposite direction. The system was set up by flashing a message during a visit. Thereafter a thumbs-up sign meant there was something being sent in or out in the agreed way.

In this manner we were able to send out letters to many people expressing our true feelings and opinions. I was able regularly to communicate with Robin and thereby pass on to the ANC some of our thoughts about the events leading up to our arrest. My mother or sister would copy out the messages and send them on to her using the false names and addresses I had supplied. They would do the reverse with letters from her.

Food parcels, too, permitted a ceaseless flow of contraband, although in one direction only. The first illicit substance we arranged to have sent in was booze. In one of my toilet paper letters I explained to my parents how to remove the plastic cap of a bottle of orange squash without breaking the seal by holding it in steam. Once it was removed half the squash could be emptied out and replaced with a clear spirit such as gin, vodka or cane spirits. With the cap replaced the same way no one could tell the difference. Twice a week Stephen and I would share our bottle of 'orange juice' and get totally smashed. The feeling of being drunk in front of the warders was exhilarating, to say the least, and also helped us to get through the day.

Most important of all, the food parcels enabled us to smuggle in money. Stephen managed to persuade his parents to send in a large sum – R360 in total. The money was sent in, concealed inside boxes of powdered milk which had been carefully opened and resealed. In *Papillon* the convicts hid their money up their anuses in what they called 'chargers'. These were metal tubes with screw-on lids in which the money was rolled and inserted. Borrowing this idea we 'ordered' a couple of cigars of the sort which come sealed in aluminium tubes. Neither of us smoked but our parents never questioned our requests. The tubes, about 12 cm long, had plastic pop-fit lids which on test under water were prone to leak slightly. To overcome this problem we 'ordered' two rubber sheaths, which were sent in concealed in a packet of sugar.

The money was divided two ways, rolled up, sealed in the sheaths and put into the tubes. These we then shoved up our rectums a la *Papillon*. The first time was the most scary, but with the help of a little Vaseline it went up with ease. In fact it went up so easily that I thought it was going to shoot up my bowels and get stuck somewhere in my guts. I immediately went to the toilet to try to expel it. I expected it to be a hard push and when my bowels worked with such ease I thought the tube had not come out at all. I was really worried, thinking that I would have to call a warder and explain what had happened. But then I spotted a glint in the bowl and realised that it had come out after all. The handling of the object was a bit off-putting at first but we soon overcame our squeamishness. The money remained in place for over three months, until we reached our ultimate destination.

The 'chargers' were the first practical step that we took towards effecting our escape, a step not taken on the off-chance that we might be able to escape—we were definitely going to escape. From the moment we were brought together as awaiting-trial prisoners we made a solemn pledge to each other that we would be out in six months after being sentenced. Our overriding direction of thought after installing the 'chargers' was not towards our defence but towards breaking out.

We did not hide the fact that we intended to escape, but neither did any of the other prisoners. Prisoners, especially when facing probable prison terms, we observed, talked of escaping all the time. Turning that talk into reality, into freedom, was another matter.

Many of our fellow prisoners were people who had already done time and so could relate many stories of escapes, most of them unsuccessful. Two that I remember involved the quick recapture of those involved. Both of them were daring attempts but seemed to be no more than the exploitation of minor cracks in security. Neither contained planning that extended beyond the initial breaking-out phase and were consequently doomed to failure.

One of them took place at Pollsmoor. Two prisoners had managed to find a way onto the roof of the prison, a flat walled area used as an exercise yard, and made a rope of sheets to get over the wall and down the side. The rope must have been very long as the height they had to drop was equivalent that of a five-storey building. The two must have realised that they would be seen by the guards in the watchtowers but must have banked on being able to get away before any recapturing forces could be mustered.

They managed to get over the wall and to the ground before the alarm went off. As the prison building is in the centre of a large complex comprising a number of other prison buildings, warders' houses and facilities, they had nowhere suitable to hide; they were also still dressed in their prison clothing. The two fugitives took refuge in the rafters of a garage belonging to a warder but were soon tracked down by sniffer dogs.

The other escape was more ingenious. Two prisoners in charge of packing dirty laundry to be sent out for washing hid themselves in the baskets and were driven out of the prison to freedom. I do not remember how they were recaptured but their freedom was short-lived. It appears that the attempt was more of an impromptu act than

50

a well planned escape.

The most important lesson gleaned from listening to escape stories was that once you have penetrated the outer barrier of your prison you should get away from the immediate vicinity as quickly as possible. Another point was that you must get as far away as possible in the time that you imagine you have before your escape is discovered. We heard a number of stories of prisoners who had made successful breaks but who had then gone into immediate hiding near their prisons or to whoop it up in the nearest pub. These all led to recapture as the prison staff were able to muster their strongest forces close to the prisons. At any time too there would always be some off-duty warders about who would spot you.

The authorities do not take kindly to escapes. Those who are recaptured not only have their sentences prolonged but have their legs chained together for several months. In true mediaeval style, iron shackles are riveted around the escapees' ankles. The shackles are joined together by a long chain which they have to carry in their hands. Because they can't get their ordinary trousers over the chains they are issued with special ones which consist of front and rear halves that button together up the sides.

A number of bare rooms just off the section were provided for the prisoners to consult with their lawyers. Curiously our first consultations did not take place in these rooms but in an office belonging to the commanding officer of the prison. Why this happened we never found out, but for some reason the warders at Pollsmoor treated us quite differently from the other prisoners, according us more respect. Perhaps they were acting under instructions to show us how well political prisoners were treated?

The office had no barred or frosted windows, affording us sight of the beautiful mountains of the Cape Peninsula. We'd only been cut off from such views for a month and a half, yet we found ourselves already deprived of visual relief. How would we feel after being cut off from the sights of nature for years on end?

Our consultations took place separately as Stephen's parents had appointed a separate advocate to deal with his affairs. It would have made more sense to have had a single legal representative but his parents refused to have anything to do with mine as they believed at the time that I was responsible for their son's plight.

I was bitterly disappointed with my first consultation. The lawyer in charge of my defence gave me the feeling right from the start that he believed I was guilty of the charges and that he could not really defend me, in the sense that he would try to refute the allegations or prove my innocence. All he could do was prevent an outrageous sentence being imposed.

This attitude did not inspire confidence, to say the least. Later consultations, which were held in the normal consultation rooms, were equally disappointing as he continued to display little interest in the specific acts which constituted the 'offences' with which I was being charged. My suspicion that he had very little sympathy for our cause was confirmed when he announced at one session that he thought the best approach would be for me to plead guilty and that he would attempt to play down the significance of the acts.

Foolishly I did not argue the point and even went to great lengths to provide him with information about the leaflet bombs which could be used to prove that they were not bombs in the real sense. I went along with him because he was the legal expert; I was merely being guided by my prejudices and feelings. I did *feel* 'guilty' because in their terms I was, but couldn't help feeling that I should plead not guilty and put the damn police to the bother of having to prove their rotten case down to the last petty detail.

Stephen was having much the same problems with his legal 'help'. He would come back from his consultations each time in a terribly bad mood, swearing that he had to find a better advocate. But his family would have none of it. They wanted no 'political' lawyers near their son and felt insulted that he was rejecting their best efforts to ensure that he was not going to spend the rest of his life in prison.

In retrospect, however, most of the blame must be put down to our attitude toward our trial. We viewed it simply as an obstacle between our state of being awaiting-trial prisoners and our future state as full-blown prisoners – a state we would soon relieve ourselves of by escaping. Both of us were of the opinion that the trial was just going to be a farce, a big 'show trial' – in fact not a trial at all but an occasion for the security police to swagger and boast that another threat to the 'security of the state' (i.e. to white minority rule and privilege) had been tracked down and was soon to be eliminated. We wanted nothing to do with it. They could have their trial, they could score their points, but we would show them in the end.

Politically speaking, it was wrong to adopt such an attitude, as the battle has to be continued at every point of contact, even where it appears futile. This error was not due to a lack of understanding about the nature of the political trials in South Africa: we knew that the courts were used to hide the fact that the 'security laws' actually by-passed normal law; we knew that the courts were used to give legitimacy to state action against its political opponents. Our determination to escape sapped our motivation to make the most of our trial. We also did not wish to offend our parents who believed that they were doing their best for us.

The two months before the trial went by quickly. The jail routine was monotonous but not intolerable. The day began when a warder released his frustrations on a large gong at half past five in the morning. The cells were opened at about seven thirty followed by an inspection and a count of prisoners before breakfast. The warders had great difficulty in performing this count because if they counted each individual prisoner it took too long and they lost count. To speed up the process we were required to stand in twos – then they only had to count half the number. Clever blighters! The only problem was that they were not too good at division and often detected a shortage of prisoners if there was an odd number. This would lead to an alert and a frenzied search for the 'missing' prisoners. When they could not be found a more senior warder would suggest a recount. Any prisoner who laughed was in trouble.

Breakfast consisted most days of *mielie pap*, 'coffee' and a few slices of bread. Stephen and I were never allowed out of the section to fetch our meals but had them brought to us – if we wanted them. The rationale for this, as far as we could work out, was that the kitchens were considered a prime area for smuggling. Food and other supplies were brought in daily by outsiders and perhaps they thought we were so devious that we would be able to open a channel there. If only they knew that we'd already opened a channel. . .

The mornings were set aside for cleaning cells, passages and ourselves. At about eleven everyone was taken out to one of the prison's internal courtyards for an hour's 'exercise'. Some people played soccer but most just lay against a wall and soaked up the fading autumn sunshine. Stephen and I did not accept the midday meal and instead put together our own meals from the food brought to us by our parents. After the midday meal we were locked up for the afternoon, alone or with more than two people per cell: two people might get up to something 'unsavoury'. Most of the time we spent reading, playing chess or just chatting. At about 4 pm the cells were opened and the prisoners let out to fetch their evening meal. This normally consisted of a sort of thickened liquid which they said was 'soup', a brown liquid alleged to be 'coffee' and bread smeared with a disgusting pink jelly.

At four thirty the prisoners were locked in their individual cells for the night and after eight they were supposed to keep quiet. The long evening hours gave you the most wonderful opportunity to read those books you'd always wanted to read – such as Tolstoy's *War and Peace* – but for which you'd never had the time. To overcome the boredom Steve and I would sometimes remove the water from our toilet bowls so that we could talk to each other through the pipes. The sound carried remarkably well and we were able, after we'd each acquired a chess set, to play the game late into the night. The lights were never switched off so you could go to sleep whenever you wished, although official bedtime was 11 pm.

The straw mats which were our beds were rolled out on the floor. They were required to be immaculately made in the morning and not slept on during the day. As with most things over which you have no choice, you soon got used to your 'bed' despite it being extremely hard and cold on the concrete floor.

The cells were almost completely inhospitable. The tiny hand-basin was practically useless except as something on which to stand to look out of the window. The tap operated by pushing a knob, but as there was no plug in the basin it was almost impossible to wash yourself as one hand had to keep the knob depressed. And when you pressed it the plumbing throughout the whole prison would judder and make the most frightful noise. For this reason hardly anyone used their taps at night and instead drew their water from their toilets. These were flushed by pressing a button on the floor with your foot, sending endless torrents of water into the bowl. Everything, including plates and bodies, was washed in toilet bowls and after you had overcome your inhibitions they also became the main source of drinking water. It seemed a shame to have to use them for other purposes.

We were sustained through the two months before our trial by the visits, bottles of laced orange squash, illicit letters, newspapers and the determination not to stay in prison longer than was absolutely necessary. Our morale sagged a little at times but a sudden flood of solidarity letters that arrived in our last days cheered us no end. The letters came from Britain–the result of our 'Defence Committee's' good work. They proved to us that we were not forgotten, as had been alleged by the security police, and that people far away were concerned about our plight. The authorities must have realised this too, for after a few days the flood dried up as suddenly as it had begun. No matter how much we pleaded they insisted that there were no more letters and took offence at our suggestions that they were deliberately withholding them.

We had not yet got used to our powerlessness.

5
Trial

Our appearance in the Cape Town Supreme Court on the 1st of June was a bit of an anticlimax. We'd had our best clothes sent in, geared ourselves mentally for the start of the trial, and then nothing happened. No charges were read out, we were not asked to plead and the case was postponed to the 6th of June. Why, we never found out. The judge mumbled something, our advocates acknowledged him in some kind of bookies' code and we were led off to the cells below the court and then driven back to Pollsmoor. Quite clearly we were still remanded in custody.

On the 6th of June the same thing happened, but the court had an altogether different appearance. The spectators' gallery was packed with people, many of them friends. At least 15 senior security police were present and at the front of the court a mountain of exhibits: the recovered leaflet bombs, the banner, piles of leaflets and envelopes all neatly tied together with string, steel trunks, tool-boxes, banned 'communist' books, cardboard boxes, typewriters, the duplicator, and sundry items of furniture, bedding and kitchenware. A toaster took pride of place on top of the trunks.

Our parents were allowed to sit on the benches immediately in front of the dock, enabling us to chat to them before the trial started. My mother eyed the piles of exhibits and said: 'What's my bedspread doing there? And my kitchen chair? And my . . . ? So that's where my other toaster got to.' She had forgotten that she had lent me the items or thought I had been using them in my 'above-ground' flat.

A fat charge sheet with two detailed schedules was made available. It listed the activities which comprised the 'offences' we had allegedly committed as well as each incidence of dissemination of leaflets – by post and leaflet bomb. Ten different leaflets distributed by post and seven spread by leaflet bomb were mentioned. Twenty six leaflet bombs were listed as well as one banner.

Again the charges were not put and we were not asked to plead. The State Prosecutor, Tielman Louw, applied for a postponement to the next day because, he said, there were matters to be 'straightened out' between the State and the defence. The defence agreed to the postponement. We were never told what these 'matters' were but the easy agreement between the two sides made us feel uneasy, as if they were colluding in our prosecution. The court was dismissed after a few minutes and we were taken back to Pollsmoor.

In London meanwhile – although not to our knowledge at the time – a picket organised by our Defence Committee was being held outside the South African Embassy to demand our release and the release of all South African political prisoners. Hundreds of leaflets were handed out to passers-by giving details of our case.

Such actions are widely appreciated by political trialists and prisoners. When they get to hear of them morale is raised to a high level as they are reminded that they are not forgotten and that people far away are concerned with their plight and fighting for them.

After breakfast on the 7th, as happened the previous times, they marched us out of the awaiting-trial section to a sort of internal garage in the prison where several armoured prison vans were parked ready to take the prisoners to court. The two of us were locked in a special compartment toward the front of a van and separately from the other prisoners – we were not to be allowed to contaminate them.

At the court the procedure was the reverse. The van passed through a set of very solid gates into a yard at the side of the court. First the black prisoners were removed and then we were briskly led through a couple of sets of heavily barred grilles and into a small cell below the courtrooms.

The cell was without windows and a weak yellow light lit the room which was empty save for a slop bucket and a narrow bench along one wall. The walls reminded us of the interior of an Egyptian tomb, covered from floor to ceiling in graffiti, drawings, verse and nonsense. Since there was nothing else to do we scanned the walls: 'Fifteen years for rape – Mogamoet' . . . 'I was here for shit' . . . 'Sweet Lord have mercy' . . . 'I love you Mary, I didn't mean it' . . . As we read this pitiful record left behind by countless victims of the racist legal system we spotted in a hole in the wall a tiny stub of a pencil. A trap! we thought. They must want us to write revolutionary slogans on the walls so they can charge us with more offences – we're not falling for that one, oh no! But what the hell! If they want to charge us further, that's OK. We're going to escape so it doesn't matter! Stephen extracted the pencil and with much delight drew a huge hammer and sickle above the door, urging the workers of the world to unite! Wherever else there were gaps we boldly wrote in ANC slogans.

After an hour in the dungeon we were driven upstairs and seated in the dock. When the judge entered an orderly shouted *'Staan in die hof!'* – 'Stand up in court!' – but we had decided that there would be no standing for us: standing meant recognising the legitimacy of the court. Our tardy arousal was met with agitated prods in the back and angry shouts from another orderly: *'Staan op!, Staan op!'* – 'Stand up!, Stand up!' Slowly we lifted ourselves, realising that it would not be productive to refuse to stand each time.

Along with the judge, Acting Justice Nel, entered two assessors – the South African equivalent of a jury. There is no trial by jury in South Africa and in most cases only a judge is present. Assessors are obliged to be present when the death sentence might be imposed. In our case this was a possibility and provided for under the Terrorism Act. At that time when assessors were present they were not allowed to decide on any questions of law but final judgements were based on a majority decision. This has now changed slightly.

We looked at these honourable gentlemen as they occupied their positions on the bench and could not help wondering where South African courts had got their reputation for being impartial and independent? Here were three so-called legal experts about to interpret what we had done in terms of a law which was so obviously political and partisan and which overturned the normal legal principle that you are innocent until proved guilty. The onus was going to be on us to prove that our actions were not intended to have any of the effects of 'terrorism' (i.e. virtually any anti-state activity) – we were guilty and had to prove that we were innocent. By willingly sitting there these gentlemen were saying that they agreed with the law they were to apply, that they believed they were about to dispense 'justice'.

The charges were read out by the prosecution and we were asked to plead. Before either of us could respond to the judge's call our 'defence' leapt to their respective feet and declared that they would be doing the pleading for us. This seemed out of order to us, but how were we to know? My advocate managed to get the first word in, telling the court that the defence was 'purely technical' in that there had been an improper duplication of charges etc., and that therefore I was guilty on count one, namely, of 'taking part in terrorist activities', but not guilty on count two, which alleged contravention of the Internal Security Act. Stephen's advocate pleaded for him in much the same way. So that was it: we had no say. We looked at each other in disbelief but not knowing what we could do just shrugged our shoulders.

State Prosecutor Louw handed in a list of exhibits to the judge – 'because there were a rather large number of them' – and announced that he would be calling five policemen and a 'Mr X' for the State, whose name 'for security reasons' would not be published.

Spyker van Wyk was the first state witness to be called. He told the court that his investigations began on 10 December 1975, being on that first occasion an investigation into the distribution of subversive pamphlets through the post. He went on to detail each pamphlet intercepted and each leaflet bomb his team had to investigate. He gave the number of pamphlets intercepted in the post each time and the number of leaflets recovered after each leaflet bomb.

This was of great interest to us as it gave some indication of the effectiveness of our distributions and of their counter-actions. Of the first three mailings only a handful of pamphlets ended up in their hands – in one case no more than two. Most of these were probably ones they had intercepted on the way to several banned people who were on our mailing list; others were handed in by people who had received them. Admittedly our mailing list held only a few hundred names on those first mailings but it showed that the police had no regular methods of detecting or intercepting the posted matter. After the first three mailings the number which they intercepted increased more and more rapidly until the last one, of which they intercepted about 80 per cent. Our conclusion was that our failure regularly to change our addressing system had made it easy for them to identify the envelopes and our failure to post from other centres permitted them to keep a small number of sorting offices in one area permanently on the alert.

The details also belied police claims that they had recovered most of the leaflets after leaflet bombings. The most that were ever recovered was 272; on average they only found about eighty. An 'expert' who later appeared told the court that a leaflet bomb – or 'ideological bombs' as they called them – could only lift 300 leaflets. We were sorry to disappoint them, but the number was always 500 – one ream.

Spyker claimed that the police had kept us under observation from 22 February 1978, the date of our last posting. This was highly unlikely as it would have been too much of a coincidence that they just happened to start watching us on the day we decided to do a posting. Our suspicion was that they had been watching us for much longer – what about all the strange phonecalls and suspicious characters? – and knew when we were about to do the posting. How otherwise could they have intercepted practically all the pamphlets of that posting?

Our defence responded to Spyker's testimony with some pathetic cross-questioning about the nature of 'real terrorists'. The point they were trying to get across to the court was that we were not 'terrorists' in the normal sense of the word and that our cell did not have the usual aim of 'terrorist cells' which is sabotage. Spyker responded that our activities during a period of unrest would, in his opinion, have had 'a helluva effect'.

The next day a police 'explosives expert', a Major J G van Tonder of the police bomb-disposal unit, gave details of the components, construction and working of the leaflet bombs. The 26 'ideological bombs' were 'neatly built, the work of a perfectionist' and made by someone 'obviously proud of his work'. In a cool and informed manner he held up one of the 'bombs' and described to the court how the parts fitted together, how the timing mechanism worked and how the platform shot the leaflets into the air when the explosive was detonated. Anyone in the spectator gallery would have been sufficiently informed to go home and make their own. Van Tonder spoke about the books on explosives that had been found in our trunks. He was convinced, he said, that our knowledge of explosives and detonators had been obtained from these books. Why then had they interrogated us about our training, we wondered.

In characteristic manner our defence attempted to get the court to view the leaflet bombs not as 'real bombs' but rather as harmless little 'leaflet launchers' – kind of Jack-in-the-boxes. Under cross-examination Van Tonder had to concede that the 'bombs' would not have damaged property or harmed anyone. One of the assessors awoke from his slumbers at this point and commented with raised finger that as far as he could see the leaflet bombs were not much more dangerous than a large firecracker. My advocate thought he had scored a major victory; we were not impressed.

And so it went on for several days. One state witness, a Lieutenant Deon Greyling of the police bomb-disposal unit, told how one of the 'bombs' had gone off in his hands while he was attempting to defuse it. Unfortunately the point he was trying to make – that the leaflet bombs were dangerous and unpredictable devices – backfired on him as he was forced to admit to the judge that he had not been harmed. The monster Van Aggenbagh displayed to the court the mailing lists and addressing equipment that we had used. The police had printed out all the names using our addressing machine to confirm that they corresponded to the envelopes they had intercepted in the post. Sure enough they did. He proudly demonstrated the piles of letters that had been intercepted, intimating that he personally was responsible for stopping the material from spreading to its unsuspecting victims and thereby had prevented a revolutionary situation from developing.

On one of the mornings my parents brought my prison food parcel to the court and it was handed to me in the cell below the court before the day's proceedings started. The bottle of laced orange squash was there as usual so we thought we'd have a little swig before being called up. Of course the swig turned into a drinking party and in no time the entire bottle was polished off. Everyone must have wondered why we sat in court that day with contented smiles on our faces!

As the morning dragged on nature had its revenge, pressurising us to ask one of the court orderlies standing behind us for permission to visit the toilet. He reminded us that the accused had to be present in court and that if we wanted to leave the room the trial would have to be adjourned. Being too embarrassed to expose our simultaneous need before all those people, there was nothing we could do but cross our legs and hope they would not carry on for too long.

A big-shot from security police headquarters in Pretoria, a Colonel Broodryk, testified on publications of the ANC and South African Communist Party (SACP). He was the 'expert' on 'communism' and banned organisations such as the ANC and SACP, one of whom usually appears in South African political trials. The racists are of the opinion, at least at the propaganda level, that every manifestation of resistance against apartheid is the result of a communist plot. Basically, they believe, blacks are happy with their lot and if they raise their voices against apartheid it is only because the Kremlin has sent its dupes to incite them for extraneous political purposes. Colonel Broodryk went to pains to stress the point that we were either witting or unwitting agents of 'Russia' – they've not heard of the Soviet Union – and that the ANC was no more than a front for the Communist Party.

He explained that our activities, most of which took place during the period of the 'Soweto uprisings' starting on June 16th 1976, could only have served to fan the fires of revolt. The implication was almost that we had been responsible for the events of that time and were a major factor behind the 'riots'. Our defence objected that he was exaggerating the consequences of our activities because the number of pamphlets we had disseminated increased many fold after 1976 and had in fact corresponded to a decrease in unrest.

Colonel Broodryk was called again by the State to support an application for the identity of the next witness, Mr X, not to be revealed. He said that in the past state witnesses testifying in similar trials had been threatened and in some cases assassinated. A quotation was read from one of our leaflets which supported his point: 'Smash the traitors and stooges – we shall harass the enemy, its police and its spies.' At least they were admitting that Mr X was a traitor and stooge.

The courtroom was cleared of spectators, the press and our parents before Mr X was brought through a back door of the court to the witness stand. He eyed the court like a frightened dog to make sure no one would recognise him and then stood to attention to obey his masters' instructions. He began his pitiful tale of how he had gone to Maputo to seek work. There he had been press-ganged by the ANC to join its 'terrorist wing' (Umkhonto we Sizwe). From Maputo he was sent to Tanzania where he claimed he had fraternised with the ANC leadership. Oliver Tambo, the President of the ANC, and Joe Slovo, the alleged mastermind behind all communist plots against South Africa, he knew well. So far Mr X had got his lines right.

From Tanzania he claimed to have been sent to Russia where he was taught 'terrorism': how to make bombs and shoot with an AK-47 rifle. In Russia he had also learnt to speak Russian. We were surprised when he did not reveal that he was mates with Brezhnev. Next he was sent to Angola where he was given explosives, guns and money. From there he was infiltrated back into South Africa through Botswana, but as soon as he got into the country he realised that what he was doing was futile and that he could not beat the police. He suddenly 'saw the light' and as a responsible citizen gave himself up and handed in his weapons. Now he was working for the police and making life better for his people that way!

The story was so transparent and close to the usual propaganda tale that it was doubtful whether Mr X was taken seriously by the judge and assessors. It was no wonder that his testimony was given *in camera* as the press would have made mincemeat of it. However, the point of the appearance was merely to emphasise to the court the State's contention that the ANC was really just a gang of nasties and that all its operatives were acting in the interests of Russia and not in the interests of South Africa's black population.

I wrote on a slip of paper the words 'I do not understand Russian' in Russian and handed it to my advocate with a note asking him to give it to Mr X to test whether he could actually speak and read Russian as he'd claimed. But he felt that such a step would not be necessary as he believed the judge did not accept Mr X's story. This was probably true, for when the judge asked Mr X to tell him what the devices in front of him were used for (the leaflet bombs), Mr X, after contemplating the objects for a good few minutes, replied that they were for 'demolishing installations'. He was promptly hustled out the door from which he'd appeared. I wonder if he was awarded the few pennies he'd been promised.

The day following Mr X's testimony there was a lot of whispering from the galleries below. Apparently some new 'evidence' had turned up and the State wanted to make another point before closing their case. Before announcing the new 'evidence' Prosecutor Louw summarised the State's case and argued for our conviction on the grounds that we had admitted to preparing the documents before the court, posting them and constructing and placing the leaflet bombs. He selected and read out the most juicy quotations from the leaflets to show that we had without doubt incited people to commit acts promoting the aims and objects of unlawful organisations. Needless to say he was not impressed by our 'literature' and considered it to be bordering on treason. One leaflet dealing with the defeat of the apartheid army in Angola in 1975 he called a 'poisonous bit of literature'. Clearly he was a victim of the propaganda which turned the racist army's defeat into a victory.

And then he announced the new 'evidence': a letter I had written (to Robin) had been intercepted in the post. The letter contained sure evidence that I was not the least bit remorseful for my conduct, pre-empting what they assumed would be the strategy of the defence which was due to present its case next.

The letter was one I had smuggled out in my prison washing and had been rewritten by my mother. I had written the letter in Robin's name because my mother had informed me that a friend of hers was going to Britain and would post it there. But at the last moment the friend had postponed the journey and could not take the letter. Not understanding the dangers of doing so and in good faith my mother put the letter in the post. It might not have been intercepted had she not also enclosed a bunch of press clippings of the trial.

My mother, naturally, felt terrible and started to blame herself for ruining my chances and for probably adding many years to my sentence. I tried to console her by explaining that the letter was but a mere pinprick compared to what I was being tried for and would not adversely affect the judge's opinion. It was just the State trying to score a political point. I'm not sure if she understood.

Having made its points the State closed its case. Our defence declared that it was not calling any witnesses to lead evidence in answer to the charges and thereby closed the defence case. Then followed a lot of legal nonsense. Something about duplication of charges, something else about the two charges being the same transaction showing the same intention etc., etc.

Stephen and I had indicated to our legal 'advisers' that we wanted to be called to answer the charges but they thought that our doing so would only worsen our case. They were not interested in political statements and were only concerned with ensuring that we received the minimum sentences. Politics, slogans and raised fists would only annoy the judge and add years to our sentences.

Instinctively both of us felt that it would look bad if we made no political comment at all. Although we knew that we were no longer allowed to make statements from the dock, we felt that they could have thought of some way to get us up front. It was not that we wanted our words recorded for posterity, it was just that we had the psychological need to say something. We could not go through a whole trial without uttering a single word as if we no more relevant to the case than the wood panelling on the walls.

Unfortunately, as I've already explained, our desire to escape left us insufficiently motivated to press the point and resist our lawyers' appeals for moderation. We should have known from our studies of political trials that length of sentence is not determined so much by what you say in court but mainly by legal precedent. If someone else before you got x years for doing more or less the same things and that had not served to deter you then your sentence was calculated by the formula $x + 20$ per cent of x.

The trial was postponed for a few days after the two sides had closed their cases. When the court reassembled, the State Prosecutor summarised the State's case: From 1st August 1975 to 2nd March 1978 the accused did 'wrongfully, unlawfully and with intent to endanger the maintenance of law and order in the Republic' commit certain acts. These were listed in detail: so many pamphlets sent through the post, so many leaflets disseminated by leaflet bombs, and the displaying of an ANC banner.

To prove that the pamphlets and leaflets had or would have had one or more of the all-embracing effects of 'terrorism' as defined by the Terrorism Act, long sections of most of our publications were read out in the court. This went some way towards helping us overcome our shame of not having said anything to the court – they were doing it for us. We felt proud of what was being read out to the large crowd gathered there, although we knew that it could not be reported in the press. Nonetheless, many people heard the message and that was what was important.

The State's object was to prove that by the dissemination of the documents, we had 'without doubt incited, instigated and encouraged others to commit acts to promote the aims and objects of the ANC, the SACP and Umkhonto we Sizwe'. This object they achieved, for immediately afterwards Acting Justice Nel pronounced his verdict: both guilty on count one and not guilty on count two. The not guilty verdict on count two was a purely technical matter relating to duplication of convictions, or something.

We were now statutory terrorists!

After judgement Prosecutor Nel took centre stage again and asked the court to impose a 'heavy sentence' on both of us but a particularly heavy sentence in my case as I was the 'leading figure' in the events that led to the trial. He described the offences as 'very serious indeed' and as amounting to high treason. Treason! Taking part in a struggle that has the support of the majority of the people and against a system of society that has been declared a crime against humanity, is treason? These servants of apartheid are the traitors; they're the ones who are really guilty.

The court was handed over to the defence to call witnesses to give evidence in mitigation. My advocate in his opening speech reiterated that we were not 'terrorists' in the 'ordinary sense of the word'. We had to be sentenced for what had been set out in the indictment, and 'this boiled down to pamphleteering and nothing else.' The pamphlets contained 'crude political claptrap' which did not call for specific acts of violence and for the most part 'fell on deaf ears'. The word 'bomb' was an emotive word and inappropriate to describe the devices exhibited.

While agreeing that he had to play down the significance of the pamphlets, this was going too far. We were proud of those damned pamphlets and took offence at the crude insults of someone who was supposed to be on our side.

The first witness to be called was a cousin of mine who was a psychiatrist at a Cape Town hospital. He was persuaded to plead on my behalf at the last moment because my lawyers thought it would not be a good idea to call my father in the light of the intercepted letter posted by my mother. Initially several people, including my boss from ISD, had offered to give evidence on my behalf but when it became clear what the charges were about they all got cold feet. That left only my father.

The cousin was a total embarrassment. He explained in his psychiatrist's jargon that my 'burning desire to help the underprivileged' was the result of a 'personality defect'. The 'extreme views' which I 'vehemently held' were common among insecure people who sought social security. As my personality needs changed so my views would 'settle' and, presumably, I would then be cured of this affliction and revert to being a 'normal', apathetic, racist white South African.

What an insult! So your beliefs and actions spring from dark psychic and emotional sources and have nothing to do with any genuine political motives; to throw in your lot with the oppressed and join the struggle against apartheid is an illness, a perversion, abnormal.

Thank goodness I only had one 'witness'. Poor Stephen had to contend with both his parents, a Roman Catholic chaplain and a family friend. The parental plea was shameful. Stephen's father explained that as a young lad Stephen was sent to boarding school because he was in danger of becoming a 'softy'. At university he was corrupted by the 'left-wing radical element' and his previously strong religious views were destroyed. The anti-capitalist tendencies he picked up there were expected to wear off and appeared to do so as he matured. But this never really happened as he merely began to harbour his views secretly. Stephen was 'over-anxious to please whatever group he found himself in and adopted the attitudes and mores of any group in which he found himself in order to be popular'. Stephen's normally ruddy complexion turned bright red; he could not lower his head far enough below the dock railing.

The very strong implication in his father's plea was that I was the ring-leader and had influenced Stephen to break the law. Mr Lee finished with an impassioned plea for leniency as a long sentence would turn his son into a 'hardened, bigoted terrorist'.

The other witnesses pushed much the same line: Stephen was basically a decent sort of bloke who used to attend mass regularly but who had been corrupted by others because he was an idealist and easily influenced. By the end Stephen's face had turned bright scarlet. The security police must have been laughing in their jackboots.

Sentence was passed on the 15th of June. The judge's summing up was brief: Accused number one had carried on his illegal activities for two years and seven months and accused number two for about two years; In that time they prepared and disseminated different seventeen different pamphlets with the clear intent of undermining law and order; They were mindful of what they were doing and of what sentences others who had engaged in similar activities had received; There was no evidence that accused number two felt any remorse for his conduct while it was obvious from the intercepted letter that accused number one was wholly unrepentant. Without a pause or change in tone of voice he sentenced me to twelve years' imprisonment and Stephen to eight.

That was it. All over. The court turned to see our response, but it had not registered. I could hear the words 'twelve years' ringing in my ears but could not associate them with myself. I swore at the judge under my breath and looked at Stephen. He was looking at me. Suddenly we were grabbed from behind and jostled down the stairs by abusive orderlies; we were *bandiete*, prisoners, and cluttering the court. We had not even been able to raise our fists in defiance or shout a slogan. Our reticence was partly influenced by the adjurations of our lawyers not to do such things after being sentenced as they would only jeopardise our chances of appealing against the sentences.

In the cells below, the two of us felt sick. Not because of the sentences just imposed upon us, but because we'd failed to raise our fists and shout *Amandla!*–'Power!'–as is fitting and proper for political prisoners to do when sentenced. Why had we succumbed to the appeals of our lawyers?

The security police graciously permitted us a few brief moments with our families to say good-bye. Weeping mothers were consoled and the hands of shocked brothers, sisters and fathers shaken. It was an unhappy scene as we all knew that it would be a long time before we'd be able to see each other again without physical barriers between us. It would also be a long time before the two of us would be able to have physical contact with a loved one. I tried to cheer my mother by saying that we'd soon be out because we were going to escape, but it was the wrong moment. She feared that we would be caught and then our sentences would be prolonged and she would not be able to bear the consequences. I assured her that it was only 'prisoner-talk'; I would do nothing foolish.

To make sure that our valuable 'chargers' stayed in place in case we were immediately carted off to Pretoria where we expected to be sent, I relieved my mother of her supply of aspirins which we swallowed to make ourselves constipated.

The cops called an end to the sad little party and cleared the cell. They handcuffed our hands behind our backs and led us out to the awaiting police cars–they were taking no chances that we would defiantly raise our fists to the eager press photographers waiting outside.

The security police accompanying us back to Pollsmoor feigned surprise at the severity of our sentences but couldn't refrain from remarking that we should have expected what we got. Why had we done it? Just look how we had ruined our lives now. Couldn't we see how much the government was doing for the blacks–more than the ANC could ever do!

The money-filled torpedoes in our guts gave reassurance at that heart-sinking time.

Now we were real prisoners and joining the more than one hundred and twenty thousand others who daily inhabit South Africa's prisons. It has been said that South Africa has the highest per capita prison population in the world. From corner to corner the country is criss-crossed by a network of prisons, filled mostly with the victims of apartheid. There are very few black South Africans who do not at some time visit one of these institutions for having infringed one of the multitude of apartheid laws that govern their lives.

Included in the one hundred and twenty thousand are the hundreds of political prisoners who officially do not exist. The regime claims that there are no political prisoners in South Africa, only what it calls 'security prisoners'. These it says are ordinary criminals who have been found guilty in the courts of law for crimes against the security of the state. In practice, however, they are forced to recognise the existence of a group of prisoners who are different from other prisoners. These prisoners are kept strictly apart from all others and have their lives governed by a different set of regulations from those applied to ordinary prisoners.

The attitude that met us in the prison reception office was completely different from what we had experienced up to then. No longer were we unconvicted prisoners who could demand a modicum of respect; we were now prison property and they were free to do with us as they wished. After signing our names in a register we were told to remove our clothes and hand in all possessions for safe-keeping. The warder in charge pointed to a pile of rags on the floor and told us to get dressed. The rags were our 'uniforms' and probably the cast-offs of some prisoners who had just been released. The shoes were four sizes too big, the shirt and trousers about double my size. Too bad, you'll just have to get used to them.

Fortunately they did not search us as they do black prisoners who become convicted prisoners: they are forced to dance the 'thawusa', an undignified naked leap into the air with legs apart to show that they have nothing concealed up their rectums. This does not happen to white prisoners, especially those considered to be 'respectable' prisoners as we were.

First task – haircuts. A large, brutal-looking convict found much pleasure running a pair of clippers through our hair. He left only stubble. Stephen's beard was shorn off like sheep's wool and he was made to remove the rest of it with an implement that he did not know how to use – a razor. When they'd finished he looked like a young boy.

We were shoved into large adjacent cells that were completely bare. In mine some workmen had been welding closed the windows that looked onto the passage and the area surrounding the plumbing below the two sinks in the one corner. The workmen had obviously taken a break as their tools were still lying about and the job had not been completed. Out of curiosity I looked below the sinks to see why they were welding there. The space was ideal for hiding things and it appeared that they were removing the wooden panelling which formerly covered the area and replacing it with sheet metal. As I looked closer my eye suddenly caught sight of a glint from the pool of water that had collected in the concrete surround below one of the sinks. I put my hand through a gap in the panelling and grabbed hold of a heavy metal object. It was a large hand-made dagger, complete with leather sheath. I put my hand in again and pulled out another, and another, and another – five in all.

The knives were beautifully crafted and had obviously just been hidden there by the prisoners who had been turfed out of the cell to make way for me. I quickly hid them in the metal lockers attached to the wall. The welders returned after a short while and completed their job. An hour later a bed, a real bed with a foam-rubber mattress, was brought in by a gang of Coloured prisoners. They must have wondered who this *lanie* – white guy – was who was getting a real bed, alone in a ten-person cell.

The next day when the head of the prison looked in on his inspection round I beckoned him toward the lockers. I opened one, took out a dagger and placed it in his hand. He stared at it speechless. The sergeant in charge of the two of us, who was standing behind the chief, stood there completely stunned with his mouth hanging wide open. The chief rebuked him for not searching the cell properly but he swore that he had checked all the lockers. I assured the chief that the cell had not been properly checked and to prove my point I went to the second locker and took out the second dagger. The sergeant's mouth dropped even further open. The chief became agitated and asked if there were any more. I opened the third locker and removed the next one and then the fourth and the fifth. The sergeant just stood there not believing what he was seeing. How could he have missed five large daggers in five separate lockers?

I gently reminded the chief that he had to be careful of us 'terrorists' as he could not tell what we'd get up to with a set of daggers. No, he assured me, they trusted us and did not believe we would use daggers in the prison, only *skollies* – delinquents – did that. To cap it all, the sergeant immediately launched another search of the cell and found a sharpened spoon hidden on a ledge inside one of the lockers which I myself had missed. I was surprised that he was allowed to keep his job after that.

The incident shook our minders so much that every day after that the sergeant came into both our cells and tapped every bar, window frame and pane of glass with a little hammer to check that we were not cutting our way out. Every hem of each sheet, blanket and item of clothing was checked and the lockers, especially, checked for dangerous weapons. They could not underestimate the deviousness of us 'terrorists'.

They kept us in those cells for about two weeks before transporting us to Pretoria. It was a lonely period much like being in solitary confinement. We saw each other for only half an hour a day when taken for exercise on the roof of the prison. Otherwise we could not communicate. Our toilet pipes did not connect and our outer cell doors were kept locked. We thought of developing a code so that we could tap messages on the wall between our cells like prisoners did during the war but then decided it was too romantic. In any case we would soon be together and then we could talk as much as we wished.

As newly-sentenced prisoners we were allowed only one visit by one person for half an hour per month, which we both took in those two weeks. At his visit Stephen's father brought the bad news that the regime had just announced that it was to introduce a new set of currency notes. This meant that after a time the notes we had just smuggled in would no longer be legal tender. It was as if they knew we had the money and had deliberatly decided to change it so that ours would be rendered useless!

There were of course no more food parcels and no way of smuggling in any more contraband. The only 'entertainment' permitted during those weeks was three books that were brought to us from the prison library each week. The rest of the time we spent having showers or just pacing madly round and round our oversized cells.

The trip to Pretoria was a nightmare that we'll never forget. Without prior notice they told us late one afternoon to pack our few things. This was no reason to suspect that we were about to be taken away; a move to other cells seemed more likely. The issuing of a blanket and a brown paper bag containing two pieces of dried-out chicken, two boiled eggs and a few slices of bread confirmed that something more significant than a change of cells was about to take place. They led us through the administrative section and, very curiously, out of the front door of the prison to an armoured prison van parked in the street outside.

Each of us had a long chain shackled between our ankles and then they pointed to an open door at the rear of the van. We looked through the door and thought that they were pointing to something they wanted us to get out of the tiny compartment behind it. No, we were to get in. We looked at them disbelievingly, thinking that they were playing a game with us. No human being could surely be expected to travel all the way from Cape Town to Pretoria in a tool locker! *'Nee! Dis jou plek. Klim in!'* – 'No! It's your place. Get in!'

Against the back wall of the compartment was a narrow ledge on which we were meant to sit and at neck height a square metal tank with sharp edges protruded beyond the ledge, making it impossible to sit up straight. The door was slammed shut and we could hear them locking padlocks on the outside. There was barely sufficient space to turn around and to make matters worse there were two large milk-churns on the floor: one containing fresh water and the other nothing. Presumably the empty one was for relieving ourselves. From the main compartment of the van we could hear the voices and chains of other prisoners.

The van set off immediately and through a small chink in the door we could see that we were being followed by a small Prisons Service panel van. The sun was beginning to set but against the red winter sky we could still see the beautiful outline of Table Mountain. Both of us sadly acknowledged that it would be a long time before we saw that sight again.

As it grew darker it became colder. It was midwinter and we knew that our route to Pretoria, if indeed that was where we were being taken, passed through the Karroo, the dry central plain of South Africa, which becomes bitterly cold at night. Temperatures often drop to well below zero. We sat close to each other for warmth and wrapped ourselves in the single blankets we'd been given. They were not very effective in keeping out the cold as above us in the roof was a ventilator that blew a stream of cold air directly onto us. To make matters worse the water in the milk-churn splashed over the brim every time the van braked, cornered or accelerated and in no time our blankets and clothing were dripping wet. The problem was partially solved by removing some of the water with the metal dixies we had been allowed to bring along.

The cold became so intense that I felt like vomiting. Stephen developed diarrhoea and was forced to use the churn directly in front of me. With one hand he had to prevent his 'charger' discharging into the depths of the churn and with the other he had to grip onto the cabin's framework to prevent himself falling over. He was most embarrassed but I assured him I was out of the room under my blanket.

The van travelled very fast and stopped a number of times at distant police outposts, but the prisoners were never allowed out to stretch their aching limbs. Several times I almost knocked myself unconscious on the sharp edge of the water tank above our heads as the van lurched from side to side. On through that icy night a van-full of frozen prisoners were crying out.

It didn't warm significantly for a long time after sunrise. By that time our bodies were racked with the intense pain of sitting in that cramped space coiled up in a ball to conserve warmth. The van stopped for an hour at a prison somewhere where the drivers and guards got out – probably to stuff their pot-bellies with hot breakfast and morning coffee. The prisoners got nothing. Then on and on it went and Stephen's stomach grew worse and worse. He began to worry if he would ever get his 'charger' back in place.

After midday the van passed through Johannesburg and sped on to Pretoria. We wondered where they would eventually deposit us. All long-term white male prisoners usually first went to Pretoria Central Prison for assessment. From there they were sent to other prisons depending on the nature of their crimes. Would they send us there or would we be offloaded immediately at the special prison for white male political prisoners?

PART TWO: GETTING OUT

6
We Meet the Comrades

It was to be Pretoria Prison, 'New European Section'—the special prison for politicals. We thanked our stars they were not taking us to Pretoria Central; we couldn't face another bout of solitary. And we had a prison to get out of.

When they opened the back of that prison van and we dismounted, uncrinkling ourselves from being cooped up in that damp, icy cage, we immediately felt that something was strange, at least as far as our limited prison experience could inform us. At Pollsmoor most boarding and alighting of prison vehicles had been done inside the prison, behind massive steel doors. Now we didn't appear to be in a prison at all. We were standing in a street exposed to all the world and in front of us stood a building that did not look very much like a prison at all. True, there was a high wall to our left but in front of us was a door, a varnished wooden door, which would not have looked out of place in any suburban home. There were no barred windows or other signs that the building we were about to enter was a prison.

Two warders received us in the street. The chains were unshackled and thrown back into the compartment out of which we'd just emerged. The sunshine felt marvellous on our frozen bodies and pale faces. They led us through the front door of the building, which wasn't even locked, but once inside we could see that indeed it was a prison. In front of us was a long passage with a great number of metal grilles across it. The first opened magically by itself; it was electrically-operated—another new experience. We passed through several more grilles and finally into a small room near the end of the passage.

In the room a Lieutenant introduced himself and asked us to sign our names in the register. He took our details and in return assigned us our prison numbers, which he explained were to be used in all official and other communications. My number was to be 393/78; Stephen's 394/78.

The atmosphere was relaxed and almost welcoming after Pollsmoor and the nightmare journey from Cape Town. There were no queues of black prisoners waiting to be signed in, no shouting and swearing, no rude warders rushing to and fro and no rattling of keys. It almost felt homely, quite unlike what we had expected.

The warders standing around eyed us up and down with curiosity, as if they'd never seen any prisoners before. It was seldom that any new prisoners were admitted to that prison and all who were came for a long stay.

They asked us what size shoes and clothes we wore. Stephen and I looked at each other in disbelief. At Pollsmoor there was no asking. What seemed the right size to them was just thrown at you and you had to fit the item rather than the other way round. A warder brought our clobber from the store and deposited two neat piles of clothing on the table in front of us. We discarded the badly-fitting Pollsmoor 'uniform' for what appeared to be a much cleaner, newer and better fitting outfit. Someone scooped up the stinking Pollsmoor rags from the floor, put them in a bag and was told to take them out to the waiting van. We dressed in our new rig, thinking to each other that this, dear friend, is how we are going to look for the next so many years. Get used to it!

The Lieutenant gave a brief lecture about prisoner-staff relations. We were to address all warders, irrespective of rank, as *Meneer*— Mister. *'Ja Meneer!'* Relations were good and if we left them alone they would leave us alone; if we caused trouble they would too. As simple as that. 'Yes, yes. Sounds reasonable enough. We have no reason to cause you any trouble.'

Then a snorting monster shuffled into the room, handlebar moustache and all—the notorious Captain Schnepel, the head of the prison. Disrupting our lesson he shouted: 'Stand up straight! *Ja Kaptein!* when I speak to you, do you hear?' A few more strange gruntings and snufflings and then the beast disappeared again. Obviously just some old fool trying to show who's king around the place.

They took us up to our cells on the first floor. On the way we passed a door through which could be heard the sounds of cowboys shooting at Indians. They told us that the other prisoners were watching a film but that we would not be able to see any for three months and then only if we behaved ourselves.

A door was flung open and before us was our section—our home for the next so long. It was quite unlike Pollsmoor: the corridor was short and light with cells only on one side. I was put in cell 17, the first cell in the section and Stephen in cell 18, the second. A warder asked if we'd had anything to eat, to which we replied that we hadn't. A short while later a relatively decent meal of chicken legs and vegetables arrived. I shouted to Stephen that maybe things weren't going to be so bad after all.

We inspected our cells. They were light and airy, although a bit cramped: about three metres long by two metres wide. They were larger than the ones we'd had at Pollsmoor but not really large enough for pacing up and down—an important consideration for prisoners. Pity. The roof was high: about three metres. The door was to the one side of my cell and as Stephen's cell was the mirror image of mine our doors were close together and we could pass things to each other through the bars of our grilles. As at Pollsmoor, our cells also had

72

outer, panelled steel doors, but they were left open that afternoon.

The bed was hard, but not uncomfortable. At least it was a proper bed, not a mat on the floor. It was neatly covered with a blue bedspread. At the foot of the bed was the toilet. It was the type we had grown accustomed to, with two curved pieces of wood fastened to the rim of the bowl on which you sat, but on which you could not sit for very long. The only difference was that it had a cover. On the wall was a push-button that flushed endless waterfalls of water – very handy for getting rid of contraband. Next to the toilet on the far wall was an ordinary porcelain handbasin with two taps. I wonder what the second tap is for? Real hot water! What next! It feels hot enough to make coffee.

A shoulder-high cupboard was fixed against the one wall. Out of the middle of it projected a shelf which could be pulled out and used as a table if you sat on the edge of your bed. Above the bed was a bookshelf and in the corner next to the basin a stool. That was all as far as 'furniture' and 'conveniences' were concerned.

At the far end of the cell above the basin was a large window and next to the door looking into the corridor another, but smaller window. There were no bars in the windows as such: a number of narrow vertical windows closed onto frames which served as the bars. The windows could individually be swung open but the space between the frames was too narrow to fit your head through. Rumour had it that inside the frames were uncuttable tungsten bars, but this was probably just a story circulated by the prison authorities to stop prisoners trying to find out. We were amazed at the thickness of the outer wall. There was enough space to crouch sideways on the window ledge on the inside and an equal space on the other side of the window.

Outside was an extraordinary sight. Instead of just bare concrete as there had been at Pollsmoor there was a well-tended garden with a central concreted area marked out as a small tennis court. On either side of the court were large patches of well-trimmed lawn. At the far end were several trees, one so tall that it obscured the view of the warder pacing up and down a roofed catwalk on top of a high wall. The left-hand end of the catwalk was glassed off, forming a shelter for the warder on duty. The warder carried an automatic rifle. Along the right side of the yard was a high corrugated-iron wall – it appeared to be a temporary structure – and about half way along its length a door. The way out! was our simultaneous first thought.

We were left to survey our new world for about two hours before we met the comrades. With a loud clang the section door flew open and in they trooped. The comrades congregated in front of our grilles to take a look at the 'new guys' in their cages. We shook hands through the bars and exchanged names with each of them in turn. They were clearly excited to see some new faces but we were a bit apprehensive because we weren't sure who they were and how many there would be. As it turned out most of those whom we had expected to be there were there. Only two we had never heard of.

The person who had been there the longest was Denis Goldberg, one of the 'Rivonia Trialists' who was sentenced with Nelson Mandela and other ANC leaders in June 1964. He had received no less than three life sentences for allegedly 'campaigning to overthrow the government by violent revolution'. Denis, like us, was from Cape Town and had been an engineer before his capture. He was a young man of 30 and father of two at the time of his arrest in 1963. When we met him that first time he was 45.

Next was Dave Kitson, who had been inside just a few months less than Denis. He was sentenced to 20 years in December 1964 for his part in the early sabotage campaigns, for furthering the aims of 'communism' and for being a member of the High Command of Umkhonto we Sizwe. Like Denis he was also an engineer, but came from Johannesburg. He was now 59 and had divorced his wife when he was imprisoned, 'to give her her freedom'.

John Matthews was sentenced to 15 years in the same trial as Dave Kitson. It was alleged that he assisted in obtaining materials for making bombs. In his trial he had grounds for appealing against his sentence but refused to do so, claiming that he was proud to be sentenced along with his co-accused. Johnny had been a bookkeeper and father in Johannesburg and was 65 years old.

After them in line in date and length of sentence was Alex Moumbaris. He was sentenced in June 1973 to 12 years' imprisonment for, among other things, 'conspiring with the ANC to instigate violent revolution in South Africa', aiding guerrillas to enter the country, distributing ANC literature and reconnoitering the Transkei coast to find places for the seaborne landing of guerrillas and arms.

Alex was 40 when we met him that first time. He was the only prisoner who was not South African and as such was to South African propaganda the archetypal 'communist'. According to this view all communists are, firstly, white, then foreigners or acting on behalf of some foreign power (usually Russia) and thirdly, but not necessarily, Jewish—which Alex wasn't. He was born in Egypt of Greek parents. His family emigrated to Australia when he was young, but he left the place when he was sixteen because, in his words, it was 'the arse-end of the world'. After that he spent a number of years in France where he married his wife, Marie-José. He then moved to London where he worked for about nine years before getting involved with the ANC.

He was arrested in 1972 with Marie-José while trying to enter South Africa from Botswana. Because she was pregnant at the time and because of pressure from the French ambassador, Marie-José was not charged but was promptly deported to France.

Raymond Suttner was sentenced to seven and a half years in

November 1975 for 'taking part in the activities of an unlawful organisation' by distributing ANC literature, and 'undergoing training or inciting or encouraging others to undergo training, or obtaining information which could be of use in furthering the achievements of any of the objects of communism or any unlawful organisation'. Before his arrest he was a senior lecturer in law at the University of Natal in Durban. He was 32.

David Rabkin and Jeremy Cronin, who were mentioned earlier, were sentenced in September 1976 to ten and seven years respectively. David, who was 30, was working as a sub-editor for the *Argus* newspaper in Cape Town when he was detained with his wife Sue. From here on Dave Rabkin will be known as Dave R so as to avoid confusion with Dave K.

Jeremy, who was 28, had been a lecturer in political science at the University of Cape Town. His wife, Anne-Marie, died shortly after his imprisonment due to a brain haemorrhage and he was denied permission to attend her funeral.

The person last sentenced before us was Tony Holiday, who has also been mentioned before. He was given six years in November 1976 for establishing an underground cell with three others, receiving money from the ANC, publishing ANC literature, receiving 'subversive' training while working in Britain, training recruits to evade surveillance, all with the aim of 'promoting the policies of a banned organisation'. Tony had been a senior reporter on the *Cape Times* at the time of his detention and before that a political reporter for the Johannesburg *Rand Daily Mail*. He was 38.

In a way the comrades were heroes to us. They were all people who had inspired us with their dedication to the cause and with their selfless actions which had got them into prison. They had reminded us while we were working underground that there were other white South Africans who were prepared to cast aside their privileges and throw in their lot with the oppressed; that we were not mad and that there were others doing the same sort of work as us.

The older comrades, Denis, Dave K and John, were all imprisoned before we became politically involved. They were of another generation. But Denis was one of Mandela's compatriots and as such one of the names we held in greatest esteem. The detentions and trials of the others we had followed with great interest and had been inspired by the brave statements they made from the dock. The trials of Raymond and Dave R and Jeremy had provided us with much information about how they had run their cells and how the police had tracked them down. Their imprisonment had angered us no end and spurred us on to even greater activity.

We had expected the comrades, especially those who had been in prison for 15 years, to be somewhat oppressed by their condition. But not so. Although obviously not happy to be where they were they were a group of people full of spirit and as committed to the cause as the day they were arrested—some of them probably even more so.

Denis in particular was an inspiration and made us feel ashamed of feeling sorry for ourselves. He'd been in prison since we were young teenagers and had no date of release to look forward to. People had come, served long sentences, and gone out. He would still be in prison after we'd served our sentences, yet the prospects did not undermine his strength and commitment. It should have been us helping him but it was he who helped us by reminding us that our sentences were just 'parking tickets'!

★ ★ ★

Pretoria Prison is part of a large prison complex known incorrectly as 'Pretoria Central'. In this complex there are actually three separate prisons or prison clusters: Pretoria Central Prison proper, Pretoria Prison and a third known only as 'Maximum' or 'Beverley Hills'. Also in the complex are warders' houses, a prison shop, a shooting range and sporting and other recreational facilities for the warders.

Pretoria Central proper consists of a number of separate prison buildings, in keeping with South African 'tradition': one for white males, one for black males, one for white females, one for black females, and so on. Central is a 'national' prison and a reception centre where many prisoners start and end their sentences. Pretoria Prison is Pretoria's local prison and consists of 'non-white' sections for ordinary prisoners, possibly separate 'white' sections for ordinary prisoners, and a maximum-security section, where we were housed. 'Maximum' is a special high-security prison for recidivists, habitual escapees, the 'State President's patients' and those condemned to death.

Ours was not a large prison. It was a single building consisting of only 52 cells and built in the late 1960s specifically for white male political prisoners. At no stage had there ever been more than 22 political prisoners in the prison, with the average complement being about 10. For this reason the remaining cells were used for housing awaiting-trial prisoners, known in prison language as 'stokkies', from the Xhosa word isitokisi, meaning 'prison'.

The prison building was 'L' shaped (see Diagram 1) and three storeys high. The ground floor of the long wing of the 'L' consisted of administrative offices; the short wing contained our dining-room, store-room, workshop and a toilet. The door to the street—through which we had entered the prison—was at the far end of the administrative section. Apart from the gate leading out of the prison yard—which actually led into prison property next door—there were no other exits from the prison.

The first and second floors consisted of cells. Ours were on the first floor of the short wing; the stokkies' occupied the rest. Each wing of

76

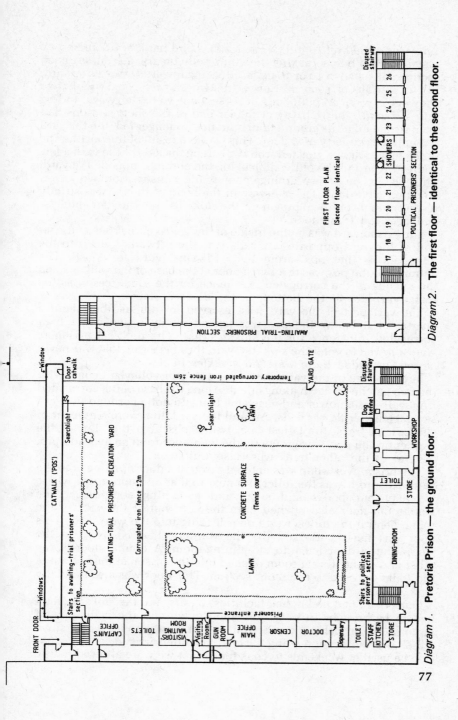

Diagram 1. **Pretoria Prison — the ground floor.**

Diagram 2. **The first floor — identical to the second floor.**

FIRST FLOOR PLAN
(Second floor identical)

POLITICAL PRISONERS' SECTION

AWAITING-TRIAL PRISONERS' SECTION

17 18 19 20 21 22 SHOWERS 23 24 25 26

Disused stairway

Temporary corrugated iron fence ±6m

YARD GATE

CATWALK ('POS')

Searchlight

Stairs to awaiting-trial prisoners section

AWAITING-TRIAL PRISONERS' RECREATION YARD

Corrugated iron fence ±2m

Searchlight

LAWN

CONCRETE SURFACE
(Tennis court)

LAWN

Door to catwalk

Window

FRONT DOOR

Windows

CAPTAIN'S OFFICE

TOILETS

VISITORS' WAITING ROOM

Visiting Room

GUN ROOM

MAIN OFFICE

CENSOR

DOCTOR

Dispensary

TOILET

STAFF KITCHEN

STORE

Prisoner's entrance

Stairs to political prisoners' section

DINING-ROOM

STORE

TOILET

WORKSHOP

Dog kennel

Disused stairway

77

cells was sealed off from the other wings and parts of the prison by panelled steel doors, making them into self-contained sections. Each section consisted of 10 or 16 cells, all facing inwards toward the yard. In the middle of each section were two shower rooms with two showers in each. At both ends of all sections were stairways leading into the yard. The stairway at the far end of the short sections had been sealed off as its ground floor entrance no longer led into the yard but into the property next door. This was as a result of the positioning of the temporary corrugated iron wall along the side of the yard a few metres inward of the old wall, leaving the entrance outside the yard. This was a temporary arrangement while construction work was going on next door. The stairway in the bend of the 'L' was strictly reserved for us political prisoners; the *stokkies* used the stair at the far end near the front door.

The prison yard was on the inside of the 'L'. As explained, at the far end of the yard opposite our cells was the catwalk, known to the prisoners as the *'pos'*—from the Afrikaans word for 'post'. The entrance to the *pos* was through a door at the base of the wall, also on the outside of the corrugated iron fence for the same reason as the sealed-off door at the bottom of the disused stairway.

The vast part of the yard was reserved for our use but about a quarter of it below the *pos* was fenced off by a two metre high corrugated iron fence for the *stokkies'* use. The political prisoners were allowed to enter the *stokkies'* yard through a gate that was never closed, provided there were no *stokkies* in it.

In the centre of the yard was our tennis and volleyball court with the two patches of lawn alongside it. Along the base of the corrugated iron wall was a flower and vegetable bed and dotted around the yard several smaller flower beds. Around the yard, too, were a number of shrubs and trees, the tallest one, which obscured the view of the warder on the *pos*, was grown by the comrades from an avocado pip. Several of the other trees were also fruit trees.

The prison workshop was entered through a door opening onto the yard. Next to it was the toilet and next to that our store-room where we kept our books and sport and gardening equipment. The store-room door also opened onto the yard but at the back of the room, behind the toilet, was a door leading into the workshop. This door was never unlocked (by the warders, that is). Next to the store-room a door led into our dining-room. A double door at the other end of the dining-room opened into the prison at the bottom of the stairs we used to reach our section. This door was also normally kept locked.

Our prison had no kitchen facilities so ours' and the *stokkies'* food had to be brought in pots from the kitchens in the main part of Pretoria Prison behind our prison. In our dining-room was a stove which was meant for heating the food that often arrived cold. It could also be used at weekends to cook foods that we were allowed to buy

78

with our allowances.

The only other objects in the yard worthy of mention were a dog kennel for the dog which was placed in the yard at night and two searchlights – one mounted on the *pos* wall and the other on a tall pole in the middle of one of the patches of lawn.

The prisoners' day started at five thirty in the morning when a bell rang and the night-warder switched on the cell lights. The prisoners had to be up, dressed, shaved and with their beds made and cells tidied in time for inspection at 7 am when the cells were unlocked. The section was not opened at the same time because we were required to sweep the passage, empty the dustbins and dust the window ledges before being released into the yard to await the arrival of our breakfast at half past seven.

To pass the time until breakfast most of us would run around the yard to keep fit, or otherwise walk up and down the tennis court and discuss the day's prospects.

Breakfast was followed by workshop duty for most of us. Our work consisted of assembling and finishing various items of prison furniture which had been prepared at the main workshops at Central – things like bookshelves, tables and benches. Those who did not work in the workshop were responsible for tidying and cleaning our part of the prison.

At about ten the warder on duty in the workshop would shout 'time'. This oft-repeated and much-hated word would signal the start of the ten minute morning break when we would drink the weak black tea prepared for us by Denis. A similar 'time' would signal its end. At eleven thirty a gang of black prisoners with a white warder in attendance would arrive with our lunch carried on trays sedan-car style.

After lunch we would be locked in our cells from twelve to one while the prison staff took their lunch break. During this period a heavily-censored recording of radio news was relayed to us over loudspeakers mounted in the passage. Later the speakers were mounted inside our cells so you could turn them off if you didn't want to listen to the 'news'. Back to the workshop until two, when there was another tea break, and then at three thirty 'time' was called to end the day's work session. Up to the section again for a quick shower and back down to the yard to await supper which arrived at about four. At supper-time letters, library books and study assignments would be handed out. The final 'time' of the day was called just after half past four when we were locked in our cells for the night.

Shortly after lock-up the day-warders knocked off duty and a single night-warder took over. He played us another 'news' broadcast and, until 8 pm, a selection of music from our large collection of records on our record player in his office. Lights out for the *stokkies* was at 8 pm, when the night-warder would make an inspection tour of the prison, and for us at eleven, marking the end of the day. At ten a guard came on duty on the *pos* and at midnight there was a change of night-warders.

There were some variations to this basic routine. On Fridays there was no workshop duty. Instead, in the morning, we were required to scrub down our part of the prison. On a rotating basis some comrades would wash the passage floor of the section while others would wash the floor of the dining-room. This did not take long and for the rest of the morning we would be locked unguarded in our section with our cell doors open. During this time we were meant to clean our cells but since most of us maintained them in a respectable state it became a much-valued period for holding discussions, playing cards, chess, scrabble, other games and for doing 'other things'.

Friday afternoons were set aside for the showing of films. During our first six months films were only shown once every two weeks, but later this changed to every week. When there were no movies we played tennis in the yard or just lay about reading and chatting.

Saturdays and Sundays were reserved for sport – mainly tennis. We were allowed to remain in the yard until the lunch-time lock-up and after that until supper-time, which was an hour earlier than on week days. Lock-up was also an hour earlier. There were occasional variations to this routine if there was a shortage of warders or someone in authority visited the prison, but in general this was the pattern of daily and weekly events.

7

First Approaches

It was on our fourth day in Pretoria Prison that we decided to tell the comrades about the money we'd brought in. Before our arrival we'd decided to wait until we had 'sussed' everyone out before revealing our secret: we did not want to have someone go straight to the authorities with the information. But it was soon obvious to us that the comrades were not sell-outs. They conducted themselves with integrity, seemed to be united and there were no obvious antagonisms. As Denis appeared to be the most senior of the prisoners we decided to tell him first. He would be able to advise us when or if the others should be told and how and where to hide it. To avoid losing all our cash if it went wrong, we decided that Stephen should reveal his stash first; if it worked out OK then I would reveal mine later.

During the pre-breakfast walk up and down the tennis court Stephen broke his news to Denis. Predictably Denis was amazed and excited; probably a bit suspicious too. But that was to be expected for it must have seemed a bit odd to an old lag to have a four-day-old prisoner come sidling up to him and claim to have a couple of hundred rand stashed away in his guts. After Denis had recovered his composure, Stephen asked him for advice on how to hide the money. Probably thinking it best to test Stephen's credentials, Denis offered to take the money and hide it himself. After all, if Stephen had been given the money to trap Denis, it would have been a bit difficult for the authorities to claim that he'd been sitting with it for the previous 15 years.

Denis took the money and concealed it inside a spare tube of toothpaste he had in his cell. To us this seemed a bit dicey but he assured Stephen that as far as he could remember his toothpaste had never been violated. Denis also spread the news among the other comrades.

A few days later, after deciding with Stephen that it was safe to do so, I too approached Denis. We were walking in the yard and when I revealed my secret he came to an abrupt halt and stared at me in astonishment. What are these new guys up to?, he must have been thinking. Money in prison, as he knew full well, is used for three things only: bribing, smuggling and escaping.

Three hundred and sixty rand would have seemed a lot to any prisoner at that time, but to Denis it must have sounded even more as he had never had a chance to come to terms with current notions of inflation. In his amazement at the revelation he could do no more than advise me to do the same with my money as he had done with

Stephen's. The toothpaste tubes turned out to be good hiding places: as long as the money was kept in them it was never discovered.

In the course of our first days Stephen and I discussed with each of the others the question of escaping. This did not raise their suspicions as escaping is the most natural thing for prisoners to talk about, especially new prisoners. All the comrades said that they had of course thought about escaping, but none of them came up with any concrete or viable ideas of how they thought it could be done. This amazed and disappointed us as we had expected them to have some pretty thoroughly worked out plans, or at least some good ideas, as some of them had been in captivity for a long time. It made us think that perhaps we had been naive in imagining that we would be able to escape from one of South Africa's most secure prisons. Perhaps we really would have to serve our full terms. The thought was demoralising in the extreme.

Denis in particular had given the question a lot of thought and had attempted an escape while in detention just before he was sentenced. The only time a collective escape had seriously been considered, many years earlier when the comrades were at Pretoria Local, the first prison in which they were kept, it had been betrayed by one of the prisoners, Raymond Thoms. Thoms was the only white political prisoner who was thoroughly broken by the prison experience. He went a bit mad and started narking on the others, who naturally sent him to Coventry. He committed suicide some time after his release.

Denis himself considered the chances of getting out of the prison to be fairly good but did not hold out much to getting away from the prison, off the terrain and out of the country without outside assistance. Any thinking he had given the problem involved making an exit via the prison yard. He had suggestions, but no thoroughly worked out plan. Quite understandably, he appeared to accept that the security situation around the prison might be thoroughly sewn up.

I approached Alex separately because he appeared to be a little aloof from the others. Surprisingly he was not aware that we had brought money in with us. I told him of the money, how we'd brought it in and what we'd done with it, but did not say that our intention was to use it for an escape. Later that same day he came back to me and said that if any escape plans were being hatched he would 'definitely like to be one of the chickens'.

His response singled him out from the others, none of whom drew the conclusion that we had brought the money in for the specific purpose of escaping. I asked Alex if he had any bright ideas how an escape might be pulled off, but he didn't have any. He did point out, however, that whatever plans were contemplated they would all involve the making of keys. How we could make these he didn't know as there were no obviously suitable materials around out of which to make them. I said to him that I had been thinking of making a key out of wood but he rudely rejected this idea. The giant prison locks, he insisted, would require keys of a much more robust material to turn them. I believed otherwise.

In our first weeks at Pretoria Steve and I carefully studied the layout of the prison to see if there were any obvious cracks in the prison's security. From our initial observations all escape routes had their origin in the prison yard. It was reasonable to think this, for once you were in the yard the only barrier between you and freedom was the yard wall. Any other starting point meant that you were placing more barriers in front of yourself, not fewer. You could take your cell as the point of departure but once out of it you had to get out of the prison building, and that meant into the yard. There were only three exits out of the prison building and two of these led directly into the yard. The third, the front door leading into the street, could not even be considered. The only way to get to it was by passing clean through the administrative section and opening a great many doors and gates on the way.

How to get out of the prison yard was another question. The yard gate, although it led out of our prison, opened into prison property next door – into the site of the old Pretoria Local which was about to be knocked down. This was not much good, but as the demolition progressed we thought it might begin to offer some prospects. Otherwise it might be possible somehow to get over or under the yard wall into the street. There had to be some way. We would eventually discover it – it would just take time.

The security arrangements that had been installed indicated that the prison authorities also recognised that if an escape was to be attempted it would have to start from or go through the yard. There were searchlights that lit it at night like a football stadium, and after lock-up a large, ferocious guard-dog was placed in it. The dogs were of the sort that would not have hesitated in tearing apart a loose prisoner. The *pos* with its armed guard eliminated the possibility of prisoners making a dash for freedom during the day.

However, we did notice a few cracks in the security: the dog was never placed in the yard exactly at lock-up (4.30 pm) and sometimes not until an hour later; between lock-up and 10 pm there was no warder on the *pos*. This meant that if we could get out of our cells shortly after lock-up and into the yard before the dog arrived it might be possible to scale a wall to get into the street. The prospects did not look brilliant but there was some hope. One thing was clear: we could not rely solely on cracks in the security arrangements to get out – we had to develop our own capabilities to exploit the weaknesses.

To be able to get into the yard after lock-up, or to be able to do anything at all for that matter, we would need keys. But how could we make them? How would we get the measurements? Between us we knew very little about how locks worked. I had only a vague idea, having once picked the back door of my parents' home with a piece of bent wire. The giant prison locks looked more formidable than anything we'd experienced in civilian life. Still, we couldn't allow ourselves to be intimidated by their size. Inside they were probably the same as any ordinary lock.

For many nights I sat on my bed and stared at the lock on my grille. It was completely accessible, just bolted to the frame. You could even see right through the keyhole and get your hand around to the other side of it because there was a fair space between the grille and the outer door. I *had* to make a key for it, but I didn't know where to start. Since the warders never left their keys lying about for us to take measurements or impressions so there was no alternative but to work it out for myself.

I dared not tell anyone apart from Stephen that I was planning to make a key, for we had no idea what sort of response we would have received from the comrades had the subject been mooted first. We knew that it would be a different matter to announce that we'd made a key that worked.

After two weeks I decided to stop staring at my lock and to get down to the business of finding out its secrets. I lit a match to see what was inside it, but all I could see were the scrape marks against the inner faces where the key had turned. Then it occurred to me that simply by measuring parts of the lock I would be able to work out some of the dimensions of the key. By measuring with a ruler the diameter of the round part of the keyhole, I would get the diameter of the key shaft. The width of the head, or the 'bit' in locksmith's lingo (*see Diagram 3*), and the shape of the ward cutaways in the side of the bit, I could establish by pushing a piece of paper through the keyhole and pressing it with a knife against the interior of the lock. The measurements I could then take directly from the impression on the paper.

The final and most crucial measurements were the heights and relative heights of the 'cuts' in the bit. These, I knew, were the working part of the key as they lifted the levers inside the lock to the correct heights so that the bolt could slide in and out. I'd noticed that there were five cuts on the warders' keys, but as the outer two were always equal in height and the inner two always equal in depth there were in fact only three measurements I had to know.

To find the height of the two outer cuts was the easiest: I could simply measure the distance between the outer edge of the shaft hole to the outer radius of the scrape marks inside the lock. Once I knew this, finding the depths of the inner three cuts was made easier because I would only have to know their depths relative to the height of the outer two. Fortunately, on this first key the cuts were all of the same depth relative to each other. In other words, the middle cut was

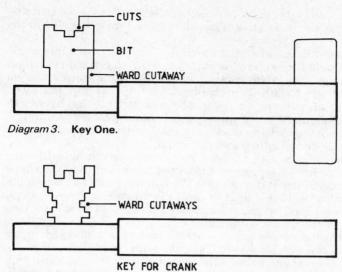

Diagram 3. **Key One.**

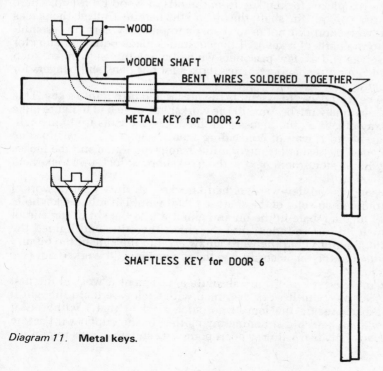

Diagram 6. **Key Two.**

Diagram 11. **Metal keys.**

as deep relative to the inner two as these were to the outer two, the key being symmetrical so that it could be used from either side of the door.

The only way to establish the actual depths of the three inner cuts was by staring at the warders' keys and making an estimate based on eye judgement. This might sound fantastic but there simply was no other way short of waiting, probably forever, for an opportunity to physically measure them when a warder inadvertently left his bunch of keys lying about. At every opportunity I would stare at the warders' keys, and there were plenty of these as they derived a sense of power by displaying and jingling them in front of us.

I estimated the cuts to be 2mm deep and then drew a life-size diagram of the key on a piece of card. I cut it out and tried the shape in the lock. Of course it did not turn the bolt but it did not jam in the keyway, indicating that at least some of the dimensions were correct. The key looked good on paper but how to turn it into a real, working key was another matter altogether.

In the absence of any other suitable materials I decided to try making the key out of wood. I searched the workshop for some suitably hard wood and found a number of off-cuts from an earlier job carried out by the comrades. Between Stephen and me, we roughly cut out the pieces for the key from the bits of wood I'd found. There were three pieces: the shaft, the bit and the handle. Cutting the pieces in the workshop did not arouse suspicion as they bore no resemblance to the parts of a key. All the comrades made odds and ends for themselves and as new prisoners we had many things to make, such as stands for our shaving mirrors, boxes for our pens and hangers for our clothes.

The next step was to assemble the pieces and turn it into a key. This could obviously not be done in the workshop so we had to figure out a safe way of getting the pieces and the necessary tools up to my cell. Having found a way of concealing them as we took them up, one afternoon I hid a small triangular file, some wood-glue and the pieces of key in the store-room next to the workshop. At lock-up I took them up to my cell.

As soon as the day-warders had knocked off duty I set to work. I first rounded one end of the shaft so that it would fit into the keyhole. Then I filed a rebate in the bit and glued it into the slit in the end of the shaft I'd just rounded; into the slit at the other end I glued the handle. Finally I filed the ward cutaways into the side of the bit and the cuts into the top according to the dimensions I'd worked out (*see Diagram 4*).

Then I tried it out. To my absolute amazement it worked the first time. Not only did it work, it turned with such ease that I thought it had broken inside the lock. I got such a fright that I withdrew it immediately and hid it among my clothes in the cupboard. I sat on the edge of my bed with my heart pounding and my hands trembling.

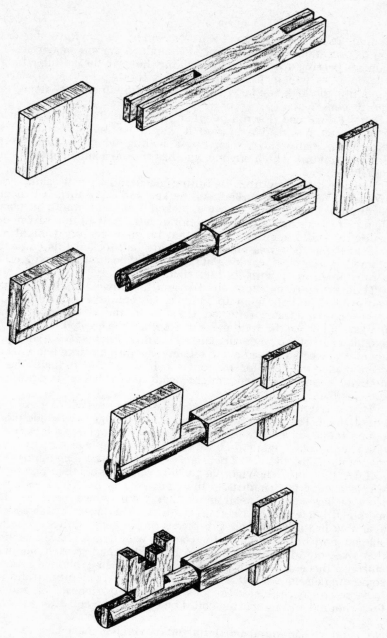

Diagram 4. **Stages of making a wooden key.**

Soon there will be a troupe of warders marching up to my cell to drag me off for attempting to escape, I thought. I started imagining TV cameras peering down at me through tiny holes in the ceiling, hidden microphones which had heard the lock turning and secret alarms signalling the lock had been tampered with. Such are the effects of a 'guilty conscience'.

After I'd calmed down a peculiar sense of defiance and achievement began to creep over me. It was a feeling we were all to experience many times later on, a feeling which is difficult to describe but one which anyone who has cocked a snook at authority will know.

I retrieved the key from its hiding place and tried it again. True enough it really had worked. As the key had to be turned two full revolutions for it to be properly unlocked, I turned it round once and then half the second turn. I dared not turn the bolt all the way in and swing the grille open as I feared that for some reason it might not relock. If the lock was found to be only half-locked this could be blamed on a careless warder, but there would be no way of explaining a fully open door with its bolt right in.

The next morning I took the key and file downstairs in the same way as I had brought them up. I hid the key behind a bookshelf in the store-room and later returned the file to the workshop. In the workshop I broke the good news to Stephen – he greeted it with such excitement that the others demanded to know what we were so happy about. But we had agreed not to tell anyone until key number two had been made – the key for the outer cell door. We thought that a premature announcement might lead to us being regarded as provocateurs.

The success of the first key proved that it was possible to make keys out of wood. The reason why we had at first thought that wood might not be suitable was because whenever a warder opened a lock it was done with such vigour that we were led to believe that the lock mechanism offered a lot of resistance to the turning. The opposite in fact was the truth. The vigorous turning was no more than part of the warders' need to demonstrate their power over us. The keys could have been made of metal (and later were as we perfected our methods) but wood had certain distinct advantages: it was readily available in the workshop; the pieces of the keys could be roughly shaped more or less openly – the warders would never have imagined that a key could be made of wood and if they had spotted one of us cutting a piece of wood it could easily have been explained away as something else; a wooden key operated relatively silently; it did not leave scrape marks inside the lock; it was easily disposed of; and the final shaping and measuring could be done in the cell after lock-up.

Now that we had found a material out of which to make keys and had developed a method of constructing them we could proceed with the next ones until we had all we needed to get ourselves into the yard and out of it. It was not quite as simple as we had first thought because the double-locking action of the locks confused us. As far as we could see the doors could be locked with two completely different sets of keys: one set by the warders during the day and one set by the night-warder. According to our comrades the day-keys were master-keys which could turn the locks both turns while the night-warder's could only turn them once. The logic for this, they explained, was to make it pointless for a prisoner to attempt to persuade the night-warder, through force of collusion, to let him out as his keys would not be able to unlock the mastered cell doors. The section doors through which he needed access were not mastered. The night-warder was in fact locked inside the prison by the departing day-warders and was let out the next morning when they came back on duty.

The second key turned out to be a much greater obstacle than the first one. Door two was a panelled steel door with only one keyhole—on the outside (*see Diagram 5*). As such, the major dimensions of the key could not be obtained in the same way as the first one's. But as both keys looked pretty much the same in overall size we guessed that some of the dimensions would be the same. These were the diameter of the key shaft, the length of the bit and the depth of the neck. As can be seen from Diagram 6, the ward cutaways were extraordinarily complicated and the shape of the cuts also much more complicated.

The main problem with door two was that we seldom had access to the outside of it. When we were to be locked into our cells we were usually brought smartly from downstairs and locked up immediately. The only times we could get to look at the keyhole was during shower-time when we were usually left unattended in the section, and on Friday mornings when we were locked in the section to clean it. Shower-time was not really suitable as the time was short and a warder could come into the section at any moment; Fridays were a better prospect as we were left in the section unattended for several hours with our cell doors open. The other problem was that if Steve or I started peering into locks the others would see straight away what we were up to, and we didn't want to be seen doing anything surreptitiously. It was clear that to proceed the others had to be told.

After making a blank key for door two based on the measurements of the first key and on guesswork, I broke the news about the first key to Dave R one afternoon in the workshop. I told him of the problem we faced with door two and asked him if we could test the new key in his door the coming Friday. It was the last in the passage and furthest from the section door; mine being the first and hence the worst. Dave agreed.

Before the Friday I also told Alex about the first key. He found it hard to believe that a wooden key had worked but was most excited

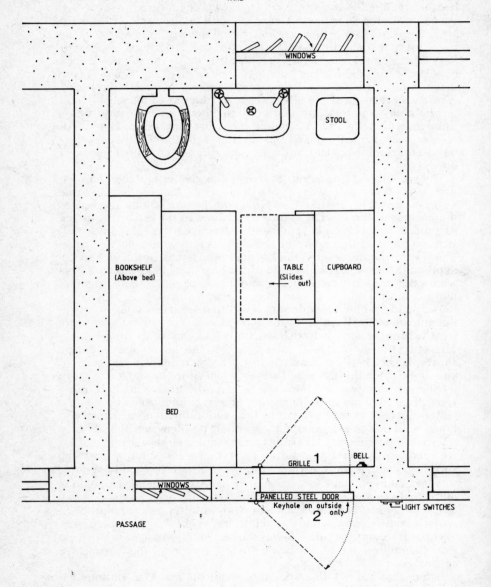

Diagram 5. **Plan of cell.**

YARD

WINDOWS

STOOL

BOOKSHELF
(Above bed)

TABLE
(Slides
out)

CUPBOARD

BED

GRILLE 1

BELL

WINDOWS

PANELLED STEEL DOOR
Keyhole on outside only

2

LIGHT SWITCHES

PASSAGE

about the prospects. To prove it for himself he took the key from me and tried it in his grille at lunch-time. Clearly it worked as well in his lock as it had in mine, for that afternoon, with a broad grin on his face, he hollowed out a piece of wood, put the key in it, glued another piece of wood over it and planed the two pieces to make it look like a single block.

The number two key was tested that Friday but it did not turn at all because the ward cutaways were incorrect. At this early stage we were not entirely sure of the function of ward cutaways and did not realise that they were there only to clear ridges (wards) in the keyway which blocked the use of incorrect keys, and that the bit could simply have been cut away on its side to clear all the wards.

I was bitterly disappointed at the failure as I'd expected the key to work the first time like number one. I was planning to tackle the third door – the section door – that weekend and for us be out in the next few weeks. After the first success it was difficult to reconcile myself to the thought that the job of making keys was not going to be as easy as I had at first thought and that it would be longer than a mere few weeks before we were free. It was also difficult to cope with the knowledge that there was absolutely nothing that could be done with door two until the next Friday. I had still not adapted to prison time, which is different from outside time in that it lacks the distance dimension. The next Friday seemed eternally far away.

Testing with a new key the following Friday resulted in our first disaster, and also our first experience of extreme good luck. Having become bolder and because everyone now knew, I tried out the key in all the number two locks. It turned part of the way in all of them, indicating that the ward cutaways were correct, but did not bring out the bolt in any except mine. I should have realised that this meant something was wrong but the excitement of seeing the bolt move blinded me – I wanted to see it come out and go back in again. At first I was worried about turning it all the way out for fear that it might not return, but I could not contain my curiosity and gradually turned it out completely. I then tried to turn it the second time to master lock it but it would not turn any further. The realisation of what I had done suddenly hit me like a punch in the chest. I tried to turn the bolt back in but it would not budge. I began to panic and tried to force it in, but all that happened was that the key broke. Fortunately it did not come to pieces inside the lock and I was able to extract the damaged implement. Fortunately too the door was open – it would have been difficult to explain a door that had locked itself closed. Unable to do anything about it, there was simply no option but to leave the door with the bolt sticking out and hope for the best.

Luckily, when the warders locked us up after lunch they said nothing about the bolt being out and even started to blame each other for not being able to unlock doors properly. All that we could conclude from the incident was that it must have been possible for an overzealous warder to jiggle his key out of the keyhole and accidentally turn out the bolt. The key had worked in my lock and not in any of the others' because when I turned it my bolt must have been partially out and the levers already lifted up. Turning the bolt fully out caused the levers to latch, preventing the bolt from moving in again.

After this near-disaster it was unanimously decided that all future testing of number two doors was to be done when they were locked. This presented a mammoth problem as the only time they were locked was when we were inside our cells and thus when we had no direct access to the keyhole. The narrow panes of the cells' passage windows opened sufficiently to allow you to stick an arm through but at full stretch your hand was still at least a metre from the keyhole. Obviously we had to make some kind of device to enable us to reach it.

Several schemes were devised. The first were inordinately complicated and would have involved using a series of pulleys and ropes. These proved too difficult to implement and were unrealistic in that they would have involved bringing a load of equipment into our cells. We finally hit on an idea that was, like all good ideas, remarkably simple. It was to construct a simple crank mechanism out of a broomstick, a block of wood and a screw.

Each cell had a broom in it and all we had to do to turn one into part of the crank was to drill a hole at the end of the broomstick ('so that it could be hung up'). To assemble the crank you removed the broomstick from the brush by unscrewing the holding screw with a knife. You then passed a long screw through the hole and screwed it into one end of the wooden block. The square end of the key shaft you inserted into a square hole that had been chiselled into the other end of the block.

The block and key dangled at the end of the broomstick and to reach your keyhole you passed it out of your window. To see what you were doing you held your shaving mirror at the correct angle with your other hand. The key was simply inserted in the keyhole and then cranked around with the broomstick like a steam-engine crankhandle (see Diagrams 7 and 8).

This method of unlocking our number twos proved very successful, mainly because it was so simple and did not require us to bring anything special into our cells. The block with the screw sticking out of it could be left openly in a cell as a 'clothes-hook' and it could be attached to the broomstick quickly and with the minimum of fuss.

It was about August 1978 when I started attempting to open my outer door by this method. I did the testing at night after the eight o'clock inspection round when the music had ended. This was the best time as it was easier to hear the movements of the night-warder after quiet had set in. Fortunately my cell was in the best position for

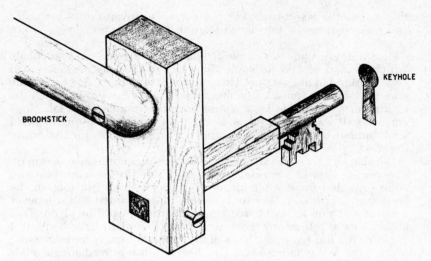

Diagram 7.   **Crank mechanism for Door Two.**

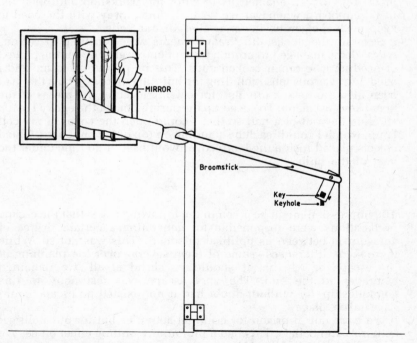

Diagram 8.   **Opening Door Two.**

93

this as I could easily hear when the warder moved out of his office and passed through the doors leading to our section.

At this time Alex one day presented me with a piece of hacksaw blade which he had picked up some time earlier after the plumbers had been working in our section. He had kept it for a rainy day and in the end it became our most valuable key-making tool, without which the making of the wooden keys would have been much more laborious and risky. It was a short piece, about eight centimetres long, which I kept hidden between the sole and heel of my shoe for the entire duration.

We also had access to all the files any prisoner could ever dream of. These were kept in a special steel tool-cabinet in the workshop and were provided for use whenever we needed them (for jobs in the workshop, of course!). The tools were seldom counted and whenever a count was due to take place ample warning would be given. This allowed us to return any 'borrowed' tools we might have had out. I kept one file hidden in the hairs of my broom for many months while making the first wooden keys. This hiding place proved adequate for the most thorough of *'skuds'*—shake-ups (searches). Later on we made keys which enabled us to enter the workshop and open the metal cupboard whenever we wished, doing away with the need to keep such dangerous items as files in our cells.

Several other locksmith's requirements were procured in various ways. Denis managed to order a pack of epoxy glue under the pretext of needing it to repair broken cups. This he passed on to me and I used it for various jobs including the building up of key-cuts that had been filed too deep and, later, for glueing together the pieces of the metal keys we made. To speed up the curing time of the epoxy I made an allen key out of a nail so that I could open the cover of my cell lamp, which I could reach by standing on top of my cupboard. Glued objects placed inside the lamp cover would set in no time under the heat of the bulb.

The impression might be given in the following pages that the escape preparations were responsible for generating a certain degree of antagonism between us political prisoners. This was not so. While there were differences—some of them severe—over the planning of the escape or whether it should go ahead at all, we remained comrades to the end. The very escape was testimony to this comradeship, for without doubt had it not existed no escape could have taken place.

We were not in prison for criminal activities but for our political activities and beliefs. This had a profoundly uniting effect on us. We were all members of the ANC and therefore shared the same views on the political situation in our country and bore the same attitude toward our jailers. Most important of all, as members of a revolutionary organisation we were disciplined and shared in our suffering collectively. No one sought advantages over another or sought privileges that others did not have.

Our unity was the prime reason for our being kept separated from other prisoners. If we had been brought together with ordinary prisoners our example of struggling collectively for improvements would have undermined prison authority. The only way the prison masters can maintain control in an ordinary prison is by promoting individualism and competitiveness. Although prison, because it is such a personal experience, naturally brings out the worst forms of individualism in a prisoner, disunity has to be ensured by additional institutional measures. In South African prisons this is chiefly brought about by having a system of rewards in the form of a grading or classification system and by promises of parole and remission. Prisoners who behave themselves are promoted to higher categories which confer increased privileges in the form of more letters, visits, spending money and the like; persistent co-operation is rewarded with remission and parole. To us these things meant nothing as those who had earned greater privileges shared them with those who hadn't. And for us there was no remission or parole.

Had we been placed among ordinary prisoners we could never have considered escaping. At that time there was a standing reward for information leading to the prevention or exposure of an escape attempt. In ordinary prisons there was little need to apply this as there would always be some prisoner wanting to ingratiate him or herself to the authorities in the hope that it would bring remission. From us they had no hope of getting to know of a planned escape. For us an escape was a political act, not an individual flight for freedom. It was this implicit trust in each other as comrades that made the escape possible.

Our comradeship also gave us the strength to withstand the conditions imposed on us. It was not easy to live at close quarters with nine or fewer people for years on end. Inevitably small things about your fellow prisoners got on your nerves. In an ordinary prison such irritations and frustrations would be relieved through aggression but in our prison a structure had been developed by the comrades to deal with them without resorting to violence or personal attack. This was our 'recce' – short for 'recreation committee'.

'Recce' consisted of a democratically elected committee of two, each member of which had the responsibility of discussing with four others matters of mutual concern. It served as an conduit for complaints by one or more prisoners to the others. It was also the body through which our collective demands were formulated and presented to the prison authorities.

The prisoner who wanted to raise something would speak to his representative who would in turn discuss it with the three under him and pass it on to the other 'recce' representative. In this way we could pass on complaints and make demands and requests without holding open meetings. If there were any matters that required thorough and urgent discussion then general meetings were held. These were frowned upon by the officers, but never in my time did they openly intervene and stop one. They kept having our favourite bushes and trees uprooted, which forced us to hold our meetings in the often unbearable sunshine, but this never deterred us.

While we were at Pretoria Denis was the accepted 'leader' of the prisoners when it came to approaching the authorities. He had over the years won their respect and they considered him the most senior of the prisoners. The commanding staff in any case preferred to deal with one prisoner rather than face a united front because they liked to think that requests were coming from an individual rather than from a collective: they never wanted to appear to be giving in to group pressure.

While our unity and comradeship was our greatest source of strength it was also the source of the controversies that arose over the planning of the escape. A failed attempt, everyone knew, would lead to severe disruption and threaten the unity which gave us our strength. The differences arose out of this: some felt that the preservation of unity was paramount; those bent on getting out found it difficult to accept that others did not display the same drive to get out.

But despite the agonising over the escape plans we remained good friends underneath it all. We shared in each others ups and downs and offered each other comfort and advice. When a prisoner was refused a visit, did not receive a letter or had a problem with a girlfriend or wife, we all knew about it and commiserated with him. The strength of our friendship was such that at no point was there any fear that our plans would be compromised. More than anything else it was this that made the escape possible.

8
The Escape Group Expands

By August 1978, apart from Alex, Steve and myself, only one other comrade had expressed any interest in the escape project. At that time we had not formulated any concrete plans as we wanted first to improve our ability to open locks. Some approached the matter from an altogether different perspective: they insisted that we first work out a detailed plan so that our energies were not wasted on experimenting with keys which might never be needed. This difference in approach led to considerable tension and controversy, especially after others joined the escape group.

We believed that getting out was essentially a technical problem and as the comrades professed to be believers in the unity of theory and practice it surprised us – perhaps wrongly – that some of them looked on it as an intellectual problem. Theory, as we understood it, was to inform practice but practice had to serve as the basis on which the theory was to be constructed. Many of the comrades believed that the entire escape could be planned beforehand in the mind without knowing if or how it could be achieved in a practical sense.

Without wishing to divide ourselves into 'pragmatists' and 'intellectuals', our approach proved in the end the folly of trying to concoct complete escape plans before knowing everything that lies before you or the limits of your own capabilities. In August 1978, and for many months after, no one would have dreamt of escaping in the way that we finally did. The route eventually taken was not even considered as a remote possibility; it would have seemed a total fantasy. It was only after a long, frustrating process of experimenting and testing that we were able to overcome the barriers across our path. Our developing technical abilities suggested the route to take, not the converse.

Some of the schemes put forward by the comrades would have led to certain disaster. One suggestion was for us to sneak through the yard gate while the Captain was conducting his morning inspection of the *stokkies* in their yard. While inspections took place the armed guard on the *pos* stood to attention and it was thought that he might not notice a handful of prisoners making a quick getaway through the yard gate. Another plan proposed waiting for summer and a thunder-shower and then, when there was no warder in the yard and the *pos*-warder was sheltering in his enclosed corner, we would sneak out of the same yard gate.

At this early stage most of the comrades were reluctant to identify with us because they believed that our dabbling with locks and keys was but an expression of our anger at the sentences we'd been given.

They told us later that they had expected us to carry on experimenting and looking for escape routes for a short while and then either get bored or give up when we found out that in fact it was impossible to get out. Our fanaticism was expected to wear off in due course.

For this reason there were at first no attempts to formalise the escape: no suggestions of establishing an escape committee or of planning the necessary steps collectively. In a sense this made our activities 'undemocratic' because they were carried on without consultation with the others. But from very early on we realised that if we took each problem to the 'yard' (i.e. to everyone) the day of departure would have been delayed and the screws would have been alerted. Besides, our problems at that stage were purely technical and none of the others could offer much assistance.

The comrades' reluctance to participate was buttressed by the fear that these 'new guys' were going to upset things by getting themselves caught. These fears were reasonable enough, especially from those who'd been inside for a long time. It had taken them 15 years of hard struggle to achieve the conditions which prevailed in the prison. The 'privileges' which had been won over the years could easily be removed and then it would be back to square one; the stable relationship with the prison staff, which at best was no more than a precarious state of truce, could easily be reversed. All the old battles would have to be fought again.

From August until November 1978 practically all escape-related activity was spent in attempting to open door two. For more than a month I struggled for up to two hours at night to open my door. I had made about six number two keys in the hope of getting one to work by trial and error. There was no other way. I would try each key, file it a bit or build it up with epoxy and then try again, over and over. Each evening I was forced to stop, not by impending inspections, but by an aching arm caused by holding the crank out of my passage window for too long.

During the day I would make every effort to stare at the warders' number two keys in an attempt to capture a mental image which I could then 'measure'. But I couldn't see any difference: our keys looked exactly the same. After a while I began to wonder if there was some hidden secret we couldn't see. Alex persuaded me not to get superstitious.

Towards the end of October I finally managed to get key two to turn in my door. It was almost annoying how smoothly and easily it suddenly turned, as if there had been no problem all along. It could at least have jammed or nearly turned to let me know that I was getting close! The excitement combined with relief as the crank effortlessly turned the key was exhilarating. I felt dizzy with success and couldn't stop myself dancing a jig on my bed.

Keeping in mind the earlier disaster with number two, I turned the key one and a half times only and then relocked it. Fortunately it relocked all the way. If it had not done so it wouldn't have been too serious as the door would still have been locked one turn. I could not have been blamed for it being unmastered and even if the warders had suspected something there would have been no evidence that I had tampered with the lock as I would have disposed of all the keys down my toilet.

To make sure that it had not been a fluke that the key had worked I immediately filed all the other number two keys to the same dimensions as the one that had worked and tried them out. All worked with equal facility. I shouted to Alex and he stuck his shaving mirror out of his window to see what I was carrying on about. When I gave a thumbs-up — the agreed sign for a success — he shouted back to confirm that I had indeed achieved the long-awaited breakthrough. He was so overjoyed at the news that for a long time after he could be heard praising the Lord.

The excitement was short-lived though. The following night Alex tried the keys in his number two and found that not one of them worked. This had us completely baffled because we knew that the warders used the same key in his number two as in mine. Why our keys should then have worked in my door and not in his we could not understand.

I took the keys back the next day and made some alterations for him to try the next night. Again none of them worked. Disappointment on top of the recent success caused a serious ebb in morale, but we kept at it. One night Alex would try out some of the keys while I modified the others; the next night he would try out the ones I'd altered while I changed the ones he'd tried the previous night. This procedure went on for another month. It was a slow and tedious process, but eventually he got one to turn. I knew because I could hear him singing in his cell that night.

I tried the successful key in my own door the following night and found that it turned as easily as the one I'd got to work a month earlier. I then cut all the other number twos to the same dimensions as the successful one and found they worked in both our doors. At last we were certain that we'd got the measurements right.

The problem as far as we could work out was caused by not having the overall heights of the key-cuts correct, the relative heights having been established when the first one worked in my door. There seemed to be some tolerance in the overall dimensions but there was no way of knowing this at the time, forcing us to employ the trial and error methods that we did.

It had been discovered early on that not all the number two doors used the same key. Starting from my cell at the beginning of the section, each alternate cell used the same number two key which had given us so much trouble; the others used a number one key. Why this was so we could never figure out. Perhaps it was to confuse new warders who found it inordinately difficult to get the sections unlocked.

This duplication of keys actually simplified matters for us because it allowed us to use our number one keys, of which we'd made several. They were of a much simpler and robust design than the complicated number twos. It was also possible to test them during shower-time and on Fridays from the open-door position. All appeared to work, but as experience had taught us, there was no certainty they would work from the door-closed position.

Stephen's was one of these number one key number two doors but the prospect of having to go through the same rigmarole to test a key in it that we'd gone through to test our own drove us to think of an alternative scheme.

During October those prisoners who were allowed to study could remain in their cells over weekends to complete their studies before exams. Alex was one of these 'students' so he requested one Saturday to be locked in his cell 'to catch up on some work'. The usual practice when this happened was for the grille to be locked but for the outer door (number two) to be left open. Stephen happened to 'fall ill' on the same day and asked to be locked in his cell. He requested that his outer door be locked 'to prevent draughts'. I remained in the yard—the normal place to be on a Saturday—to signal to Alex when it looked like the warders were relaxing and unlikely to enter our section. When I gave the all-clear by lifting from the ground the book I was reading, Alex opened his grille with the number one key he had with him, crept down the passage to Stephen's cell and tested his number two lock with the same key. It worked perfectly.

After we had successfully opened our number twos Denis and Dave K wondered if the keys would work in their doors. We were sure they would but our earlier experiences informed us that to be certain they had to be tested.

Since both had doors which used the problematic number two key, they had to be tested with the crank from the door-closed position—i.e. at night. We gave Dave K the crank and a couple of keys to try out one evening. Our hearts thumped when he missed the keyhole trying to get the key in with the crank. Eventually he managed to get it in but he could not get it to turn. I was sure that he was trying to turn it the wrong way but he swore that he wasn't. Alex and I watched with our mirrors as he struggled for a long time to get the key out. After what felt like a heart-seizing eternity the key suddenly shot out and he pulled the crank back through his window and into his cell. Almost as he did so the night-warder came into the section on an unscheduled inspection round.

After that we decided it would be less risky for Alex or me to come out of our cells one night and test the locks directly. As Denis's and

Dave's cells were closest to mine and because I'd gained the most experience in opening doors the task fell upon me.

It was not a difficult mission but it required more courage than I imagined I possessed. Actually coming out of my cell was altogether a different matter to sticking a broomstick out of a window. If a warder came into the section while I was out of my cell it would be the end: there would be no way of turning it into an escape.

But all went well. I opened my doors after the music had stopped, as I'd done many times before, came out when I could hear no movements from downstairs and headed down the passage towards Denis's and Dave's cells. It was an eerie sensation as I stood in the passage: I was experiencing a situation which many prisoners had dreamt about but which no prisoner in that prison had ever experienced. I tried the key in Dave's door first and then in Denis's – it worked perfectly in both. Then back into my cell. I'd never felt happier to be in my cell than I did then. The whole operation had taken less than a minute, but more than a year off my lifespan.

By the end of 1978 there was a feeling among some of the comrades that we were just messing around and not concentrating on developing a proper plan. Perhaps in an attempt to ensure that the escape planning took a more collectively-inspired course the 'Washing Committee' ('WC') was set up, ostensibly as an escape committee to co-ordinate activities and liaise with the comrades. A point had been reached where it was evident to all that we were serious about our intentions and doubts about our motivations had been dispelled. It was therefore decided by the yard that a committee should be set up to bring our activities under the mantle of the yard democracy. This did not mean that henceforth every move had to have the blessing of the entire yard, but that the yard wanted some connection with the escape group and some say in affairs which would affect everyone. It was never clear exactly what the mandate of the WC was and it seemed to vary with time and depending on who was considering its functions. However, after a time its functions became accepted and its mandate became structured by practice rather than by a formal constitution.

Alex, Steve and I, at first not too pleased that our wings had been clipped, eventually welcomed the formation of the WC because it seemed to give our activities, if not approval, then at least an air of acceptance.

The committee finally accepted by the yard consisted of Alex and Dave Kitson. One member of the Committee had to be one of the three of us and this fell upon Alex because he was the most vociferous. I was more involved with the technical side, and as everyone knew, not much of a negotiator.

Despite what was ever intended for it the WC served in practice a vital function, especially at a later stage when more people were involved in the plans. It served as a focus for ideas and suggestions and for spreading these to other members of the escape group.

Before going on to discuss the first concrete escape plans which were contrived before the end of 1978, it is worth describing in more detail how we went about making our keys, how we managed to smuggle the necessary bits and pieces into and out of our cells and how we concealed the contraband.

Only seven of the ten of us worked in the workshop. Dave K was the official gardener so was excused from workshop duty. Denis used to be one of the best carpenters and even passed a trade test in carpentry while in prison, but was excused by the doctor because he had a gammy back. He had injured it in his youth while playing rugby and standing behind a bench for several hours gave him severe backache. He was the chief dishwasher, tea and milk maker and cleaner, but these were not particularly arduous tasks. He was assisted in this important work by Tony, so the chores were quickly done and the two of them were able to get on with the more important job of keeping themselves amused. Tony was excused from workshop duty because he had a co-ordination problem and could not handle tools at all. A short test proved that he would have severely damaged prison property, that is, himself.

In the workshop were four workbenches. Raymond and Dave R worked at the first next to the door and to where the warder usually sat; I worked alone at the second; Jeremy and Johnny at the next and Steve and Alex at the last. Alex, fortunately, had the best position for making illicit articles. Not only was he against the back wall of the workshop but between him and the wall was a tall rack of shelves on which were kept the parts we had to assemble for the prisons. The shelves and piles of wood gave him excellent hiding places for contraband.

Each bench had its own locker of woodworking tools that was unlocked at the beginning of the day by the warder on duty and in theory should have been relocked by him at the end of the day after checking that all the tools had been replaced. In practice it did not work like this. The prisoners closed their own lockers and seldom were there checks for missing tools. The 'security' cupboard containing the files and hacksaws, amongst other things, stood in the corner next to the door leading into the store-room. This would be opened on request if anything was needed out of it, but it was easy enough to return less to it than had been taken out.

While the rest of us dutifully sanded our items of prison woodwork, Alex was more often than not busy cutting out the bits of wood needed to make the keys. He would prop up the piece of furniture on which he was meant to be working in such a way that it would obscure what he was really doing. He also had an uncanny ability to appear to be doing the prison's work while actually doing something else. He did take twice as long as everyone else to complete his quota but he had always been the slowest so they did not suspect he was up to anything.

None of the objects Alex made on the side were recognisable to the warders, so even if he had been caught there would have been no serious consequences. In fact he, and for that matter all of us, were regularly 'caught' by the warders making personal things. So long as you had a good excuse, such as that you were making chess pieces or a pen holder, they didn't mind. Sometimes they would even get us to make or mend things for them. Johnny, who had proved himself over the years to be a competent fix-it-all, spent most of his time repairing damaged prison items and doing odd jobs for the warders.

Workshop duty for the warders was a singularly boring task as it involved sitting doing nothing for three hours in the morning and two and a half in the afternoon. Usually the sessions were totally uneventful: only occasionally would one of us speak to them and then only to comment about rugby, the cost of living or some other inane topic. We were generally well-behaved and got on with the work, which was probably not the case in most other prisons.

Most of the warders took a turn at workshop duty but one particular warder was assigned more or less permanently to the post. His name was Van Loggerenberg, or 'Loggie' as we called him. He was a fat, lazy hulk of a man with a drooping moustache and pointed pixie ears. I always said that if one were to attach an electroencephalograph to his head there would be an absolutely straight line, except for a slight bump now and then when he sucked on his pipe. He is the only person I've ever known who could sit dead still looking into space for three hours. He must have been asleep with his eyes open. Sometimes in the workshop his eyes would shut but he had a well-tested method of ensuring that this had no serious consequences. He would sit in front of the door and hold onto the door handle, and when he collapsed into his empty stupor his hand would drop off the handle and it would snap up and wake him. Loggie was totally uninterested in what was going on, and for his 'assistance' in this way we are eternally grateful. Thank you Loggie.

The bits and pieces Alex made during the day would be taken out of the workshop before the end of the afternoon work session. They would be deposited either behind the flush tank of the toilet next door or hidden behind some books in the store-room. At supper-time I would retrieve the pieces and conceal them in order to take them to my cell at lock-up. I was able to hide the pieces of key as well as sandpaper, files and whatever else I needed for an evening's keymaking session. Sometimes when there was too much to carry up in the usual way I would make 'key sandwiches' out of the five or so slices of bread we were given at supper. In the mornings the reverse procedure applied: I smuggled the items from my cell and then hid them in the store-room or downstairs toilet for later dispersal.

Sandpaper and other debris I flushed down my toilet.

At first I kept the completed keys behind a book rack in the store-room, then in a tin of sugar or bottle of lavatory cleaner in my cell. These were not very good hiding places compared to some of the places we were later to open up, but they proved adequate at the time. When there were too many keys for these hiding places I hid them in tins of sugar in the dining-room and in 'unopened' boxes of soap powder. When there were just too many for all these places Dave K buried some of them in the garden. They were first sealed in plastic bags, then placed in old jam and coffee jars and buried under particular plants so that they could be found again later.

★ ★ ★

The peaceful relations that existed between prisoners and prison staff were an important factor in the success of our escape. As I've indicated, a *modus vivendi* existed based on the principle of 'you leave us alone and we'll leave you alone'. Had any other form of relations prevailed it is doubtful whether an escape could have been pulled off. As the authorities had not for a long time been given cause to suspect that the prisoners were up to anything mischievous, they had allowed their watchfulness to diminish. Relations had been peaceful for so long that they were under the impression that all we wanted to do was read our boring text-books and talk our intellectual and unintelligible things. They had observed that when they left us alone we gave them no problems and responsibly got on with our affairs.

This state of affairs had not always existed. In the early sixties when the first comrades were brought to Pretoria Local, relations between the prisoners and staff were very strained. Vindictive warders made life as difficult as possible by rigidly applying a multitude of petty rules and regulations. The policy was to make the prisoners' lives hell and it appears that to a certain extent they succeeded. Political prisoners were kept for years in the very lowest classification grades, conditions were harsh, 'privileges' few, and hours out of cells, short.

On Robben Island the black prisoners were frequently beaten, overworked and starved. Conditions were never quite so bad for the white prisoners, mainly because they were white, but also because most had access to prominent lawyers and the press. The publicity for the authorities would have been too negative if they had violated the prison regulations too seriously. In any case, because of their prejudices they found it more difficult to assault and mistreat white prisoners than black prisoners – not that they had any great sympathy for 'communists', as they saw us.

Over the years the warders' attitudes matured. They learned that by being harsh on the prisoners they made life more difficult for themselves. Bad publicity resulted and the working day was unpleasant. As far as my experience goes, warders are generally lazy creatures and only join the prisons to get out of military service or because they can't find employment elsewhere. To spend the time chasing prisoners meant less time to read comics and newspapers, to sit and smoke pipes or do nothing. They also learned that if they were more relaxed the prisoners were more relaxed, caused fewer problems and were less inclined to want to get out. A relaxed atmosphere also meant that the prisoners would get on with their affairs openly and not resort to underhand activities.

None of us kowtowed to our jailers but neither did we seek confrontation. Our policy was to maintain a relationship of distance and least contact. This meant seeking a balance between compliance and outright defiance. Some of us tended more towards the one extreme and some to the other. But on the whole we obeyed the prison regulations and related to our captors in a spirit of firmness and dignity.

In prison situations where the conditions are extremely harsh there is a case for confronting your jailers aggressively and defiantly, especially if there is nothing to lose by doing so and those outside can derive succour from your stand. But where the conditions are not so severe or there is little chance of the outside world hearing of your struggle, a permanent state of war becomes counter-productive. No one's nervous system can take the strain of confrontation for years on end and anyway there is no point in destroying yourself for your jailers' delight.

As disciplined members of a revolutionary organisation our duty was to do whatever was best for our organisation, and this was not to destroy ourselves for publicity's sake. We had to ensure that we would be of value to the movement when we got out and this meant keeping ourselves healthy both physically and mentally. We had to keep ourselves informed of the current situation as best we could and advance our knowledge in such ways that we would be useful to the revolution later on.

Our attitude towards the prison staff paid dividends in that they accorded us a certain measure of respect and treated us as partly-civilised humans rather than as animals, which was how they treated ordinary prisoners, especially black prisoners. They knew it was unlikely that they would ever be assaulted by one of us and for this reason some of the usual security measures that applied in other prisons did not apply in ours. Searches, for instance, were rare and perfunctory. Sometimes the only sign that they'd been through your cell was a ruffled bedspread. They never found anything illicit so searches became a matter of mere routine. Never, while I was there at least, were we subjected to a thorough or humiliating body search. Occasionally they would go through our pockets, but even when they did there would be indications beforehand that something was afoot.

This trust in us had other small consequences which made life just that much more bearable. Ours was probably the only prison in the country where the prisoners were allowed to eat with knives and forks off proper china plates. In other prisons the prisoners were forced to eat with spoons out of steel dixies and in some of the most dangerous prisons even the handles of the spoons were removed. We were allowed to prepare food for ourselves from purchases made from our allowances and generally possess all manner of objects and substances normally considered dangerous.

As we were generally well-mannered and well-behaved, the warders did not find it necessary to watch over us very closely. In the mornings after opening our cells they would leave us alone in the section before letting us out into the yard. This gave us time to hide any contraband that we'd had out for the night. Most times while we were in the yard there would only be one or two warders in attendance. They paid scant attention to what we were doing and preferred to spend their time talking to each other or dreaming about their cars and girlfriends. In the workshop only one warder watched over us, and as they were not required to give any advice or assistance—and were usually incapable of doing so anyway—they invariably fell into a trance or stood in the doorway looking wistfully into the yard. There were seldom warders in attendance during meal-times and if there were it was not because they were intent on watching us eat but because they got bored watching nothing in the yard. At shower-time and on Friday mornings when we were cleaning our section there would be no warders in attendance at all. These periods on our own provided us with ample opportunity to get on with our 'illegal' activities.

Our 'good' behaviour fooled our jailers into thinking that we were all totally reconciled to our fate. Some of them even believed that as 'communists' we were proud of being in prison and were using our imprisonment to show the world that we were strong and could cope with any adversity. Stephen and I attempted to appear more resigned than the others: in doing this we had an advantage in that the warders had no previous knowledge of us. We kept our cells clean and tidy, dressed neatly and generally avoided giving the warders any cause to criticise us. It was important to make them feel that you respected and feared their authority. The urge to tease and taunt had to be suppressed and responses of anger, rudeness and arrogance avoided. When they spoke to us we attempted to appear intimidated and obediently carried out orders or instructions given to us.

Alex, unfortunately, had a bad reputation among the warders and officers. He was often rude and would visibly display his reluctance to respond to orders. He would laugh at new warders who attempted to throw their weight around or who tried to discipline him. He refused to keep his cell clean and tidy and his appearance was generally scruffy. For this reason he had never been promoted beyond

'B' group in his six years in prison; other prisoners had reached 'A' group within two. Not that this mattered a damn to Alex but his attitude had to change if he was going to give the impression that he was at last 'settling in' and not thriving on thoughts outside the prison.

After the escape idea had taken hold of him, Alex pulled up his socks: he began to dust down his cell. Within a few months his change of heart was noticed and he was 'rewarded' with a promotion to 'A' group. They thought that their magnanimous gesture had won him over, that he had been reformed, that he was going to give no more trouble. Little did they know . . .

For the first nine months of our sentence Captain Schnepel was the head of the prison. He was a bumptious old dog who imagined he instilled fear into everybody, but whose bark was worse than his bite. He was so grossly overweight and unfit that he had to take a break to catch his breath when he walked across the yard. His face would turn red and his handlebar moustache would twitch up and down in time with his panting. You could often not make out what he was saying under his snorting and puffing. To get across his message he would shout, but his mind was slower than his voice. He could never tell whether the comrades were having him on or not.

Captain Schnepel – 'Schneppie' we called him – was of the old school of warders. He believed that a *bandiet* was a *bandiet* and a 'communist' was a 'communist'. He had only contempt for the young guard who believed that you could look at a prisoner other than as a *bandiet* and a 'communist' other than as a 'communist'. He had been in charge of the politicals more or less from the start and had only become more lenient towards them because it was in his own interest, not because he had softened towards the 'communists'.

Why Schnepel was placed in charge of political prisoners I could never understand, because the question of political prisoners was a very sensitive one for the regime and he did nothing to make it easier for them. He had an abrasive personality and had annoyed countless visitors with his caprice, unreasonableness and irrationality. Perhaps his tenure had something to do with the internal politics of the Prisons Service, a residue of the old guard in a battle for ascendancy by the new school with their degrees and university theories.

In the first half of 1979 Schnepel was replaced by a sour-faced dwarf of a Captain by the name of Venter. Captain Venter had a face that had spent most of its life contorted into a scowl. The grimace had become permanently engraved so that even when he was smiling he looked miserable. He was a more constant personality than Schnepel and for this reason Steve and I guardedly welcomed the change. We had found it almost impossible to communicate with Schnepel, but the older guys said that they'd learned to handle him and that they preferred to stick with the devil they knew.

107

The advent of Venter brought rumours of 'big changes'. We wondered what these would be. Had he been brought in because the authorities had got wind of what we were planning? Would he scour the prison to start off with a clean sheet? Would he introduce new security measures? Only time would tell.

Within a month or two it became clear that nothing of the sort was about to happen. The atmosphere became more relaxed and the governors became more responsive to our demands and requests. While Venter tried to appear firm and in control he was really a weak man. Clearly he had personal problems, for he would often reek of alcohol. It did not take long for the prison staff to nickname him 'Half-Jack'.

The change of Captains was not the only change in staff during our time: there was a tremendously high turnover of warders. Twice a year there would be an influx of pimply-faced youngsters fresh from prison college. Some of these new recruits were only 18 years of age and found it difficult to address us by the stipulated surname only. Sometimes one of them would preface a name with a 'Mister' and we would laugh them out of our presence.

Warders who served in our prison were thoroughly briefed on how to handle the 'communists': there was to be no talking to them except to give instructions and they were to be watched extra carefully because they were *slim* — treacherous. It took a few months for them to learn that we were not monsters but ordinary people, not at all like the criminals and gangsters they'd been taught about in college.

This high turnover of staff had both advantages and disadvantages for us. It took a while to get to know the whims and habits of particular warders and consequently we felt more at ease with those who had been around for longer. New warders were unpredictable and some would deliberately do things to try to catch us out. The obverse applied from their perspective: older warders knew our behaviour better and were able to detect changed patterns; new warders would not know what to expect. We were able to use both these factors to our advantage. For instance, we would only test our number twos at night when warders whose behaviour we knew well were on duty. Later on we took advantage of newly-arrived warders to do things which we would not have contemplated had older warders been on duty.

It is probably true of warders throughout the service that they are not the brightest of creatures. This is no doubt due to the fact that the job is one without much status and hence does not attract towards it the nation's geniuses. Some of the specimens who worked in our prison were close to borderline cases. There was one warder, unfortunately named Van der Merwe (a butt of dunce jokes in South Africa), whom Alex nicknamed 'Mongo' after a particularly thick character who rode an ox in the American comedy-western, *Blazing Saddles*. Van der Merwe was definitely half-man, half-brute. When he was on duty on the *pos* he would march up and down with his arms flailing to the accompaniment of his own voice shouting 'left, right'. He was once discovered in the toilet attempting to see from how far back his stream of piss would still reach the wall. It must have been a world record. Another time he was found having fisticuffs with a grille and challenging it to hit back.

On the whole it was difficult for us to judge the warders correctly, as they were not really in their element. Most of them were Afrikaans-speaking and could not understand English properly. Although most of us were fairly fluent in Afrikaans we were not familiar with their everyday topics of conversation. Also, ours was not really a prison in the sense in which they had been trained to serve. They were instructed to treat us differently to ordinary prisoners and to avoid human contact as far as possible. As such the job was extremely boring and soul-destroying, which accounted for the large number of resignations and transfers.

Although the warders were just doing a job they were wittingly or unwittingly playing a political role which one day they will have to account for. This applies especially to the officers who knew what the game was all about. They in particular have been responsible for keeping some of our best people behind bars for so long. How many years of lives have they wasted? How much have they contributed to the continued existence of the apartheid regime? . . . We know.

9

First Plans

It was towards the end of 1978 that we began to think of escape routes which did not start from or pass through the prison yard. The initial observation that there could be no other departure point than the yard had strait-jacketed our escape-thinking up till then; the realisation that there could be another way brought forth an explosion of fresh ideas. Although we neither had the technical means nor could visualise how to do it, our recent successes suggested that a route taking the front door as the departure point was not entirely inconceivable.

We had looked over all possibilities involving the yard, but none of them was very satisfactory. Any escape going this way would have involved either going out through the yard gate into the prison property next door or scaling a wall.

The prospects of using the yard gate had improved slightly from the time when Stephen and I arrived, as the old Pretoria Local Prison next door was being knocked down and excavations for a new building had started. As such 'next door' was a deserted building site at night, not a well-guarded prison precinct.

It was common knowledge that the yard gate used a number one key but the main problem was in deciding when the best time would be to get out through it. During the day when we had access, getting out would have been impossible because the warder on the *pos* would have used us for target practice. After lock-up we would have had to break out of our cells, capture the night-warder, tie him up and then make our way outside. Within an hour of lock-up the guard-dog was placed in the yard, introducing another obstacle which would have had to be overcome. In the yard we would also have been in full view of the *stokkies* in the other wing who undoubtedly would have raised the alarm.

These were not seen as insurmountable obstacles. We could have made our exit before the dog was placed in the yard or, if it was already there, it could have been lured inside the building or poisoned. And if we were dressed in suitable clothing we would have looked like *stokkies* to the *stokkies*, not as escaping political prisoners. These were, however, complicating factors which could easily have caused the plans to go awry.

To escape over the wall into the street presented the same problems. There was one weak link, however. This was the short piece of wall next to the front door which joined the main building to the *pos*. Here the wall was not as high as the rest and once over it you

110

were in freedom and not still on prison property as would have been the case had we climbed over anywhere else. The problem of the dog could have been solved by closing the *stokkies'* yard gate, which we would have reached by passing through their section and out of their yard door.

A serious problem with this plan was that if there had been any *stokkies* in the cells above ours they would have seen us in their yard and scaling the wall – they could not be trusted not to raise the alarm. When there were only a few of them signed in, the cells above ours were not used but it was difficult for us to find out if they were in use or not. If we could have found a way of answering this unknown this route may have become the chosen one. However, this option was only realistic while there was no guard on the *pos* in the evening and was later eliminated when one was placed there permanently.

Considerable thought and experimentation was devoted to some of these plans. Alex and I carried out a number of tests to find out if the dogs would accept food thrown to them because it was claimed that they were trained not to accept food from anyone other than their handlers. This seemed to be partially true but there were some dogs that accepted whatever food was thrown at them. As only a limited number of dogs were used, we could simply have waited until they used one that we knew would accept food. Then we could either have poisoned it or lured it somewhere where it would have been out of our way.

But it was in the face of all these problems and in the light of the confidence we'd gained from our practical achievements that we started to turn our attention towards getting out through the front door. The initial plans involving this exit were a bit wild, but that was to be expected because we did not know exactly what lay in front of us – forcefulness substituted for thoughtfulness. One scheme involved capturing the night-warder, tying him up, taking his keys to get out (we did not realise at this stage that he was locked into the prison and only had keys to enable him to move from section to section), taking his car keys and weapon (if any) and making a getaway in his car which he parked outside.

Although we assumed that the night-warder would have the keys to enable us to open all the doors on the way to the front door, we could not be certain. We realised, for instance, that the keys might be locked in a cupboard – for which he might have no key. So, to avoid finding ourselves in an embarrassing situation on the day we escaped, we decided to develop our door-opening abilities to the extent of being able to open any door, even when confronted by it for the first time. This meant perfecting our lock-picking skills and making keys for the workshop so that we could at any time get hold of the tools we might need: hammers, levers, chisels, screwdrivers, hacksaws and so on.

We took advantage of Loggie's laziness here. Most days he found it too much bother to get up from his seat to open the metal

111

tool-cupboard where all the 'security' tools were kept. Many times he would, against the rules, hand us his bunch of workshop keys and allow us to get out whatever tools we needed. On the bunch were the keys for the metal cupboard, the tool lockers and the two workshop doors. It was easy enough to take impressions of them on a piece of soap while pretending to be searching for something in the cupboard, and then to make our own keys.

The key for the metal cupboard was a small Yale-type key while the two for the doors were ordinary small mortise lock keys—miniature versions of our cell keys. It did not require much skill to make a replica of the cupboard key out of a small piece of aluminium found in the workshop. The two door keys were made out of wood, in much the same fashion as the larger number one and two keys.

Having these was a tremendous boon because we then had access to the workshop and all the tools we could possibly want, whenever we needed them. We could get into the workshop through the interior door at the back of the store-room, out of the sight of the warders. One of us would sit at the entrance to the store-room and watch for signs of approaching warders while the other would enter the workshop and help himself to any tools that were needed. We did not bother making keys for our own tool lockers because we could simply leave out during the day any tools we needed from them and then retrieve them on entering the workshop after it was shut. Our bench lockers did not in any case contain much of value for keymaking or door-forcing.

The tools I required for evening keymaking sessions were usually retrieved from the workshop at supper-time. I would take them secretly up to my cell in the usual way and replace them the next morning before breakfast while the comrades were getting dressed for their morning run and exercise.

After making keys for the workshop we made keys for every other door to which we had regular access. These were the two doors to the dining-room, the door leading into the yard at the bottom of the stairs to our section, the store-room outer door, the visiting-room door, the awaiting-trial prisoners' yard door and door number four (the metal grille at the start of the administrative section). Door number three, our section door, used a number one key, obviating any effort there.

The measurements of the keys for the dining-room outer door, the door at the bottom of our stairs and the awaiting-trial prisoners' yard door were obtained by taking soap impressions when warders inadvertently left the keys in the locks. The warders did not bother too much about the security of these doors as they did not lead anywhere of importance and were just ordinary wooden doors with small mortise locks. The measurements of the key for the store-room outer door were obtained by removing the lock from the door one Saturday while the others were playing tennis. The lock was opened and a prepared blank cut to the correct measurements there and then. This I did in the dark recess at the back of the store-room while Alex or Steve stood guard at the entrance.

The measurements of the key for the visiting-room door I obtained one day by catching a quick glimpse of the key when I entered the room for a visit. The key was in its lock and when I entered there was no warder or visitor in the room. I quickly pulled it out, looked at it, and put it back. Its measurements were simple: like a number one key, only smaller. I made a key from our large stock of blanks and one showery day while there was no one in the yard, Dave K and I took shelter in the doorway. Behind my back I inserted the key and turned it. I pulled the door handle and the door opened.

The key for the dining-room double-door at the bottom of our stairs was normally handed to Dave K on Fridays so that he could open the door to bring through the film equipment which was kept in a small cupboard under the stairs. The only measurement that needed to be taken was the height of one of the outer cuts relative to the key-shaft; the rest could be obtained by sight.

Key four was also a cinch as it had a very simple shape. We frequently got a chance to see it when taken into the administrative section. Its bit was flat along the top except for two shallow cuts about 1 mm deep. I prepared a key to the same basic dimensions as keys one and two, filed the cuts as I had seen them and tried it out one day while passing the grille on the way down to the yard. It failed to work the first few times but by lowering the overall heights of the cuts a fraction each time I eventually succeeded. Key four was also the key for door five, the next grille down the passage on the way to the front door.

Regular trips out of and back into the prison by the comrades helped us build up a thorough picture of the number and types of doors on the way to the front door. Quite often someone would go out – either to the dentist, the doctor or the optician – and be issued with instructions to look for this or that crucial detail.

Having made the key for doors four and five we knew that we only had to make two more of the large-type prison keys – for doors six and seven. Door six was a panelled steel door the same as our outer cell doors; door seven a grille. Door eight was also a grille but was electrically-operated. We knew that the button to open it was in the main office where the night-warder sat during his shift – you could see the warders pressing it as you were taken out. Doors nine and ten were ordinary wooden doors like the others in the prison and used the small-type mortise keys. Door ten was the front door, the door to freedom.

The door that gave us the most worries was door six because no one had ever seen its key. Whenever we went into the administrative section it was open and hooked back against the wall. But Denis remembered from an occasion some years previously when he was brought back from hospital very late one night that door six had been closed. From this piece of information it made sense to assume that it was only locked at night, by the departing day-staff, to lock the night-warder into the prison. This turned out to be the case, as we later found out.

Key seven we would occasionally see, so we had a vague idea of its shape. But this door did not worry us much as we knew that we could, if necessary, tackle it another way—by cutting the bars or dismantling its lock. That left only keys six, nine and ten about which we knew nothing.

If you do not have the key for a lock the only other ways to open it are to smash it or pick it. Smashing doors was not our style so we set about training ourselves to become master lock-pickers. Our knowledge of how locks worked had grown considerably so it was not too difficult to figure out how to make lock-picks. The greatest advance was made one night when I managed to smuggle a shifting-spanner and screwdriver into my cell and then used them to remove and open my number one lock. The lock was held to the frame by four bolts, the ends of which were hammered over to stop the nuts being turned off. But with the help of a small triangular file from the 'security' tool-cupboard I was able to restore the thread and loosen the nuts. I removed the lock from the frame, dismantled it and measured its internals in minute detail. To help us understand the geometry of the lock and to reveal possible hidden secrets I also made accurate tracings of the levers onto a piece of paper.

If I may say so myself, we made some quite ingenious lock-picks from pieces of bent wire after that. We spent hours practising how to use them on the inner workshop door and on our number one locks, and in no time became quite adept at picking the prison's locks. One of our picks was actually a special shaftless key with adjustable cuts for opening the smaller locks in the wooden doors. Once the vague shape of the key was known this device worked as easily as the real key. What were formerly barriers became openings; what was solid became paper.

In the end we had more keys than our jailers, which presented us with a massive security problem—where to hide them all. With such a vast amount of equipment it became vital that we found some better hiding places than the ones we were using.

As luck would have it, fate presented us with the perfect hiding place just when we most needed it. One day, after the plumbers had been to repair one of the hot water geysers in our shower, we noticed that the door to the closet in which it was housed had been left unlocked. Inside the closet, behind the geyser, was the perfect place for storing our contraband. If we made keys for the closets—there was one in each shower—we would have two massive and secure storage spaces.

114

So, one shower-time I removed the lock of the unlocked door and hid it in my cell over supper-time. Risky? Not at all. The warders never had a shake-down during supper: the time was too short and they were in any case readying themselves to go home. That evening I took a blank that had been prepared beforehand and cut a key to work the lock. The lock was replaced the next morning before we were let out of the section for breakfast.

The following Friday we picked the lock of the other closet and left the door unlocked to see if it would be noticed. It wasn't, so a few days later I made a key for it in the same way as I'd made the first one. All our gear was then placed in a sack and dropped down the triangular space between the geyser and the corner of the closet in which it stood. A piece of string was attached to the sack so that it could be pulled up again. To keep the string out of sight a piece of black cotton was tied to the end of it and led over the pipes at the back of the geyser and hidden there. To retrieve the sack you first had to find the piece of cotton, then pull up the string and finally the sack.

The geyser closets proved to be the ideal hiding places and were used to the end. They did give the occasional problem, such as the time when a leak occurred in one of them and the plumbers had to be called in – but that story is for later.

Also at this time – the end of 1978 – our thinking began to turn towards getting our hands on some civilian clothing. So far the only non-prison garments we had were two pairs of short socks – not exactly enough for a whole gang of convicts to break loose in. These had been retrieved from the rubbish bin in the *stokkies'* yard.

Alex in his usual pioneering way put in an order for two white T-shirts for 'sports use' – the first time anyone had done so. Inexplicably the order was granted without question and two more items were added to our wardrobe. I ordered some coloured drawing inks via Denis to dye one of the shirts for myself. After this everyone ordered T-shirts for themselves – for both legitimate and illegitimate purposes.

For trousers I took one of my voluminous pairs of prison trousers and modified them to look like a pair of khaki bell-bottom jeans (they were in fashion at that time and khaki was trendy!). Everyone had proper running shoes (trainers) which were quite suitable for escaping in. Alex, who was always scratching around in rubbish bins, later found a pair of shorts in one of the *stokkies'* bins. Only the fly zip was missing but he soon replaced this with one from an old tobacco pouch. I made three belts from an old piece of canvas someone found in the workshop and Alex carved three buckles out of wood for them. We made these openly and Alex even wore his belt to assist in the everyday job of keeping his oversize prison trousers around his waist. Steve and I made ourselves caps – modelled on Denis's tennis cap – out of surplus prison shirts and a few pairs of gloves and some balaclava-style 'terrorist' hoods out of surplus vests. All this was ultimately stored in our cache behind the geysers.

Prison is not good for much, but I'm thankful for the various skills I learnt during my short stay. I picked up a few tips about carpentry, but most of all I'm now a proficient seamster and locksmith (read: lock-picker).

★ ★ ★

According to traditional penological theory, a prison sentence is supposed to serve five purposes: it is *punishment* for the offender; it is to *rehabilitate* the prisoner; it is to act as a *deterrent* to others; it *prevents* the offender from committing the same or other offences, at least while he or she is in prison; it *protects* society from the offender. In political cases there are two other purposes in imprisonment: the *political* purpose and the *retributive* purpose.

Starting from the last: the vengeance inherent in political imprisonment is not aimed at the individual; it is aimed at the organisation which has had the temerity to challenge state authority. To the state the individual prisoner is nothing, just a number. Vengeance is closely allied to the political purpose of imprisonment.

The political purpose itself has several dimensions. First of all, the state uses it to demonstrate to its enemies that it still has power and that it will use that power when and how it likes in order to preserve its authority. It also uses it to demonstrate to its followers that it is still in control; that its enemies will not get far.

Political imprisonment in South Africa, while it 'protects' whites from the 'offender', does not protect the majority of the people—for they do not want to be 'protected' from those imprisoned for political reasons, but rather from the state itself. Political prisoners are seen as freedom fighters and those who have been involved in armed actions against the state in particular, are seen as heroes and protectors of the people.

Political imprisonment does of course prevent prisoners from engaging in the activities for which they were imprisoned, but in the long term it serves to encourage others to take up where the imprisoned left off. In the same way political imprisonment fails as a deterrent. While it does deter some, others take the imprisonment of their comrades as added cause to challenge the state.

There is no way that political imprisonment can serve to rehabilitate a political prisoner. For a political prisoner 'rehabilitation' means re-education and in South Africa this means adopting the ideology of apartheid—hardly likely even for a prisoner broken by the experience. Had the authorities attempted to 'rehabilitate' prisoners it would have been resisted with everything at the prisoners' disposal. They knew this and it is for this reason they did not try their hand at it. All they could hope for is that the experience would serve to

116

mellow the prisoners or sap their resolve to fight apartheid when they get out. It usually did the opposite.

Finally, for imprisonment to serve as a punishment it has to be perceived as such by the prisoner. The prisoner must show some remorse, feel guilty and at the bottom of it recognise that what he or she has been committed to prison for is considered by society to be 'wrong', a crime, anti-social and deserving of punishment. In political imprisonment the prisoners show no contrition. Their imprisonment convinces them that they were absolutely correct in doing what they did and only makes them regret not having done more. In South Africa, only supporters of 'the system' agree to the imprisonment of the opponents of apartheid; to the oppressed majority those con-victed for fighting apartheid have committed no offence at all. The only offence is the imprisonment of the alleged offender by the state.

The punishment inherent in imprisonment is the loss of freedom itself. Anything over and above this is vindictiveness. For this reason we as political prisoners could not help feeling victimised. Our punishment went way beyond the normal loss of freedom associated with imprisonment. Special conditions applied to us which made life very difficult. This was intentional as our captors wanted to inflict their vengeance on us. We were the political enemy, 'communists', and in their eyes not worthy of recognition as human beings. They knew that we could not be 'rehabilitated' and so had to ensure that when we left prison we were broken and no longer desirous of 'making trouble'. The only way of doing this, they thought, was by ensuring that we were kept permanently demoralised; that we were cut off from events in the real world as effectively as possible by being denied all 'news' of everything. They knew as well as we did that our morale was based on developments in the political world, not on the conditions of our immediate existence.

What this meant in practice was at first a total black-out on news, and later, as they became more sophisticated, only the transmission of news which they considered to be good news, that is, what we interpreted as bad news. The total ban on news applied until 1978. Before that time there were no newspapers, no radio broadcasts, no news magazines – nothing. The prisoners were not allowed to discuss anything apart from family news with visitors and the same applied to letters. The authorities were so obsessed about this that the only periodicals they allowed were a handful of family and entertainment and sports magazines. Even these were subject to rigid censorship and often had vast sections removed from them. The censor would meticulously search through everything in the pursuit of anything which smacked of 'news', or 'sex' – the other bogey. If something was found the whole article would be excised, not just the offending line or paragraph.

The lengths the censors would go to to remove the news drove the comrades to desperation and in 1977 they made a court application for an order to ease the restrictions placed on them. The prisoners' request was that they be allowed to receive newspapers and magazines of their own choice, to have less censorship of their letters, and to have freer conversations without interference during visits. In their application the comrades claimed that the deprivation of news was 'cruel, inhuman and unnecessarily harsh treatment'. They asked no more than that they be treated in the same way as other prisoners.

During the court case, which the comrades were not allowed to attend, the prison authorities confirmed that the witholding of news was their way of 'rehabilitating' political prisoners. The state representative said that 'the individual propensities of these so-called political prisoners could be cured by not allowing them to know what is going on'. The comrades' lawyer argued that to live without any real knowledge of the world was cruel, vindictive punishment.

The comrades' application was dismissed by the judge. In summing up he said that to grant the order would fetter the discretion of the censors and would mean the end of the prison authorities' right to exercise the function entrusted to them. He clarified the state's view by commenting: 'News is not necessary for me. The last thing I want to do is look at the news'.

The comrades appealed against the judgement and lost that too. In the end, however, they won a moral victory because the absurdity of the efforts to keep political prisoners in the dark were exposed to the world. Shortly after the appeal the rigid censorship began to break down. Within a short time letters began to be left largely intact, interference in conversations during visits became less frequent and the comrades were allowed to receive a wider range of periodicals. Not only had they achieved an actual improvement for themselves but the prisoners on Robben Island, who had been conducting a similar campaign over the years, were granted the same 'privileges' as well.

By the time that Steve and I arrived at Pretoria heavily censored SABC news broadcasts – which were highly censored versions of the truth in the first place – were being relayed over the loudspeaker system twice daily. Virtually all news about South Africa was cut out except for sports news and the most trivial items which displayed the regime in a good light (from their point of view). Foreign news was also heavily censored but the censor, not being too bright, would often not know what was 'bad' news and what was 'good' news from their viewpoint. Sometimes the most startling things would come through. For instance, for long periods we'd hear about the advance of the revolution in Nicaragua and about events in Afghanistan. The censor had obviously never heard of these places.

The radio broadcasts were a step forward – not a big one – but a foot in the door. Like all 'privileges' they could be removed or their removal could be used as a threat against us. But through attrition we gradually wore down the rigidity of the censor. In 1979 we were allowed to receive *Time* magazine – censored of all references to South Africa – and shortly after we escaped political prisoners were allowed uncensored daily newspapers.

Despite the blanket ban on news the comrades had managed to keep themselves amazingly well-informed over the years. One important source of news was from new prisoners who came to the prison. They were 'debriefed' by the others and every ounce of information squeezed from them. Another source was the representatives of the International Committee of the Red Cross who visited us, and all other political prisoners in South Africa, once a year. They would fill us in on events during the preceding year and give us their analysis of current developments. The major source of news, however, was smuggled newspapers. Extraordinary as it may seem, for long periods we read newspapers, or parts of them, every day.

The smuggling worked like this: the administrative section of our prison was cleaned by black prisoners who were brought to the prison each day from the black section of Pretoria Prison. Part of their work was to empty the rubbish bins inside the prison into the main bins in the *stokkies'* yard and to take these out of the prison for emptying. The bins would be taken out through the yard gate, emptied somewhere, and then returned through the same gate. The cleaners often found newspapers, thrown out by the warders or *stokkies*, in smaller bins inside the prison. This we knew because occasionally we would find a piece of newspaper in the bins in the *stokkies* yard, where we emptied our own bins. They could also, presumably, bring newspapers from their own prison.

To initiate the smuggling act one of us would go to the toilet next to the workshop while the black prisoners were waiting in front of the yard gate to be let out with the bins. From there he would mimic the action of reading a newspaper and point to the *stokkies'* bins, meaning that if they got hold of any papers they should leave them in the bins. He would then mimic smoking and point again to the bins, meaning that we'd exchange tobacco, the prison currency, for any newspapers.

The black prisoners understood exactly what we wanted and would indicate agreement of the trade with a thumbs-up disguised as a scratch of the hair with a thumb. They were obviously skilled smugglers and understood prison sign-language and needs even better than we did. Sometimes they indicated that they wanted other things apart from tobacco, such as a pack of cards, soap, aspirin or other medicines. We were amazed – and shocked – that they could not get these basic items which we took for granted.

The system worked perfectly for months at a time. The tobacco would be wrapped in a piece of dirty brown paper and be deposited in the *stokkies'* bins by Denis or Tony when they emptied our kitchen bin each morning; the newspaper would be retrieved later in the

119

morning when the kitchen bin was 'emptied' again. If it was a good chunk of newspaper the reward would be greater the next day: half a bag of tobacco for a page or two, a whole bag or more for several pages or a whole paper.

The newspapers were hidden in the store-room during the day and taken up to the cells at shower-time. At shower-time the paper was split in two, one half to the five cells on the one side of the shower and the other half to the other five. The papers were passed on to the next comrade by means of an ingenious device made from two long rulers. The rulers were joined together with a rubber band and then pushed under the door in the direction of the next cell. The rubber band would cause the first ruler to spring under the next door instead of just following the bottom of the wall. The next comrade would then grab the end of the first ruler and pull in the second, to which was attached by a piece of string an envelope containing the folded pieces of newspaper. The following night the two halves were swapped over. The last comrade on each side to receive the piece would finally dispose of it down his toilet.

In this way we were able to keep ourselves reasonably well informed, but the system had its dangers and broke down several times, sometimes for as long as two or three months. When this happened we really felt the pressure of our enemy's attempts to 'rehabilitate' us!

Occasionally the warders would discover a piece of newspaper on one of the black prisoners, or find the tobacco or piece of newspaper in the *stokkies'* bins. Then there would be pandemonium. Although nothing happened to us, the entire gang of black prisoners would be punished or changed for a new group. Each time a new group of prisoners was brought in the system had to be set up again and if the prisoners had been threatened not to engage in smuggling with us they would be very reluctant to co-operate.

Nevertheless, practically the whole time we had newspapers to read. The authorities probably knew that we were smuggling but could do little to stop it. They were reluctant to tackle it from our end as they didn't want to upset relations – constant searches would have fouled the air too much. If one of us had been caught, punishment could only have been imposed after an internal 'trial'. Since it was within our rights to request a lawyer on such occasions – the comrades had always done so in the past – the bother and embarrassment of having to hold 'court' with a skilled lawyer present was usually too much for them.

We knew their feelings on this matter and for that reason took no extra-special precautions about transporting and reading the papers. They were carried up to the section after lock-up when there was little chance of being caught. If you heard a warder coming while you were reading a paper you simply threw it under your bed. If he did manage to catch you reading, you could calmly tear it up and flush it down the toilet in front of his eyes as he had no access to the cells. If there was a 'trial' it would only be his word against yours. However, it was not advisable to get caught as it would only make it more difficult to keep the system going.

There were other ways of getting news of the world and details of our immediate surroundings – these were from visitors, letters and warders. Strictly speaking, the only matters that were allowed to be discussed with visitors or written about in letters were family affairs and news of friends. But all of us got around these restrictions by developing code-words with our most regular visitors and correspondents which referred to certain political figures or countries. Stephen and I were ahead of the others in this respect as we had agreed with our parents while awaiting trial on a set of code-words to refer to various countries and political organisations. For example: Angola was Angela; Mozambique was Mary, and Frelimo was 'her boy-friend'; Rhodesia – Roger; Namibia – Nancy, and SWAPO 'her boy-friend'; ANC – Anthony; Britain – Aunt Bertha; USA – Uncle Sam; and so on. Although the need to use this code seldom arose, it came in useful when the newspaper smuggling broke down or if there was an urgent need to know the latest on some major international development.

Denis and the others had established similar codes with their visitors over the years. Denis's code in particular was sophisticated enough to enable him to make contact with the movement in connection with the escape.

Stephen and I had other letter codes which we had set up while awaiting trial. One of these could be used to describe conditions in the prison and our own treatment. It involved writing the letter according to various formats, each configuration conveying information about the degree to which the food was edible, of the nature of our treatment, and so on. Another less descriptive code could be used to convey a short, accurate message. We never used any of these codes as the clamp on talk about conditions was not as tight as we'd imagined it would be and we never thought it advisable to inform our families about our real intentions.

The prison staff themselves were a major source of information about the prison and surroundings. Although they were instructed not to talk to us about such things, some were quite willing to answer questions which seemed totally innocuous and were fond of bragging about the 'impenetrable' security barriers on the terrain. From warders we were able to extract information about such things as dog patrols, dog handlers and their dogs, security arrangements, sentry duties, shifts, changes in routine and security, morale, who hated whom, which warders were corrupt, and other things such as whether the old currency (like that we'd brought in) was still legal tender.

These questions could be asked in much the same way as we would

121

ask them of our visitors – not directly but as requests for comments on something about which you pretended to know already. For instance, we would often hear dogs barking at night and to try to find out where they were stationed we'd say something like: 'I can't work today, *Meneer*, because the dogs were making so much noise last night. Why must they have dogs in the empty yard next door? They just keep us awake.' One particular warder named Moreby, who was much hated by the prisoners, was also hated by the other warders. To ascertain the level of antagonism towards him we'd say to another warder: 'It's good when you're on duty in the workshop, *Meneer*. You know, when *Meneer* Moreby is on duty here he walks around looking at our work so much it puts us off and we can't get on with the job.' Inevitably they'd also have something disparaging to say about him.

The warders were also a source of news about the world in general, although not a reliable one. Sometimes after reading something in a smuggled newspaper and then not finding out the outcome we'd ask a warder, provided it was not the censor, to comment on the matter. For example, we once read that there was going to be a by-election but then never found out the result. Someone then asked a warder what he thought about a particular party – the party thought least likely to have won – winning the election. The warder responded indignantly that the traitorous party just mentioned had not won the election. The Nationalists, the party he obviously supported, had scored a landslide. To clear the matter the person who had asked the question then said: 'Oh, I must have heard it wrong on the radio'.

10
First Escape Date

By the end of 1978 the first plan of escape had taken shape—the product of countless hours of debate and dispute. With hindsight it can be said that the plan contained a large element of adventuristic ideas, but at the time we weren't aware of the many pitfalls that lay before us. It was not a complicated plan: it involved leaving our cells shortly after lockup (at 5 pm to be more precise), quietly moving downstairs, passing through door four, jumping the night-warder in his office, tying him up and taking his prison and car keys.

Door six remained a major problem but we'd thought of various ways to tackle it. We hoped that one of our many keys would fit its lock or that we would find the key for it in the possession of the night-warder. If not, there was a contingency plan which involved going out into the yard, entering the visiting-room, smashing the window separating the two halves of the room and then re-emerging in the passage beyond door six but before door seven.

Door seven wasn't considered much of an obstacle because we could cut through its bars with a hacksaw, or dismantle its lock with a spanner. Door eight we would open by pressing the button in the warder's office before going out into the yard. Doors nine and ten were wooden doors which we could smash open, or, as they opened inwards and exposed their hinges, we could dismantle these. Then we would all jump into the warder's car outside and drive off into the setting sun. Simple as that!

The plan was somewhat far-fetched and undoubtedly suicidal, but based on our knowledge of the prison and terrain at the time it seemed feasible. Getting out was a bit like making your way through a jungle: if you know the way and all the hazards that lie before you the chances of getting through are good; if you know nothing the tendency is to take chances based on intuition, with unknown results.

By January 1979 both Denis and Dave K were fully behind us and prepared to come along on the first date, which had been set for a Saturday in early February. It was understandable that Denis should have shown an interest because he had everything to gain by escaping. He'd spent 15 years in prison and had no release date to look forward to. As we began to show that the prison's doors were not as impenetrable as he'd been led to believe, his attitude grew more positive. Dave K had always shown an interest in the escape even though he had not at first displayed any keenness to participate. He looked at escaping in much the same way as we did, largely as a

123

technical problem.

Although those of us in the escape group were determined to break out, there was an air of unreality about the whole affair. We had a plan but no one we spoke to had real faith in it. Privately we could somehow not see ourselves tip-toeing down to the warder's office and pouncing on him there; we could not see ourselves tying him to a grille and fastening a gag around his mouth; we could not see ourselves casually hopping into his car and driving off to freedom. That was the stuff of movies, not reality.

As the escape date approached, Denis rightfully began to raise a number of objections and problems. Then two days before the date I was told that outside contacts had responded to a request for escape assistance and claimed to be able to provide transport, a safe house and all the rest if we would give them some time and further details. Denis had conveyed the request in a letter code which he had established many years previously and kept up to date to cover new situations.

A vote was taken on the issue and it was decided to postpone the attempt until help could be arranged. Those participating felt that in view of the increasing number of people showing an interest in escaping, our chances would be infinitely improved if we could be assured of outside assistance and did not have to rely solely on our own resources to get away. It would also then not matter so much if the actual break-out was not a neat one as we would be able to get away from the mess quickly. Only Alex voted against postponement. Looking back, it was a good thing that he was defeated on that one occasion.

We realised that it would take some time to arrange assistance and for some reason – probably impatience – assumed that two months would be sufficient. From our point of view we considered this reasonable: when you have all the time in the world to contemplate one thing only, it is difficult to understand how it could take others longer to think about the same thing. We tended to forget that those outside were planning and executing the revolution and that our little request could not have been top of the agenda. Even if it was, it would have taken months to assemble a team to carry out the task, to acquire suitable vehicles and a safe house, let alone carry out all the detailed planning.

A second escape-date was set for mid-April and a letter sent off to the contact. The reason for the choice of the April date was because the presence on duty of a certain night-warder, a Sergeant Vermeulen, was vital to the success of the then-existing plans. He was going on a two-month holiday from just after the initial (February) date and was due to return in April. The new date was on the first weekend after he was due back on duty after his holiday.

Vermeulen's presence was necessary not because we had struck an arrangement with him but because our plan involved taking a warder's car, and we knew what sort of car he had and where he parked it. Not only that, the man had been on the early night shift – at his own preference – for almost 11 years and was thus thoroughly reliable and consistent in his movements. For instance, he was supposed to inspect the cells every half hour or so but we knew that he never came into our section until 8 pm when he was required to come up to the first floor to turn off the *stokkies'* lights. And when he did come into the section he never looked properly into the cells. Most nights he would go straight to Denis's window and chat about rugby or air his gripes. Other warders, in most cases being younger and newer to the job, grew bored and restless as the evening wore on. They would perform inspections at whim, just for something to do. Some would look carefully into the cells and some would stop for a chat. Others would even play tricks by coming into the section very quietly and then trying to trap a prisoner doing something illegal or embarrassing.

During this two-month wait we made some of our greatest technical advancements. We developed our lock-picking abilities and improved our adjustable picking device to enable us to open doors nine and ten as well as all the other wooden doors to which we had access. The period also gave us time to recover from the effects of the nervous strain that the preceding months' activities had inflicted upon us. Everyone had been affected by the stress of carrying out these activities under the noses of the warders and it helped those of us intimately involved with the preparations to realise why some of the comrades had expressed opposition to the escape preparations.

I cannot speak for the others, but the strain seriously affected my sleep. At night I would lie awake for hours with my mind's cursor jumping from one idea to the next. Shapes of keys would flit across my brain, locks would be dismantled and we would escape from the prison in a hundred different ways. When I concentrated too deeply on these thoughts my heart would pound heavily as if I had just received a fright. I would break into a cold sweat and be completely unable to relax. Even during the day when I had a moment to rest, my heart would beat faster than normal, stuck in a state of chronic excitation. Memories of the university physiology class came to mind and the flight and fright system of the autonomic nervous system. What had been purely theoretical then was now being demonstrated to me in the most practical way. The hours awake were not wasted though, for mental work like this can be productive: many problems were solved during those late night insomniac sessions. And if we'd made a breakthrough it would ensure that I got no sleep at all that night.

Despite the agony caused by the fear of being caught, there was no question of reconsidering or stopping what we were doing, or of being stopped. The preparations had taken on a momentum of their own and drove us forward remorselessly. We began to live the escape, sleep the escape and see everything in terms of the escape. Nothing else mattered; nothing else existed. It forced those of us at the core of the exercise closer together, but further apart from those who were not. Our combined obsession was turned into an inexorable force.

It was during this period of waiting that David R became interested in the escape and asked if he could join the group. He joined after the February postponement because he could see that our technical capabilities had progressed to the point where the chances of pulling off an escape were becoming increasingly good and that there was a likelihood that outside assistance might be forthcoming. He also had a very long sentence ahead of him. The earlier thoughts that we were wasting time by making too many keys before working out a plan were raised no more. The keys in hand had been shown to be more effective in opening doors than brainwaves.

The added participation was welcomed by all and the new 'escapee' was integrated into the group. Although this greatly increased the logistical problems, the political impact that we would make if, more people got out of prison at one time, made it worthwhile.

This period was one of good comradely co-operation as well as intense debate. Dave R took an active part in preparing clothing for himself and others. Dave made himself a canvas shoulder bag while the others ordered some T-shirts, inks to dye them and felt pens to draw on them. After 'civilianising' them the shirts were stored behind the geyser with all the other gear.

Dave R discovered another hiding place for forbidden wares – in the space between the two sides of the corrugated iron yard wall. The wall ended just below and to the one side of his cell window. From his window he could reach the top of the wall and hang a bag down the middle from a piece of string attached to a nail. The string could not be seen from inside his cell so it was quite safe. It had two disadvantages though: it could only be reached late at night and was open to the weather. Nonetheless, the bag he made was wrapped in plastic and stored in the place until the end.

A rather amusing incident concerning the acquisition of civilian clothing happened at this time. To wash the floors of our part of the prison we needed a large supply of rags. Usually we were provided with discarded bedspreads which could be torn into useful-sized rags. One day, after a request had been made for more rags, it was found that there were no old bedspreads available. In order to avoid the floors not being cleaned – something the governors could not tolerate – some old clothing left behind by *stokkies* was given to us by none other than Captain Schnepel. Amongst the jumble was a perfectly usable pair of blue denim jeans. As they happened to be Stephen's size he took them, washed them, mended the loose hems and repaired the zip. Since the jeans were 'legal', they were washed openly and hung on the washline in the yard to dry. One of the warders saw them hanging up and asked where we had got them, thinking he had stumbled on a misdemeanor. When told that they had come from the Captain and were to be used for cleaning the floors he expressed surprise but could do nothing. The jeans soon disappeared into our cache.

Soon after this Alex made a windfall discovery of a mine of disused civilian clothing. For a long time a large wicker basket had stood under the stairway to our section. Everyone knew it to be full of old linen and blankets. One day, out of curiosity, Alex put his hand into the basket and lifted up the sheets and blankets to see if it contained anything else. At the bottom of the basket he discovered sufficient socks, shirts and trousers to dress a battalion. They were cast-offs that had been left by departing *stokkies*. Over a period of weeks we removed everything of value and hid it in the cache. The items were washed and repaired, and altered to the respective requirements of all those participating.

With a full wardrobe of escape garments we began to think of other ways of disguising ourselves. In the store-room was a shoebox-full of old spectacles discarded by the comrades over the years. Alex found a pair of weak, old-fashioned glasses which hardly affected his normal vision at all. He looked quite ridiculous when he put them on but that was the whole idea. Stephen ordered a pair of sunglasses because he found the Pretoria sun 'too bright' for his eyes.

I could not wear any of the old specs because of my short-sightedness so I set about thinking how I could get another, different-looking, pair for myself. I normally wore a pair of clip-on shades over my glasses because I really did find the Pretoria sun too bright. But I couldn't wear those while escaping because the prison staff would have got used to me looking that way. So I put in a request to see the doctor and complained to him that I was getting terrible headaches because I believed there was something wrong with my glasses. I was taken to an optician who—what a surprise—found nothing wrong with my prescription. But I insisted that I was to be given a new pair of glasses. Maybe the distance between the focal points of the two lenses had been ground in the wrong place, I suggested. After much wrangling and having to put up with accusations of complaining about headaches just to get a ride into town they eventually relented: I could choose a pair of frames paid for by the state or pay for frames of my own choice. I chose the state frames because they were dreadful—thick, dark and heavy. They thought I was mad because I had 'lots of money' and because the frames did not suit me at all (even they could tell that!). I explained that in prison it did not matter how I looked and that I would rather spend my money on records and books, when I was allowed to buy them. When the specs arrived a week later they went straight into the cache and were never worn until the day of the escape: I did not want the warders to get used to seeing me with them on.

After much thinking about the difficulty of organising help through the established codes with people who could never appreciate the problems we faced in getting out of the prison, a contingency plan was worked out in case on the day of the escape there was no help waiting for us outside.

The plan was based on the strange fact that one of us had in his possession, in his cell, his 'Book-of-Life' – an identity document carried by all white South Africans containing various licences such as driver's licence, marriage certificate, gun licence and so on, as well as personal details. Through some curious bureacratic bungle he had been handed the document by the security police so the commanding staff never questioned his keeping it. Noting that it had a driving licence stamped in it, we realised that if we could get to a place where there was a car-hire facility it would be possible for him to hire a car which we could use to drive ourselves to the border.

The plan that emerged out of this was that if we managed to get outside and there was no assistance waiting for us, we would all climb into the warder's car parked outside and drive from Pretoria to Jan Smuts Airport near Kempton Park where undoubtedly there would be car-hire facilities. There Denis, Dave K and one other would split from the rest of the group, take the airport bus into Johannesburg and fend for themselves. At the airport the rest of us would dump the 'hot' warder's car and hire a car from one of the car-hire firms. From there we would drive as rapidly as possible to the northern Lesotho border. We estimated that this would take between five and six hours, beyond the time when our absence would have been discovered, but hopefully before the police would have mobilised roadblocks that distance away. This plan had the second-level contingency that if the warder's car was not outside the prison, we would take the airport bus from Pretoria to Jan Smuts.

Only four of us would use the hire-car because it was felt that it would be impossible to drive all the way to Lesotho with six people in one car. Besides this, Denis and Dave K claimed to have friends in Johannesburg who would 'put them up' and felt it wisest anyway not to make for the border immediately but to wait some time for the heat to wear off.

Alex and I were unhappy with this plan because we felt it would be better to make for Swaziland rather than Lesotho: we considered the time factor to be more important than the intensity of the border guard. Our estimate was that it would take between three and four hours to reach the Swazi border in the region of a town called Amsterdam in the Eastern Transvaal. This would give us sufficient

128

time to be over the border before the police had been mobilised and roadblocks set up. Our objection to the Lesotho route was that it would take too long to reach the place and the police would already have been alerted by the time we got there. Also, we did not like the idea of six people climbing into one car directly outside the prison, let alone driving all the way to Jan Smuts. Lastly, we felt that Lesotho would be too vulnerable, being completely surrounded by South Africa, and from where there would be nowhere to go should we not have been welcome. By going to Swaziland we could pass immediately to Mozambique, should the need arise, where we would be welcome.

Since it was vital that our get-away be made with the warder's car and because we had to rely on the driver's licence the two of us had no choice but to go along with the Lesotho plan.

Another major dispute broke out over the question of taking arms, if we could lay our hands on any. It had been observed that when the warder who was to stand guard on the *pos* came on duty at 10 pm, he would first collect his FN rifle from the night-warder in the office. The latter passed the rifle through the office window to the other who stood in the yard, while the dog-minder held the dog on leash. There was no exchange of keys so it was legitimate to assume that the night-warder had free access to the rifle, and thus we would too. In addition we thought that the night-warder would either have a small pistol on his person or have one lying about his office, or have keys to the gun-room or a locker in the office.

Alex and I argued that we did not plan to shoot our way out of the prison, but that if we were accosted at the last moment by someone who did not represent too great a menace, the weapons could be used as a threat. We envisaged, for instance, that there might be a guard on the gate outside the prison and that we would have to force him inside where he could be tied up.

Others argued that if we got away and it was discovered that we'd taken weapons we would be regarded as 'armed terrorists' and shot on sight. This was a fair view but we believed (perhaps naively) the police would prefer to capture us alive than dead: they knew that we were not an inherently violent lot. In any case we felt that it was more important to think how we could gain our freedom rather than waste our thought-power on how they would recapture us.

Whether in retrospect the arguments for or against taking arms seem more sensible, our attitude on this point reflected our single-minded determination in contrast to the others' greater sense of caution. The arms question was finally decided by the vote and it was agreed that no weapons would be taken. We were in a minority at that time and had to abide by the group's decisions.

We had expected the outcome and had prepared ourselves for it: we had begun to construct a wooden model of a pistol which would substitute for the real thing. To this project we gave the name 'pea', short for 'pea-shooter'.

In an old *Reader's Digest* we found some really good profile photographs of a Beretta 7.62 mm pistol. The pictures were illustrating an article about a murder and were of the murder weapon. They were perfect side, front and oblique views – a bit like the pictures of a criminal from a police record. I made a tracing of the side-view photograph and a number of accurate enlargements from this using a grid. These shapes I then cut out for the three of us to study so that we could choose the one which seemed to be the most life-like. Once we'd chosen one, I cut it into its major component parts and made accurate drawings of the other smaller parts.

Alex stuck the paper cut-outs of the body and breech of the gun to suitable pieces of wood and cut out the outline shapes in the workshop. Between us we cut out all the other visible parts to be stuck to the body of the gun later. This we did not only so that the finished product would look more realistic, but also as a safety measure in case a warder found a part on one of us. The parts before they were properly shaped looked like nothing at all and could easily be explained away as something else.

The barrel was made on a 'lathe' created out of a large breast-drill. This we did openly in the workshop and explained it away as a 'pencil-holder' in the making.

The parts of the gun I carved to shape in my cell at night, one at a time. Our trusty piece of hacksaw blade came in most handy for this job but for the final details we 'borrowed' files from the 'security' cupboard. To finish them each part was sanded with fine sandpaper and then coloured with a very soft pencil. To prevent the lead rubbing off, I sprayed the parts with artist's fixative.

When all the parts were completed the 'pea' was assembled. There were many parts: the body, sliding breech, barrel, trigger, magazine, hammer-cock, safety catch and two side panels for the handle. They were all stuck in place with epoxy glue and when completed it looked extremely realistic. It even fooled the other comrades when we showed it to them. Finally, it was wrapped in toilet paper and plastic and stuck under the bottom of the metal tool cupboard in the workshop – probably the least likely place the warders would have looked for booty if they had decided to have a thorough search.

Despite the earlier opposition to arms, when the others saw the 'pea' there was no opposition to its use and it even became included in the general plans. It was to be used in accosting the night-warder and making the job of tying him up a bit easier. Some wanted the plan to include revealing to the warder after he had been tied up that the 'pea' was a fake gun and even leaving it with him so that we would not be regarded as armed fugitives. How the 'pea' was finally to be used was never brought to the vote because the 'gun question' got pushed into the background as other problems came to the fore. Later the escape plans were changed, making the 'pea' no longer an important question.

★ ★ ★

In November 1977 the prison authorities announced that political prisoners would no longer be allowed to study beyond matriculation level while in prison. Prisoners who were already studying post-matric courses (in all cases correspondence courses through the University of South Africa – South Africa's correspondence university) would be allowed to complete their courses, but no new courses could be started.

The change in policy was said to have been made because prisoners on Robben Island had abused the study 'privilege' (as the authorities saw it) by using study material to smuggle 'inciting documents' to the outside. Rumour had it that one or more prisoners on Robben Island had written revolutionary slogans in a library book from the University of South Africa. Because of this alleged abuse by one prisoner all prisoners had to pay the penalty.

The authorities are probably sorry now that they took away this right (as we saw it). The ensuing publicity was very bad for them and the first two prisoners to be affected by this ruling at Pretoria Prison decided, as they were forbidden from engaging in academic studies, to study something else – how to get out of prison. I would not like to believe that our escape was the sole or even one of the main reasons for the reinstatement of studies shortly after we got out, but undoubtedly it must have affected their decision.

The real reasons for removing the right to study had nothing to do with an 'abuse' of the 'privilege' by political prisoners. The authorities for years had been looking for a pretext to stop political prisoners studying. They knew as well as the prisoners that prison is regarded as the university of the revolution.

On Robben Island Nelson Mandela and other ANC leaders imprisoned for life had organised their fellow prisoners to study, much to the chagrin of the enemy. Many of the prisoners had engaged themselves in correspondence courses to complete their school certificates so that they could go on to study for degrees; prisoners who had been in prison for a long time were working on their umpteenth degree. It was no wonder that Mandela and other leading figures were removed from Robben Island and sent to Pollsmoor where they are now kept in isolation from the general mass of politicals.

The fascist jailers grew jealous that their captives were able to engage in studies funded by outside sources, and they were not. They despised prisoners who were more intelligent than themselves – especially black prisoners. Also, they believed that these 'terrorists' would only use their education for 'subversive purposes' when they were released. Why allow them the opportunity to advance their cause while in prison? Their imprisonment was specifically designed to remove them from circulation so that they could not 'subvert' law and order. They should be allowed to rot, to suffer for their 'crimes', to be kept completely in the dark so that when they come out they are broken and of no value to their 'terrorist' friends. These were the real reasons behind the ending of studies, not the discovery of slogans in a book margin.

It is true of course that the prisoners did 'abuse the privilege'. They did so in every conceivable way, deliberately and cunningly. This was natural for they used every opportunity to advance their knowledge not only of current happenings in the real world (otherwise known as 'news') but generally so that they could be of more value to the movement when released (just as suspected!).

One of the benefits of study was that the university had a fabulous library by prison standards. Library books were not supposed to be swapped but of course they were. At the beginning of the year it was decided collectively who would study what, so that the broadest possible range of library books could be obtained. Nobody ever studied the same subject in the same year – that was a waste. The course on Comparative Literature, for instance, gave access to a great range of top-class literary works from many countries. We read all the most famous novels of the Russian revolution as well as a number of progressive African writers. To the censor the Soviet books looked like ordinary novels and he didn't know where Mockba or the Union of Soviet Socialist Republics was – he only knew that 'Russia' was the bad word to look out for. The course on Comparative African Government gave access to virtually any books on Africa. Those who hadn't been able to keep up with developments on the continent because of the denial of news could update their understanding to within a year or two.

Science subjects were not permitted but the reasons for this were practical – there could be no access to laboratories and workshops. The only arts subjects not permitted were law and Russian language. Law could not be allowed, they said, because people who had been in prison couldn't practise as lawyers. The real reason was that they didn't want us to know too much about the legal circumstances under which we were being held. Who knows what the prisoners might have got up to had they known more about the law! Of course this prohibition was meaningless because there was usually one or more qualified lawyers among the prisoners and most of the others had studied some aspect of the law at one time or another. On top of this we had the best lawyers at our disposal so there was little that the authorities could get away with on this score.

Not everybody was engaged in formal studies while we were there, but everyone read the university library books, including those not enrolled. In addition there were a vast number of textbooks that had

132

accumulated over the years and these could also be read by all. There was even a complete set of Russian grammar books which had been purchased by one of the comrades who had studied the language before it was banned. In a way, those who were not enrolled had an advantage over those who were–they were not encumbered with essays and swotting. Everyone could also order any book they wanted–you just had to find someone whose course covered your area of interest.

We had to ensure that our years in prison were not totally wasted and that our minds did not atrophy as our political enemies wished.

11
The Second Date

The date set for the second escape attempt was the 21st of April 1979, a date we had calculated as one when Sergeant Vermeulen would be back on duty after his holiday. This was the date which Denis had conveyed by code to his contact. Our request for a car and driver were the minimum requirements. Our suggestion was that the driver should wear a yellow shirt so as to be easily recognisable in case it was not possible to park the getaway vehicle directly in front of the prison.

No reply arrived by the April date and so without confirmation of outside help there was no choice but to cancel the attempt. A deep gloom set in. Those of us who were in more of a hurry to get out were annoyed in a way that we had agreed to wait for assistance. By doing so we were in effect keeping ourselves in prison. We believed that we were in a position to let ourselves out and had now placed ourselves at the mercy of unknown people outside with whom we had no direct contact.

A message eventually arrived about ten days after the cancelled attempt explaining that we'd given insufficient time and details for assistance to be arranged. A general meeting of the escape group was called and it was decided that the onus on choosing a date should be passed to those giving the assistance. Another letter should be written explaining that we were prepared to wait until all the necessary arrangements had been made and that all we wanted to know was in which month the attempt should be made. To simplify matters we would take as the date of our first attempt the first Sunday of the month of the choice of the assistance group (a change from our earlier choice of a Saturday). If for any reason, ours or theirs, it was not possible to make it on the first Sunday, we would do it on the second Sunday, and so on. In addition, we should let them know that the escape group had expanded but that the previous arrangements remained the same, that is, the minimum requirements and the person with the yellow shirt.

Another letter was sent. Each letter stirred Alex's, Steve's and my further impatience. It took two months from the time a letter was sent off till we received a reply. It was now May—nine months after the first key had been made and three months since we had first considered ourselves ready to leave. The reply would only arrive in July and even then our helpers might not be ready. We felt somehow that we had relinquished to others the initiative of what we'd started. We believed that every step taken should be towards bringing forward our day of departure, not delaying it.

Our impatience to get out was prompted by a number of factors. After April it begins to get cold in Pretoria, and Transvaal winters can be bitterly cold. The approach of the cold season worried us because our civilian clothing was unsuitable for winter use. Our money too was becoming outdated because it was then ten months since the new currency had been introduced. Each passing day also increased the chances of our cache being discovered.

The decision to change the day of escape from a Saturday to a Sunday was another of those decisions which revealed the differences between the participants in the escape group. From an early stage everyone was of the opinion that it would be better to make a break over a weekend rather than during the week because lock-up on Saturdays and Sundays at 3.30 pm was an hour earlier than on weekdays, but the dog was placed in the yard at the same time – about 5 pm This would give us more time to put our contingency plan into operation should it be necessary. Also, on weekdays awaiting-trial prisoners were brought to the prison at about 6 pm, which meant that we would only have about an hour before the escape was discovered; at weekends no awaiting-trial prisoners were brought in because the courts only operated during the week. We would thus have about five hours before the escape was discovered. This was reduced to three or four hours on some weekends when a particular duty-bound officer would inspect the prison at about seven or eight in the evening.

The basis of our differences regarding Saturday or Sunday departure revolved around this occasional inspection. It had been noticed that if the officer inspected on the Saturday he would inspect again at the same time on the Sunday. Those who favoured a Sunday argued that if the officer came to inspect the prison before 11 pm on the Saturday then we would not go on the Sunday but postpone it to the next weekend.

Alex, Steve and I felt that the officer was irrelevant to our plans because he never carried out his inspection before 7 pm, several hours after the planned time of breakout. A Saturday departure would give us the advantage that the authorities would not be able to get our pictures in the papers the next day. (The Sunday papers were all printed on Saturdays and it would thus not be before the Monday that our pictures appeared, by which time we would be far away. TV did not count because it only operated for five hours in the evening at that time.) We also reasoned that there would be fewer warders around on a Saturday night should there be a general alert and call-up. By Sunday night most of those who had been away for the weekend would have returned. A final reason we put forward was that petrol stations were closed on Sundays at that time, due to rationing, but open until 6 pm on Saturdays. This meant that we would still have time to refuel the warder's car if it was necessary. Later this argument fell away as petrol stations closed even earlier.

These were the arguments which we had originally put forward for a Saturday departure and they had been accepted when the group consisted of only five participants. When it was rediscussed the Sunday option was again canvassed and after intense discussion it was Sunday that won the day.

Towards the end of May one of the comrades was taken to hospital for a minor operation and for a week or two after had to be taken daily to Central Prison for a bath. On one of his trips he spoke to an accompanying warder who claimed to work on gate duty in the street outside the prison. When the comrade asked him what time he came on duty the warder told him that gate duty started at three thirty in the afternoon. Some were influenced by what he had been told but others did not accept it. No one had ever seen a guard on duty outside the prison at that time of the day and we could clearly hear the gate squeaking and its chains rattling only after six in the evening.

However this new information and its effects on comrades' attitudes forced us to subject our plans to a radical re-evaluation. In particular we now felt less confident about being able to physically overcome and restrain the night-warder. It was not an easy problem to solve because jumping him meant in practice stopping him from using the walkie-talkie he wore on his belt, restraining him and tying him up. The only way we could now think of acheiving this task was the 'pea'. It would, we hoped, be sufficient inducement to persuade the warder to 'co-operate' without the need to use physical coercion. But if his walkie-talkie was fitted with a panic button which he could press to send out a distress signal, the 'pea' would make a very inadequate replacement.

The plan after we'd removed or disabled the walkie-talkie and restrained the warder was to move him either to the 'cage' between doors six and seven where we could handcuff him to a grille, or 'encourage' him to drive us out of the prison complex in his car. A bit far-fetched? Perhaps, but who would have stopped a warder in uniform driving around the area with a group of respectable-looking passengers?

There was one major shortcoming with this plan: if we could not get through door six and were forced to put our contingency plan of going through the visiting-room into operation, it would be extremely difficult to get the warder outside to chauffeur us away. This observation made us realise that it was no longer good enough to rely on the hope that one of our keys would open door six or that we would find its key in the prison – we had to be absolutely certain that we could open it.

The logical train of thoughts generated by this realisation led us to the conclusion that we had to find a way of testing door six. It seemed a total impossiblity. The administration area was sacred, totally out of bounds. Our thinking would not even allow us to visualise ourselves

The following is the text of a leaflet currently being distributed by the African National Congress inside South Africa:

PEOPLE OF SOUTH AFRICA - SONS AND DAUGHTERS OF THE SOIL -

THE AFRICAN NATIONAL CONGRESS BRINGS YOU THIS MESSAGE!

The conditions for developing our liberation struggle, smashing the Apartheid monster and winning our freedom, are greater than ever before. Nothing can hide the fact that White South Africa is in irreversible crisis from which it cannot escape. The opportunities for developing the armed struggle right inside South Africa are becoming more possible. Through armed force, with Umkhonto We Sizwe - the ANC's military wing - as the armed spearhead, we too will smash the brute force of the oppressors. But do not wait for that day. It cannot come unless the . masses are involved in all forms of struggle. The time to act - to hit back - is NOW!! Rally to the ANC - the tried and trusted organisation of all our people that Vorster and his police can never crush!

EVERYONE MUST BE A FREEDOM FIGHTER! Our men, our women, our youth - the toilers in the towns and countryside - the scholars and the professional groups. The MPLA and FRELIMO are victorious because the entire people supported them.

OUR ORGANISED STRENGTH, UNITY AND MILITANT ACTIONS ARE THE KEY TO FREEDOM! Organise wherever you are. In the factories, townships, mines, farms, schools, countryside - mobilise the power of our people and of all Genuine democrats. Intensify the freedom struggle in every possible way. We, African, Indian and Coloured people must resist Vorster's policy of divide and rule. Reject tribal politics, Bantustans, Indian Councils and all dummy institutions! Smash the stooges and traitors! Fight the unjust laws and fight for a new life!

PEOPLE OF SOUTH AFRICA - DEMONSTRATE OUR SUPPORT FOR THOSE VORSTER SEEKS TO CRUSH! It is within our power to prevent his aggression against our brothers and sisters in Angola, Namibia or anywhere else. We must not permit subversive activities against the people and state of Angola! By intensifying our struggle we will tie Vorster's army down and make it impossible for him to launch his war machine across the borders. The struggle in Angola, Zimbabwe, Namibia is our struggle - a struggle against a common enemy - racism and imperialism. Together we will win!

THE ANC SAYS: AMANDLA NGAWETHU! MAATLA KE ARONA' POWER TO THE PEOPLE!

THE ANC SAYS TO VORSTER AND HIS RACIST REGIME:
ALL POWER TO THE MPLA - LIBERATORS OF ANGOLA! ALL POWER TO THE PEOPLE!
VORSTER - GET OUT OF ANGOLA! GET OUT OF NAMIBIA!
NO INTERFERENCE IN ZIMBABWE! HANDS OFF AFRICA!
PEOPLE OF SOUTH AFRICA! The MPLA have scored an outstanding victory over the forces of racism and imperialism. Vorster's defeat in Angola is of outstanding significance to our struggle.

VORSTER TRIED TO SWALLOW ANGOLA BUT NOW HE IS CHOKING TO DEATH! The MPLA have taught him the lesson of his life. He thought he could send his army into Angola and place his stooges in power, but the MPLA thrashed him in battle and sent his White soldiers and stooges fleeing in terror. The MPLA proved that his racist arrogance is hollow, that White South Africa is not invincible, that the forces of freedom are growing in strength and will soon be powerful enough to completely destroy him.

Reproduction of leaflet distributed by leaflet bomb for 21 March 1976 — Johannesburg.

PEOPLE OF SOUTH AFRICA — THE AFRICAN NATIONAL CONGRESS CALLS ON YOU.

AMANDLA SOWETO!

BROTHER AND SISTERS: Vorster and his assassins have learnt nothing since Sharpeville. Once again he has called out his murderers to shoot down in cold blood innocent people in the name of preserving 'law and order'. Once again the racists have blamed agitators, inciters, communists and black power militants for the disturbances instead of their hated Apartheid system. They will never admit that it is their system of racial oppression that has aroused the collective fury of our people, for to do so they would have to admit that it has been a complete failure. They have shown us again that they are not prepared to listen to our grievances and would rather shoot anyone who dares stand up to register them. The massacre of our people must end. We have had enough!

THE AFRICAN NATIONAL CONGRESS calls on our people in every walk of life — in the factories, townships, mines, schools, farms, to embark on massive protests, actions and demonstrations against white supremacy, against the murder of our children, against Bantu Education, Bantustans, the pass laws and all the hated policies of Apartheid. NOW IS THE TIME TO ACT!!

SONS AND DAUGHTERS OF AFRICA; stand together firm and united and show the oppressor that we will not be intimidated. We have the strength to hit back. Our organised strength, unity and militant actions will give us more power than Vorster and all his guns. Rally to the call of the ANC - the tried and trusted organisation of all our people that Vorster and his police can never crush! United in this task we will smash the brute force of the oppressor!

DEMONSTRATE AGAINST THE BRUTAL MURDER OF OUR CHILDREN, OF OUR BROTHERS AND SISTERS IN SOWETO AND OTHER TOWNSHIPS. DEMONSTRATE YOUR RESOLUTE OPPOSITION TO THE APARTHEID STATE, TO RACIAL OPPRESSION AND THE MASSACRE OF OUR PEOPLE

VORSTER YOUR DAYS ARE NUMBERED!   IZAK'UNYATHELI AFRIKA!

AMANDLA SOWETO!! FORWARD TO THE LIBERATION OF OUR SOUTH AFRICA! AMANDLA NGAWETHU! MATLA KE ARONA! AFRIKA MAYIBUYE! FORWARD TO PEOPLES POWER!!

Leaflet spread by leaflet bomb July 1976 — Johannesburg.

<u>THE STRUGGLE CONTINUES!   VICTORY IS CERTAIN.</u>

People of South Africa – Sons and Daughters of the soil – the AFRICAN NATIONAL CONGRESS and its military wing UMKHONTO WE SIZWE has declared:

"WE SHALL AVENGE THE BRUTAL MURDER OF OUR INNOCENT CHILDREN. WE SHALL AVENGE THE RUTHLESS KILLING AND MAIMING OF OUR PEOPLE WHO HAVE RISEN IN HEROIC PROTEST AGAINST THE APARTHEID MONSTER!"

The terror that Vorster let loose in the Black townships has failed to crush the spirit of our people. Our unity and determination to struggle is greater than ever before. Africans, Coloureds and Indians, young and old, workers and parents, pupils and teachers, have stood firm against the police atrocities, and in the heroic months since June have raised the struggle to new heights.

Vorster and his cohorts must know: We shall defy their murder squads with greater determination; we shall continue to build the unity of all the Black people and reject with contempt efforts to divide us through useless concessions, dummy bodies and Bantustan frauds; we shall organise better, in secret to outwit enemy spies and informers; we shall co-ordinate our struggle in all corners of South Africa; develop our mass actions, demonstrations and strikes which mobilise our people and disrupt the economy; we shall harass the enemy, his police, soldiers, officials and spies wherever we can. Above all, we shall arm ourselves with modern weapons and hit back through our organised fighting force UMKHONTO WE SIZWE!

<u>UMKHONTO WE SIZWE – PEOPLE'S ARMY OF LIBERATION!</u>

These racist murderers who slaughter unarmed children and women, fled in panic when they came face to face with the armed freedom fighters of UMKHONTO in Zimbabwe in 1967 and 1968. Their racist arrogance shrank when our MPLA comrades thrashed them in Angola. And now the time is coming when UMKHONTO will punish the racists on our own soil. The mass struggle of our people helps to bring that day nearer. Already Vorster is trembling because last October bombs destroyed the Jabulani police station, the Mzimhlope railway line and the Tzaneen to Pietersburg railway. He knows that armed freedom struggles start in small ways as happened in Angola, Mozambique and Vietnam. The freedom fighters organise the people in the towns and countryside: the mass struggle grows side by side with the armed struggle. In this way we build a PEOPLE'S POWER that will punish the oppressor for his crimes and establish freedom and justice over every inch of our beloved South Africa!

<u>DECEMBER 16TH IS A HISTORIC DAY IN THE FREEDOM STRUGGLE!</u>

The national liberation movement, under the leadership of the ANC, formed UMKHONTO WE SIZWE in 1961 when it became clear that only through armed struggle – no matter how long and bloody – could freedom be won. UMKHONTO provides our people with the skills of modern warfare. The bomb blasts and sabotage actions that rocked South Africa in the early 1960's are being heard again. Now the conditions and opportunities for our struggle have become more favourable. The oppressor will be met bullet for bullet here in South Africa. Our youth – African, Indian and Coloured – must join UMKHONTO in ever bigger numbers and train to become skilled freedom fighters. Remember: to succeed in struggle it is essential to be disciplined, organised and correctly to identify the enemy. You must be part of an organisation, part of a revolutionary movement – the ANC with its allies and military wing UMKHONTO WE SIZWE will lead our people to victory!

<u>COUNTRYMEN AND COMRADES:</u> You have shown your courage and contempt for death. With such fighting spirit and unity our final victory is assured. Let us continue to convert our anger into revolutionary action. Let us harass the enemy on every front.

On this December 16th – HEROES DAY – the ANC dips its revolutionary banner in memory of all those comrades who have fallen in battle. To all the parents we say "Be proud for giving birth to such heroic children. They have not died in vain and we will continue the battle until victory is won."

To all of you we say: Forward brave fighters! Forward brothers and sisters! Maintain your revolutionary unity and fighting spirit. Together we will raise the struggle to more glorious heights. The blood of our people has made us stronger and more determined.

AMANDLA NGAWETHU!   THE STRUGGLE CONTINUES! VICTORY IS CERTAIN!

Leaflet spread by leaflet bomb for 16 December 1976 — Cape Town.

Policeman retrieving banner — September 1977.

1978:   ANTI-APARTHEID YEAR

BROTHERS AND SISTERS! While the racist bosses get fat over their Christmas turkeys, the working people of South Africa reel under increasing burdens, bringing many of us to the point of despair. Our militants are rotting in the racists prisons. Throughout the land, deaths, detentions, harrassments, humiliations, unemployment and starvation ruin for millions of us the so-called 'holiday season'. We cannot bear this oppression any longer. Recent events have shaken the fascists as never before, but it is vital that we step up our mass resistance to the Apartheid state.

1978 must go down in history books as ANTI-APARTHEID YEAR!

WORKERS OF ALL RACES!

A falling standard of living and the prospect of unemployment is all that South Africa's capitalist economy has to offer you in the predicted years of economic crisis ahead. Only a strong united working class can win the fulfilment of your deepest wishes. Rally behind the banner of SACTU, the South African Congress of Trade Unions. Use the powerful strike weapon to force through your economic demands and the programme of the FREEDOM CHARTER.

STUDENTS AND PUPILS OF ALL RACES!

Reject the fascist education system that is forced down your throats. Whether you are subject to Bantu Education or Christian National Education, it is 3rd rate education designed to support an unjust system. Use the boycott weapon, raise your voices and demand a single, free compulsory national education system, founded in a society which allows you to acutally benefit from what you study.

WOMEN OF ALL RACES!

For as long as the Apartheid state continues to exist, you will be faced with sex discrimination in wages, employment opportunities, legal matters and many other areas. Fight for a state where all forms of discrimination including sex discrimination and sexism will be outlawed forever.

The AFRICAN NATIONAL CONGRESS, representing the most oppressed section of our people, leads the South African liberation movement against all the sham institutions held out to us by the fascists - Bantustans, CRC, South African Indian Council, new constitutional 'proposals' and so on.

THE VICTORY OF OUR CAUSE IS CERTAIN! No power on earth is able to hold down an oppressed people forever. This country was colonized by force, the regime is maintained in power by force, and it will be thrown out by force. The use of force to achieve Freedom is not of our choosing. The strategy of armed struggle was initiated only after the ANC was declared illegal and so forced underground, and only after decades of peaceful demands for the ending of racial and colonial oppression yielded no improvement.

DIE STRYD DUUR VOORT!   VICTORY IS CERTAIN!   AMANDLA NGAWETHU!

Reproduction of our last leaflet bomb leaflet December 1977 — Cape Town.

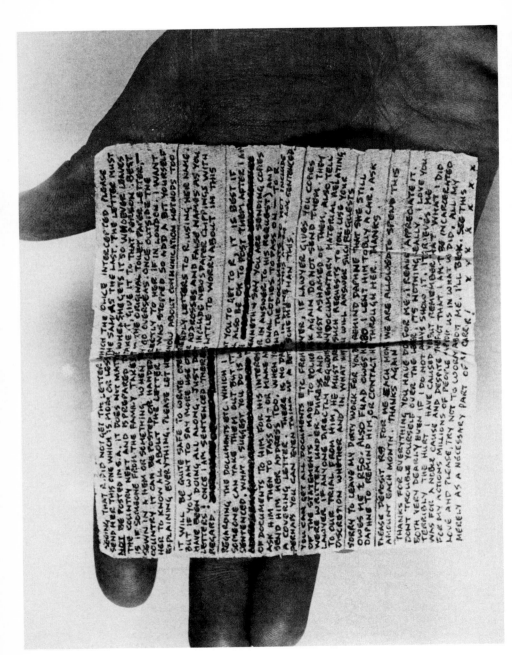

Toilet paper letter smuggled out of Pollsmoor.

Protesters, including Robin, outside South Africa House, 6 June 1978.

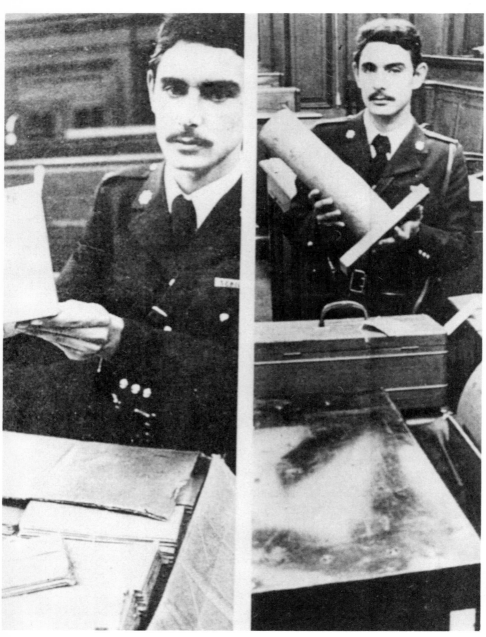

Court orderly displaying exhibits.

View of the prison from the 'pos'.

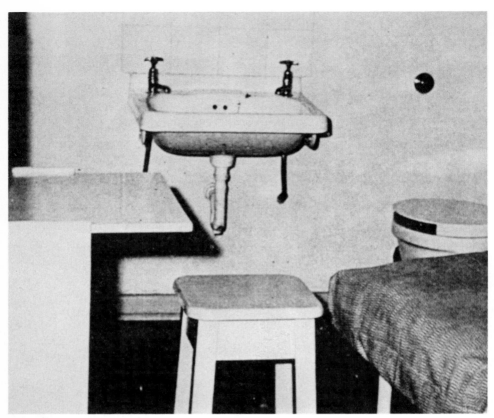
Interior of a cell.

Sgt. Vermeulen opening door Four — this picture was one of those exhibited at Vermeulen's trial.

Sgt. Vermeulen in his office.

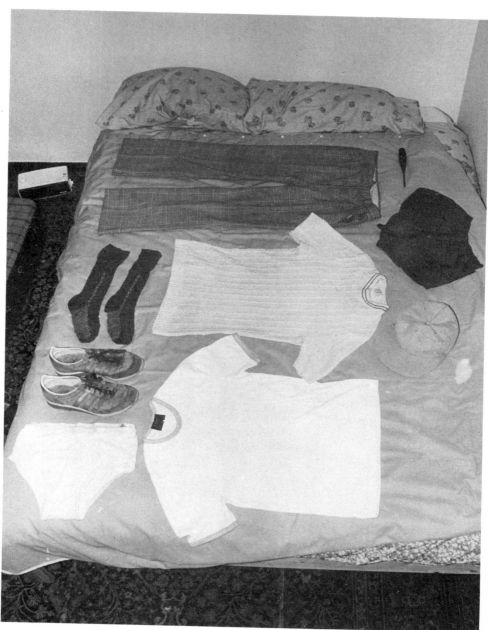

Escape clothing (and chisel).

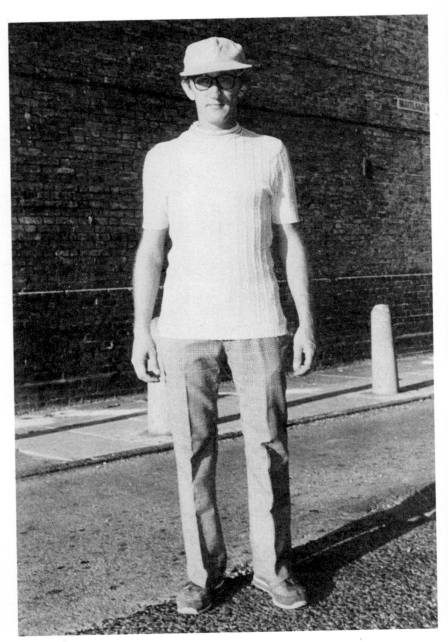

Escape outfit.

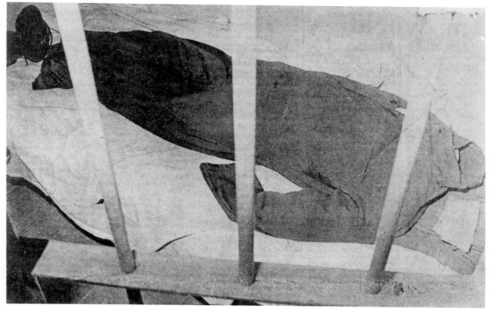

What they found the morning after — dummy in the bed.

All together in Dar es Salaam.

Arriving at Heathrow, early 21 January 1980.

walking through that area, let alone fiddling with or testing the locks. But necessity is the mother of invention they say. For days we strained our brains to bursting point and finally realised that it was just our prejudices that were preventing us from getting any further. The area beyond door four was not inviolable: there had to be a way of getting in there to do what needed to be done.

Separately and on the same night, both Alex and I thought of a plan to get to door six. It was really quite simple. If we came out of our cells shortly before 8 pm and hid in the dining-room while the warder was doing his inspection-round at eight, we could come out of the dining-room, go through door four and down the passage, open five and test six. Then we could dash back to the dining-room and wait for the warder to return to his office before we returned to our cells.

After arriving at this plan it was only a matter of time before we realised that if we could somehow get to door six before 8 pm we could pass through it and test all the doors down the passage on the way to the front door and return to our cells at eight. We could do this right under the warder's nose as door six was a solid door which would obscure us from his view. Not only that, the actual escape could be made without the need to accost the warder at all, allowing us to choose a time of departure that would maximise the time before the escape was discovered.

So ultimately the disturbing information about the warder on gate-duty gave impetus to the most profound changes in the escape plan. In the same way that it helped us overcome our fears about going down to the administrative section to test door six, it allowed us to overcome the idea of having to confront the night-warder to get beyond him. The benefits were enormous and gave the plan for the first time an air of realism. No longer did we need to resort to measures which were more in place in story-books than in reality.

The plan that emerged out of all this was not complicated, but the way we'd arrived at it reminded us that we could never have dreamt it up before we had the technical ability to carry it out, as some of the comrades had wanted us to do when the first preparations for escaping were being made.

No letter confirming that help had been arranged arrived during May and June. Alex, Steve and I became increasingly frustrated by the delay and realised that the longer we put it off the more problems we would have to face. The problems were not long in coming.

On the 20th of June I was taken to hospital for a minor nasal operation. As I was climbing into the prison ambulance outside the front door I noticed some building activity in the street. I did not give it much thought because it looked as if they were digging up the road to repair a broken drain-pipe or sewer. Denis happened to be taken out two days later and noticed that the building activity was not going downwards but upwards: a new sentry post was in the process of

137

being built, right outside the front door of our prison in the middle of the street. Several of the others were taken out at this time so we were able to monitor the progress of the new post. Even worse, they reported, the gate in the street was being moved about 20 metres closer to the front door, placing it about 15 metres from the post-in-the-making.

It was clear that the post was going to be a sophisticated one. It was being constructed almost entirely of glass and was to consist of two sections or rooms. We guessed that it would probably also be equipped with phones and sirens. On either side of it were being erected heavy booms that would be remotely operated from inside the post.

Alex, especially, became worried about this development for it seemed logical to conclude that the post was being equipped for a guard to be on duty 24 hours a day. We couldn't help thinking that our jailers knew all about our escape plans and were quietly going ahead with measures to make the prison escape-proof. Alex began to agitate that we had to make the break then, before the post was completed, because it would be our last chance. A meeting of the escape group was called and after much debate approval was given for the three of us to go if we wanted to.

The others were still waiting for word from the contact. Alex, Steve and I discussed the matter between ourselves and decided that we would make an attempt one night during the 8 pm inspection-round. The plan was based on the scheme we'd just arrived at but it combined elements of the previous plan because we were not certain if we could get through door six. We would move downstairs shortly before eight, hide in the dining-room, and while the warder was upstairs switching off the lights in the *stokkies'* section we would attempt to make our way through doors four, five and six. If we got past six with our own resources we would have all night to work our way through doors seven, nine and ten. Door eight would have been opened by pressing the button in the warder's office before going through five and six. If we could not get six open we would wait in the warder's office for him to return. Then we would threaten him with the 'pea', tie him up and take his keys if he had any. If he had no keys we would attempt to get into the visiting-room and through it as we'd planned earlier.

We realised that we would have to contend with a guard on duty at the gates in the street, but since the gates even in their new position were a short distance from the front door it would still be possible to exit without being seen. The plan was to use the 'pea' to force the sentry into the prison where we could tie him to a grille.

In the end I decided the scheme was far too risky and refused to participate in it. It was the product of panic, not reason. It would be too risky for the three of us alone to tackle the night-warder, the door six barrier had not been breached and the situation outside the front

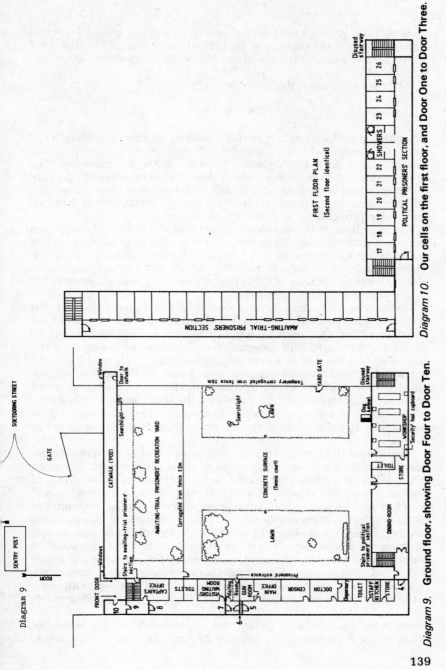

Diagram 9

SENTRY POST

SOETDOORING STREET

GATE

BOOM

FRONT DOOR

CATWALK (POST)

Searchlight

Window

Door to catwalk

Stairs to awaiting-trial prisoners' section

windows

AWAITING-TRIAL PRISONERS' RECREATION YARD

Corrugated iron fence ±2m

Temporary corrugated iron fence ±6m

LAWN

Searchlight

CONCRETE SURFACE
(Tennis court)

LAWN

Dog kennel

YARD GATE

Disused stairway

WORKSHOP

Security tool cupboard

TOILET

STORE

DINING-ROOM

Stairs to political prisoner section

10

9

CAPTAIN'S OFFICE

8

TOILETS

7

VISITORS' WAITING ROOM

6

Waiting Room

5

GUN ROOM

MAIN OFFICE

CENSOR

DOCTOR

Dispensary

TOILET

STAFF KITCHEN

STORE

4

Prisoner's entrance

Diagram 9.   Ground floor, showing Door Four to Door Ten.

FIRST FLOOR PLAN
(Second floor identical)

AWAITING-TRIAL PRISONERS' SECTION

POLITICAL PRISONERS' SECTION

17   18   19   20   21   22   23   24   25   26

SHOWERS

Disused stairway

Diagram 10.   Our cells on the first floor, and Door One to Door Three.

139

door was too great an unknown. I could not allow a plan which had been so long in the making to be hinged on the hope that the 'pea' alone would ensure our freedom. What if the warders were not convinced?

Without unanimity the plan was scrapped.

★ ★ ★

After the great burst of key-making activity in the early months of 1979, the period which followed until the next major phase of the escape was a period of reduced activity on the escape front. The activity did not stop, it just slowed down. We continued to prepare clothing, discuss options and details and work out new plans. The absence of overt preparations led to a general reduction in tensions and an improvement in relations all round.

The activities of the previous period had affected everyone, even those not participating. They were understandably growing weary of the constant fiddling with locks, hiding of gear and talk of escaping. There had been no let-up, resulting in an atmosphere of tension closing over the prison. And because everthing was so secretive it made prison life very unsettling.

Those who were less determined to get out had tolerated our activities despite the disruption it had caused. But they were not the worst to suffer. Our own merciless drive to get out rebounded on ourselves. Alex's task of generating enthusiasm, of persuading the comrades that we should all participate and that it *was* possible to get out was far more onerous than my one of making the keys. Clearly it affected him because he would often complain of sleepless nights and regularly walk on his own up and down the court with clenched jaw, furrowed brow and eyes looking down at his feet. Stephen shared Alex's task. Regular visits to the medicine man exposed his response to it all.

I welcomed the few months of calm as a period of recovery for my nerves, which were beginning to show signs of the strain. I'd never 'settled in' to prison life in the sense of finding some form of non-escape-related activity to which I could devote my attention and which would help me to relax. I'd given everything to getting out, not to making life more bearable inside. Taking an interest in something else helped me understand the unsettling effect of the escape project on some of the others. It was quite easy to become absorbed in something like reading, drawing, music or studying a subject in detail if you had nothing else to do. It also became easier to see how much intellectual and emotional investment could get tied up with such activity and how destabilising it was when it was threatened.

There were many things to do and contemplate if you were not planning and preparing an escape. Prison life was not all work, frantic pacing up and down the yard and lock-up. It had its lighter side too. There was sport, books to read, letters to write, visitors to see, and many other things. I would not like to give the impression that life was pleasant and that prison was fun, but to avoid insanity you had to find distractions to take your mind off your immediate predicament.

Each prisoner found solace in different things. I took up drawing, an old interest but one which real life had never provided me with enough time to pursue. I was not allowed to buy my own pencils and paper because I was not 'studying', but to get around this I got Denis to order the equipment for his course work so that he could pass it on to me. There was nothing to inspire artistry so I took to copying pictures from magazines and memories of better times. Drawing was very therapeutic and it helped me overcome the boredom of the long evenings and take my mind off the details of the escape. So many ideas and plans had been rushing through the recesses of my brain for so long that it was not easy to stem their momentum.

The warders did not mind me drawing, even though it was not strictly permitted. A huge portrait of Robin I'd copied from a photograph stood proudly atop my cupboard for a long time; a picture of Karl Marx I drew for Stephen—his 'grandfather' he told them—remained pinned to the inside of his cupboard for months. But when they found a picture I'd drawn of a guerrilla with AK-47 and all, they drew the line. All my pencils and drawing books were confiscated and I was put on the carpet. I tried to argue that there was nothing wrong with the picture as it was only a drawing and not a real guerrilla. But they were not convinced and threatened the most dire punishments if I drew anything more.

For a month or two I drew no more and took to reading instead. But a budding artist's urges can't be suppressed so I got Denis to order some more equipment and I carried on as before. The only difference was that I had to return the paper and pencils to his cell each morning and dispose of my works of art down the toilet before open-up.

Stephen took to writing poetry and prose, like drawing, also tolerated 'illegal' activities. The authorities believed that unauthorised writing was by definition subversive; in any case he had no cause to write anything apart from letters as he was not allowed to 'study'. Denis was a serious reader and writer but his studies took up most of his time. Tony was totally absorbed by his philosophy course and Dave K spent his time reading novels. Jeremy, Raymond and Dave R, involved themselves in deep 'extra-curricular' studies. Jeremy was also a keen poet and produced some stunningly inspirational poems, considering the bleak environment in which he had to write them. Johnny was a reader but preferred more upmarket titles than Dave K. Alex was the dreamer. He would lie for hours on his bed looking up at the ceiling and dream of freedom. Before Steve and I arrived and introduced the theme of escaping he would smoke himself to death while mulling over his predicament. He gave up that foul habit, thank goodness, when getting out gave his life more meaning.

Books were an essential part of our lives as nothing else removed our minds from our pickle as effectively as they did. But we had a problem – the supply of *good* books. Each prisoner was brought three per week from the prison's library at Central – meaning there were thirty to choose from – but most were rubbish.

To meet our insatiable demand the warder in charge of library books tried to institute a system whereby we could order what we really wanted from the main Pretoria City Library. This never really worked as there was no system of connecting our orders with the books that arrived at the prison library at Central. There was also no categorisation: the books were just arranged in alphabetical order. At one stage, the older comrades related, practically all the books were categorised under 'T' because so many titles started with 'The'. A warder would sometimes write out a list of the books on the shelves which he thought would be of interest to us. Needless to say he was not much good at judging our preferences.

There were other sources of books: the University of South Africa provided for those allowed to study; the 'A' groupers could buy three books a month; and our own library. Here there were a couple of thousand volumes bought by the comrades over the years. Departing prisoners were not allowed to take with them those they'd paid for so they became prison property. All were of a high quality – a fine collection by any standards – but long since read by those who'd been inside for years. Although our prison censor had a list of banned books it appeared that he kept no record of what had been ordered, for he never removed anything from our shelves.

We also had a vast range of magazines to read. Each prisoner could order several of his own choice and in this way we were able to provide ourselves with a comprehensive selection. The magazines were circulated and when read by all were meant to be returned to the censor, but like everything else if there was anything worth keeping it would be torn out and stored or the magazine just not returned. Magazines were important for keeping contact with the real world, for providing a feel of the times and for keeping up with them. It was no wonder the authorities for so long denied the comrades permission to receive periodicals: they helped keep us alive spiritually.

The censor's main task was to watch out for anything 'subversive' and sexually stimulating. By 'subversive' was meant anything about 'communism', 'socialism' or 'Marxism' or which was critical of the South African 'government' and, naturally, anything which could undermine security such as electronics, chemistry and locksmithing. Censors were not very sharp so there was about a 50 per cent chance that a 'subversive' book would get through if the title was innocuous enough – a chance we considered high enough to justify losing the book if it was not approved. Karl Marx's *Capital* did not get through, but several 'subversive' books on economics and political theory did.

While we never went without something to read it was a constant struggle to ensure that there were sufficient books of interest and value. Ours was political imprisonment so we had to keep fighting to keep our intellects alive and the darkness they wished to impose at bay.

On the cultural front, apart from books, there was music. Our record collection must have been one of the best anywhere and contained more than five hundred titles. Each prisoner was allowed to order one record every three months, adding to our collection 40 new records a year. Knowledge of new releases came from magazines and visitors, so we were pretty well informed of the latest developments in the music world.

The records to be played each evening were chosen by those comrades who were interested in music and familiar with our collection. Lists of a week's records would be written up and a copy given to each comrade. Every day the four or five chosen records would be given to the night-warder who would play them on the turntable in his office, in the order in which he was instructed.

Some of the comrades took the music very seriously and would lie for hours on their beds savouring the sounds. Sometimes you could hear someone dancing or singing in their cell or tapping their feet to the beat. The loudspeakers were at first mounted in the passage so if something was not to your taste it was just too bad. Later, when they were remounted inside our cells, you could turn yours off if you could not stand the particular number.

Music had never interested me much, but as paradoxical as it might seem, prison was a cultural experience. Our music collection was of such a varied nature that the comrades could arrange an educational programme to run over several nights. For instance, by selecting jazz records from various periods it was possible to assemble a history of jazz from Ledbelly to the present day.

Denis was the only one who regularly made his own music. He taught himself to play the guitar and after a few years of practice grew quite proficient. One or two of the others tried their hands – or mouths to be more precise – at the mouth organ. On the whole prison is not a good place to learn a musical instrument because you can never find a secluded spot and everyone is forced to hear your first discordant steps.

The films we saw on Friday afternoons should not exactly be placed under the heading of 'culture'. They all came from a hire-shop in downtown Pretoria: we selected the films from a shop catalogue. The films were fetched by a warder but invariably the ones we wanted to see would be 'out on loan' and we would end up seeing one chosen by the warder. Our choice was usually for films with some cultural value, films which bored the warders. They preferred junk American cop-films and would normally get their way by saying that the film they had brought was all that was left. Many of the comrades got so angry with this that they preferred to stay in their cells and read. There was nothing we could do about it as we were not in a position to question whether the film we'd ordered was really out on loan or not. Nevertheless, over the years some good films were shown and, curious as it may seem, most of us saw more movies in prison than we would have if we'd been outside. But then there are other interesting things to do outside.

Weekends were set aside for sport. Although none of us were fanatical about sports, it was an activity valued by all because it provided an outlet for releasing pent up emotions and frustrations. It also kept us fit in body and mind and provided a distraction from our cloistered little world. The main sporting activity was tennis—not real tennis for our court was only two-thirds full size and we only had wooden beach bats. Denis and Jeremy were the champions; I was the worst. Tony did not play because of his co-ordination problem, but Raymond was remarkably good considering he had only one good eye.

The tennis court also doubled as a volley-ball court: the net posts were tall enough to support the net at the correct height for the game. Despite it being a popular game we were seldom able to play because of the difficulty in mustering sufficient players to make up two equal-sized teams. Prior to Stephen's and my arrival volleyball used to be played every weekend because the prison staff, including Captain Schnepel, joined in. But they must have received instruction not to play sport with the 'communists' as they suddenly stopped participating. There was to be no fraternising with the prisoners—if friendships developed it could lead to a member of staff wanting to assist the prisoners in their seditious activities.

Everyone took to 'jogging' in the prison yard. This may sound impossible to outsiders, as jogging usually conjures up images of leisurely runs through leafy parks. Our 'track' must have been no more than 100 metres per lap and for most of the way hard concrete. Every morning before breakfast most of us would don our running shoes, T-shirts and shorts and run anything from five to 100 laps. More than that would be too much of a strain on the ankles. One week we would run clockwise, the next counter-clockwise—to prevent boredom!

The monotony of running round and round the yard was countered by the knowledge that we were doing it to keep fit—an essential prerequisite for escapers. And certainly it did keep us fit. It provided us with much of the stamina we needed to keep in sight our goal, the front door. It's surprising our jailers suspected nothing fishy in our keenness to run every morning, come rain, frost or burning sun.

Aside from the aspects of prison life which made it just bearable, there were two others which allowed you to keep your sanity: letters and visits. Without these conduits to the outside world you could easily forget you were a human being with wishes, hopes and desires; you could become thoroughly institutionalised and see the world entirely in terms of the prison. This is why for some long-term prisoners without relatives their saddest day is the day they are released. Their world collapses: they have nowhere to go, no one to receive them and everything they have built up is left behind.

Letters were a very important component of our lives as they were one of the few ways we could maintain contact with reality. Letters, university communications and library books were collected from the censor at supper-time by Dave K while the rest of us would wait expectantly in the dining-room in anticipation of what he would bring. Every day you'd hope for a letter although you knew that you only got one, two or three a month depending on your grading. If nothing arrived you'd feel miserable and swear they were deliberately withholding your post.

Prisoners who had just arrived in prison, like Stephen and myself, were classified as 'C' group prisoners and only permitted to send and receive one letter of 500 words per month. 'B' group prisoners were allowed two letters per month and 'A' groupers three. Denis was allowed four letters as a special dispensation for being a life prisoner. If more than your alloted number arrived they would usually ask which one(s) you wanted.

Five hundred words a month sounds very little but when you have nothing to write about it seems an awful lot. A 500-word letter written to you, on the other hand, seemed very short. People outside had so much to write about, did so much, led such exciting lives – they didn't appreciate their freedom!

The censorship of incoming letters was not overly severe. Perhaps this was because our correspondents had become circumspect over time. They knew that all letters, in and out, were thoroughly perused by the security police and the prison's censor. This knowledge enforced a self-censorship on the writers, in both directions.

If a prisoner wrote something 'unacceptable' he would simply be handed the letter back and told to rewrite it. This routine could be exploited if you wanted to pass a little message to the chiefs: you could write something directed at them, something you would like to say but could not do in any other way. I took advantage of this once, after a fly-past on 'Republic Day' by a formation of jets spewing out vapour-trails of the much-despised orange, white and blue colours of the apartheid republic. I wrote in a letter that the sight had made me vomit and that I hoped they would not come and pollute the clear blue sky above our prison again. The next day I was on the carpet to face the wrath of a red-faced Captain. That I had provoked such ire gave me great satisfaction.

It took them nine months to figure out that my correspondent 'Makaira Herscheli', or 'Molly' for short, was Robin (the name was concocted out of the scientific terms for the bird 'robin' and the fish 'marlin'—which was her surname). It must have come as a shock to them to find out that my letters were, in effect, going direct to the ANC office in London, where Robin was still working. I was hauled up again and told discreetly that I could no longer write to this person. I did not argue the point and meekly accepted the instruction, knowing that I'd still be able to write to her using another false name that I had for her. At the next visit I wistfully reported to my mother that I was no longer allowed to write to 'Margaret', whom she understood to be Robin, and asked her to get me the address of my other London friend, 'Sally'. A month or so later I had a new address and resumed the unbroken communication I'd had with Robin.

Prisoners were also allowed to receive photographs from their correspondents, and have photo albums to keep them in. These were not allowed to have more than 12 pages. What the authorities had in mind were albums with six leaves, with two or three photos neatly pasted on each side. When the album was full you were supposed to hand in surplus pictures so they could be held in safekeeping until your release. But everyone wanted all their pictures, not just the latest ones—old ones carried memories. So to get around this restriction the comrades, instead of ordering normal photo-albums, ordered loose, clear plastic pockets that could be put into ring binders. A sheet of white paper was inserted in each and the pocket literally stuffed with pictures on each side of the sheet. In this way you could keep dozens of pictures. Whenever the warders demanded that we hand in some of our pictures, we pointed out that our albums were the regulation 12 pages and that it was not specified how many pictures you could have on each page. Their pettiness knew no bounds (neither did our deviousness, they would have said).

For your birthday and at Christmas you were allowed to receive 12 cards. Twelve cards were more than any of us ever received for our birthdays, but at Christmas it had long been a tradition for sympathisers both in South Africa and abroad to send cards to political prisoners. The officers were never quite sure how to cope with this annual flood of greetings and salutations. They would try various ruses to prevent us knowing of their arrival and of how many had arrived. With monotonous predictability each year they would at first deny that there were any cards at all, and then let us have them very slowly to give the impression that there were very few. Some years, the comrades said, they would keep them all until Christmas day or after and then give you eight or so and say that there was none more.

But we knew that hundreds of cards arrived for us. One year the censor, after receiving a complaint of being tardy with our letters, forgot himself by complaining about the sacks of envelopes he had to go through. Another year the censor, who had resigned and was about to leave, decided to allow us to choose our own cards from the bundles that had arrived. He called each of us to his office window in turn, and read out the name of the sender of each card from the pile he held and then asked if we wanted it. Of course each prisoner said 'not that one' until he'd read out every name. In this way we were able to find out who had sent the cards and get some idea of the numbers that had arrived.

Visits, like letters, were regulated according to grading. 'C' group prisoners were allowed one visit by one person per month, lasting 45 minutes. 'B' groupers one visit per month by two people at a time and 'A' groupers two visits by two people. There were some exceptions to this rule: those who had no family in South Africa, such as Dave R, Dave K, and Alex, could receive several special visits over a week or couple of weeks if they had relatives visit them from overseas. Visits were strictly non-contact except for those who had small children (such as Alex and Dave R during our time). They were allowed short contact sessions with their children under close scrutiny in one of the administration offices. This applied until the children reached about six years old. After that – *verbode* (forbidden).

I placed visits below letters in order of preference because I found them intimidating. The visiting-room was very small: the same size as a cell but split down the middle by a chest-high counter and thick glass panes. There were three positions in the room with stools on each side. For us politicals only one visit took place at a time; for the *stokkies* three at a time. A warder sat on each side to make sure nothing 'illegal' was said and visitors were pre-warned that they were only allowed to discuss 'family matters'.

Your voice carried through to the other side via holes in the pegboard panels on each side of the window. Inside the panels microphones were hidden, recording every word spoken. We weren't supposed to know this but were aware that recording took place because Denis was once taken into the main office while the door to the small office next to the visiting-room had inadvertently been left open. In it he saw tapes turning while a prisoner was having his visit. When they saw him looking at the tapes the door was not very discreetly slammed in his face. The cryptic language used by the comrades in trying to extract news from their visitors must have confounded the warders in attendance and big brother who listened to the tapes afterwards. They must have thought they were unearthing all sorts of 'terrorist' plots and conspiracies.

This was the setting in which you had to conduct your conversations. What could you say when you knew that your every word was being listened to and then sent to security-police headquarters for detailed analysis? I also found it embarrassing to sit in front of my family in my prison uniform, with my cropped hair and in such an uncongenial environment. Others did not feel as intimidated and looked forward to their visits with great anticipation and excitement.

I said everything there was to say about the place at my very first visit; after that I didn't know what to say. Most times I would put in a few good words about the prison—to give the impression that I was quite happy and that I'd be the last person to be so rash as to contemplate anything like escaping. Occasionally I'd even 'brag' about the impenetrability of the place to make my watchers think that I was totally intimidated by the security measures. After saying my bit I would get my visitors to do the talking. Most of us made a point of saying things to confuse the warders as it was agreed that we should always take advantage of every opportunity to present ourselves in a light other than the correct one.

All visits had to be conducted in one of the two 'official' languages—Afrikaans and English. The only person adversely affected by this ruling was Alex, whose mother—who visited him twice a year from France—spoke Greek and French but only a little English. Boris, his son—who came with her—spoke only French. The Captain didn't mind this too much as he reckoned that Alex couldn't say too much to a young kid that would be a security risk.

Marie-José, Alex's wife, was permitted by the prison authorities to visit him but she could not get a visa to enter the country as she had been deported to France shortly after their detention in 1972. Every year she applied for a visa and ritually the application would be turned down. This perverse prohibition drove Alex to desperation and at the end of February 1978 he went on a hunger strike to try to force the authorities to change their minds. The prison authorities claimed to be in sympathy with him, but said they could do nothing about the visa as it was out of their hands. Alex soon realised the futility of the exercise and terminated his fast after ten days.

Denis's wife Esmé, too, had problems obtaining a visa. She had visited him once or twice but for many years had been refused entry from Britain, where she had been living from shortly after his imprisonment. Dave R's wife, Sue, had also been deported and was likewise refused a visa to enter South Africa. Dave K's ex-wife, Norma, could get a visa but she considered it too risky to go to South Africa.

There were other visitors apart from our permitted one or two per month—priests, envoys, judges, big-shot prison officials, lawyers, doctors and government ministers. Apart from the priests and doctors, these visits were not frequent.

All of us apart from John and myself, saw priests, ministers or rabbis. This was not because we wanted to atone for our 'sins' but because the visits let us see people other than our captors.

Denis, Dave R and Raymond had it best. Their rabbi seemed to be an interesting chap but the chief benefit came from the organised way the Jewish community cared and catered for Jewish prisoners in general. Twice a year each of them received huge food hampers containing cold meats, biscuits, dried and fresh fruit, tinned goods and the like. As with everything else, these were shared with everyone.

Tony, Jeremy and Steve, who saw the Catholic priest, invariably returned from their visits swearing that it was the last one they would be attending. Monseigneur McGuinness was a musty old bore who insisted on reading passages from the bible and engaging in long prayer sessions. As hard as they tried, the 'Catholic' comrades were unable to persuade him to organise food hampers.

Dave K visited a minister who was an old friend he had known outside. For Dave religious visits were like an extra visit. They would start off the session by discussing the bible and end up by discussing ordinary lay matters.

John and I did not see religious practitioners because we could not decide what religions we were and did not feel the benefits were worth it. When I first arrived at Pretoria I tried to sign on as a Jew, after the others had advised me of the advantages. But they would not fall for that one. Then I thought I'd be a Catholic because I didn't want to see a priest on my own. Finally I decided against having a religion when I suspected that the Catholic priest was a bore. When the prison chaplain came around to sort out my 'religious needs' he could not understand when I said that I had no religion. He could understand my not wanting to see a spiritual adviser but was incapable of understanding that anyone could not believe in God. He had a form to fill in and could not leave it blank. Eventually I was classified Anglican, I think, because I said my father was a member of that church at one stage.

The 'foreigners'—Dave R, Alex and Steve—were from time to time granted the 'privilege' of seeing envoys from their respective countries. The French envoy would always tell Alex that he was doing everything in his power to secure his release and get permission for his wife to visit him. Alex grew cynical about these claims since nothing ever happened, but he continued to see the envoy as it amounted to another visit from an outsider and he could ask questions about France.

Stephen and Dave R were visited by a British envoy who made similar claims of action. But no one expected much from the envoys as their respective governments had seldom shown much sympathy for the plight of political prisoners in South Africa. For a long time these governments had regularly made the misguided claim that political prisoners were legally sentenced by the courts for breaking the law and that judgements could be trusted because the South African legal system had always displayed a healthy measure of independence. They never questioned—and still do not question—the so-called laws under which the accused were charged and sentenced and under which the judges made their judgements. They never said anything about the 'security laws' which presumed guilt or about the illegitimate racist 'parliament' which passed those laws in the first place.

Judges were supposed to visit the prisons to see for themselves the implications of their judgements and the sentences they handed out. In all the time I was there only one judge came around. His visit was so brief and cursory that the impression he got must have confirmed his prejudices. The ones who didn't come must have had implicit faith in the system for which they worked.

Visits by big-shot prison officers were more frequent but were clearly just acts of duty. Probably many of the heavies from head office had never been near a prison or had not visited one for many years. Some of them were prepared to receive representations from the prisoners, but as their visits were impromptu the prisoners were not given time to formulate a list of demands, although there were always the standing demands for less censorship and for permission to receive newspapers. It is difficult to know whether these regularly-presented demands fell on deaf ears or whether over the years they had a compounding effect. On occasion we felt that they had an impact but, unlike the Red Cross, they never produced any immediate response.

Representatives of the International Committee of the Red Cross visited all South African political prisoners once a year. The Red Cross contributed significantly to the well-being of all political prisoners and were responsible for some of the greatest improvements in conditions over the years.

The authorities would never let us know when the Red Cross was coming, but we could always sense their imminent arrival by the behaviour of the warders. Demands that we had made to the Red Cross the previous year would suddenly be fulfilled and we would for no apparent reason be required to make the prison look clean and orderly. In 1979, for instance, after many years of complaining to the Red Cross that our tennis court was cracking up and that it was becoming impossible to play on, it was suddenly dug up and relaid. A few days later the Red Cross arrived.

All the prisoners looked forward to Red Cross visits. The team would arrive early in the morning and spend the day with us. They would eat our food—you could be sure we'd be served something exceptional that day—and find out from each prisoner in turn whether he had any personal problems. They would tell us about the conditions of other political prisoners in South Africa and around the world. In all ways, they told us, we were better off than the black prisoners and in some ways better off than many political prisoners in other parts of the world. In one respect we were worse off: in the provision of news, the denial of which they considered to be very serious. Without a doubt their pressure helped persuade the authorities to give in on this matter and from 1980 allow political prisoners to receive newspapers.

The only member of 'government' who visited our prison during my short stay was the new Minister of Police and Prisons (later the Minister of Law and Order), Louis le Grange. His visit was just a familiarisation exercise. The ten of us were made to stand to attention on the tennis court as this tall, close-eyed butcher with swept-back grey hair made his whirlwind inspection. The sight of the chief figure behind all the police massacres, detentions, torture and imprisonment of South African patriots was enough to turn the stomach. Perhaps the radiations of our hostility were the cause of his scurrying off so quickly.

12
Stage One

The plan for the attempt we'd just abandoned after the scare over the new sentry post became the basis for our new escape plan. We were determined now to get out without having to accost the night-warder and without leaving a trace. But before we could proceed with the plan we had to be absolutely certain that we could open door six using our own resources.

Going out through door six and without the warders' knowledge meant a total reconceptualisation of our escape plans. Out the window went all our strategies to tackle the warder as well as the need to rely on the complicated contingency route through the visiting-room. While this meant abandoning all notions of taking the warder's car, the advantages of getting out secretly were so much greater that it did not matter.

In any case, as our intelligence improved, it became obvious that it would not be so easy to simply hop into the warder's car and drive off. And after the withdrawal of the comrade with the driving licence the warder's car had no particular advantages for us as there was no point in driving it somewhere to hire a car. To get away from Pretoria we could just as easily, and probably more safely, use our money to hire a taxi; less favourably catch a bus or train. It was these observations that led us to the conclusion that if we wanted to proceed we had to find a way of getting to door six to see if we could open it.

It had long been suspected that door six used the same key as door two. We had arrived at this conclusion by a complex process of deduction. As we had never seen any keys on a bunch carried by a warder that could not be linked to a particular lock, key six had to be one of those which were in regular use. It could not be one of those on the night-warders' bunch as he was locked into the prison by door six. He had only two keys: one for the section doors (our door three) and one for door four (the same as five). His section-door key was different to the number ones we'd used to open three, but this was because his could not master them. If he had been able to do so he would have had access to half the cells, and we knew that he couldn't open the cells with the keys he carried. If a cell had to be opened at night in an emergency, someone from outside had to bring the day-keys (i.e. the ones and twos) or a key to unlock a locker containing them in the office. This meant that the departing day-staff had to leave with at least one bunch of the day-keys to lock the doors on their way out, including six. From this it was reasonable to deduce that six used a one or two key. It seemed less likely that it would be a number one as key one was related to the section key used by the night-warder, and door six just looked like door two.

Our experiences with the number two locks had taught us that it was not good enough to know that a particular lock used a particular key—it had to be tried out. But to test six was altogether a different matter from testing our ones and twos, or even three and four. The only time we could get down to test it was during the 8 pm inspection-round when we would have no more than a few minutes. This meant that we had to be pretty certain that our keys would work: there would be no time for modifications on the spot.

The project to go down to test door six became known as 'stage one' because it was to be the first part of a two-stage project to test our keys in all the doors on the way to the front door. 'Stage two' would be the testing of the doors beyond six to the front door. 'Stage three' would be the actual breakout.

Stage one, or at least the first stage-one attempt, was carried out around the beginning of August 1979. The general plan was the same as the one we had previously worked out but it contained certain refinements to make it workable. As with all our plans it relied on Sergeant Vermeulen being on duty.

We had decided against using the dining-room as our hiding place while Vermeulen passed to go upstairs in favour of the film equipment cupboard under the stairs to our section. The dining-room had the disadvantage that its door was visible from the end of the passage at door four. We could not take the chance of exposing ourselves to view while entering it. The film cupboard was set well back from view.

It was easy enough to obtain the measurements of the key for the film cupboard. I simply measured them one Friday when Dave K was given the key to get the film equipment out. When the equipment was repacked after the filmshow it was arranged in such a way that it would allow two people to crouch inside the cupboard not too uncomfortably. The key was a typical wardrobe key, simple in construction, and a copy was easily made from a piece of sheet metal found in the workshop.

A number of other details also had to be worked out. Not having watches, as prisoners do today, there was no way of knowing when it was eight o'clock or when we should go downstairs. We couldn't just go down and sit in the cupboard for hours on end—it would be too uncomfortable. This is where we took advantage of our records.

Vermeulen never carried out his inspection at exactly eight, but only after he had finished playing the records that had been selected for the night or when he came to the end of a record at around inspection time. As he was required to play them in the exact order given to him, it was possible to tell pretty accurately how near we were to the inspection. A certain record placed in the list could signal the moment for us to go downstairs; the last record when it was eight. He was so reliable and predictable that he would never leave his office if a record was coming to the end, even if he had been called upstairs by a *stokkie* who had pressed his bell. It was thus quite safe to move downstairs during the last cut of a record because Vermeulen would want to be in his office to turn it over or put on the next one. The record we chose as the signal record was *Parallel Lines* by 'Blondie', which was popular at the time.

Without any opposition Alex and I were chosen to carry out the mission. We had the most experience in practical matters and had worked out the plan; we were also the only ones who would do it. This is not to say that we were not dead scared about doing it. We'd been messing around with locks for months and both of us had been out of our cells while our doors were supposed to be locked, but the thought of having to remain out of our cells for probably more than an hour, violate the sanctity of the admin section and expose ourselves to the possibility of bumping into Vermeulen was terrifying in the extreme. The thought of it would cause us to break into shivers of cold fear; our bellies would lock solid and we'd feel weak at the knees.

This then is how the first stage one was carried out:

At around six o'clock, that is an hour and a half after lock-up, we placed dummies in our beds. These we created out of our prison overalls by placing them on the bottom sheets of our beds and stuffing them with clothes, books, towels etc. to make them look like authentic 'bodies' under the blankets. There was no need to worry about the 'head' because this was toward the wall below the passage window and out of sight from the passage. (The authorities realised this fatal error after our departure because one of the first things they did was to turn the prisoners around so they could see their heads from the window.) In the unlikely event of Vermeulen looking through our windows, we arranged our cells to look as if we had eaten our sandwiches, undressed and gone to sleep.

At around 7 pm we both unlocked our inner doors with the number one keys we'd earlier concealed in our cells. Alex unlocked his outer door using the crank mechanism, after I had signalled to him with a towel that I could hear no sounds from Vermeulen. After emerging from his cell Alex relocked his number two, turning it once only, and tip-toed down to my cell to unlock my outer door. While Alex made his way to the shower I emerged from my cell and relocked my number two with the key he'd passed me through my window. I then made my way to the shower too.

Alex had opened the geyser door and removed from the cache the keys we would need, the 'pea' and our balaclavas. When ready we crouched, one in each shower, behind the low walls separating the two showers in each room to wait for the signal record to end. Here we were out of view of Vermeulen if he had come into the section and looked into the showers from the passage. Had he come right in he would obviously have seen us but we'd reckoned that if this happened his sudden discovery of two masked 'terrorists' would give him such a fright that he'd probably drop down with a heart attack. Then we'd have the prison to ourselves.

We were dressed in our prison overalls but had decided that if we got caught we would threaten Vermeulen with the 'pea', tie him up, release Stephen, get dressed in our proper escape clothing and make our way out as best we could. Around our necks we carried our running shoes tied together by their laces.

When the 'Blondie' record came near to the end we rose from our hiding places and poked our heads out of the shower to watch for the all-clear signal from Stephen – a wave of a towel – before proceeding to door three. On the signal we crept down the passage towards the door. I peeked through the keyhole to make sure no one was standing on the other side and then slowly unlocked the door. We went through and after listening for any movements from downstairs I relocked the door and we cautiously made our way down the stairs to the cupboard. Alex unlocked the cupboard and the two of us squeezed inside. Once inside we realised that there was one detail we'd not thought about: how to hold the door closed. The small lock jutting out on the inside did not afford a proper grip. A small detail, but an important one.

From inside the cupboard we could still hear the music coming from our section. It was an eerie sound and much louder than we'd expected, but reassuring in that it indicated that everything was in order. Silence would have been much more frightening as we would have had no idea how long it was to the eight o'clock inspection round. Our thoughts in the pitch darkness, the agony of our contorted limbs and our pounding hearts flooded our senses.

As soon as the music stopped we could hear Vermeulen picking up his keys and making his way towards door four. The sound of him opening the grille so near made us shudder with fright. Alex tensed and as he did so his sweating fingers lost grip of the lock by which he was holding the door closed. The door swung open a little and a bright shaft of light entered the cupboard. He's seen us, we both thought, but Alex managed to regain his grip and pulled the door closed just as Vermeulen would have come into view of it. I swore quietly in Alex's ear.

As Vermeulen walked over our heads and up the stairs Alex's hand was shaking so much the door rattled as if there was an earth tremor. 'Oh God! He must have heard it', I whispered out loud, forgetting myself in that moment of terror. But no, he continued on his customary way up the stairs and into the *stokkies'* section. He must have been in a trance.

155

As soon as we heard the clang of the *stokkies'* section door closing we leapt out of the cupboard and made our way through door four, which Vermeulen had conveniently left open. As we turned the corner after door four, door six, the last major obstacle in our path to freedom, came into view. We stared at the solid blue barrier in awe like two archaeologists finding the entrance to some long-concealed tomb. It was closed across the passage as we'd suspected.

I unlocked door five, a grille a few inches in front of six, with the number four key. The key glided around with no resistance and we swung it open so that I could get to six. I inserted a number two key into six and tried to turn it, but it wouldn't turn – not even a little bit. My heart sank. Another long battle ahead, I thought. I tried several of the other number twos but none of them turned. I also tried a number one key, just in case, but it also refused to turn.

I remembered how long it had taken us to get our number twos to work, and then we'd had hours to test them each night. How often will we be able to get down here to test this door? How long is it going to take to get this one right? Is this really the end? Alex prodded me back to reality as I contemplated the problem: 'Take it out. There's no more time. We'll have to try again.'

I relocked five and we made our way back to the cupboard, baffled and dismayed. The wait for Vermeulen to return seemed to take an eternity. We'd arranged for Denis to detain him for as long as possible by asking him the latest on the rugby front, and obviously Denis was carrying out his task with relish. In fact Vermeulen took so long to return that we wondered if something had gone wrong: Had he discovered us missing from our cells? Had he radioed for reinforcements?

Eventually we heard him coming out of our section and his casual footsteps descending the steps above our heads. The release of tension as he closed four turned our fear into defiance and we congratulated each other by telepathy. As soon as we heard him throw his keys onto the table in his office and turn on his radio we came out of our hiding place, scurried up the stairs and made our way back to the shower. We returned to the cache everything we'd taken, apart from one number one and one number two key. After Stephen had given another all-clear I relocked Alex in his cell, returned to my own and relocked my number two with the crank.

After I had relocked my cell doors and cleaned up all evidence of the 'misdemeanour' I expected to come down from the agitated state, as one normally does after a stressful event. But there was so much adrenalin flowing in my veins that night that I remained in a high state and wasn't able to get a wink of sleep. I lay awake all night wondering if I'd be able to face another stage one: my nerves could only take so much. The keys hadn't worked and it seemed we might have to go down many times. I wasn't sure I could face it again.

The whole episode, including the days preceding the actual

operation, had been one of the most agonisingly stressful, self-inflicted experiences of our lives. It took us both a few days to come down from that high and when we did we tried to reassess the situation. Although none of our keys had worked we were not convinced that six did not use a number two key. Close examination of the keys the day after had revealed that some of them had almost turned and that the problem had been caused by the ward cutaways not matching the wards exactly. Why they did not jam in our number twos we could only ascribe to the fact that our cell doors were opened and closed much more frequently than number six, causing the wards to be more worn. One thing was sure: door six did not use a number one key.

Very shortly after our first stage-one attempt a series of disasters and near-disasters occurred. The first happened one Friday morning while we were supposed to be busy cleaning our section. Alex and I had completed our chore of cleaning the showers and for some reason had taken out of the cache one of the sacks of clothing and the 'pea'. As we were going through the sack we heard the section door open. I peered out of the shower and saw that it was Moreby, the most hated of all the warders, who had just entered. I shouted to Alex. He instinctively slung the bag into the closet and closed the door, without locking it; the 'pea' he tucked into his belt under his shirt.

Moreby must have seen my worried look and made his way directly towards the shower to see what was going on. Alex grabbed a rag and pretended to be cleaning the wall. I went to the entrance again to see what Moreby was doing. As I turned to look out, Moreby stepped into the shower and the two of us collided head on. 'What's going on here' he demanded. 'Nothing, Mister Moreby. We're just cleaning the shower as we're supposed to. What's the problem?' Alex glanced casually over his shoulder but said nothing. Moreby stood with his hands on his hips for a few seconds scanning the scene to find something wrong. Satisfied that he could find nothing, he warned, 'You just watch out', and left the shower. I guess he must have thought that Alex and I were having it off. What else could have accounted for our red faces?

After that incident Moreby kept a closer watch on Alex and me than he had before. He was a totally insecure character always out to put himself in a light flattering to his superiors, and he wanted desperately to uncover some dirty business and bring it to the attention of the Captain.

A second misadventure involving Warder Moreby occurred shortly after the shower incident. It was on a day when our usual workshop attendant, 'Loggie', was off duty and Moreby had taken his place. Alex, foolishly, started making a spanner for dismantling door seven's lock out of the handle of an old tin opener. Moreby spotted him doing something which was not required for the particular job in hand and started to walk towards Alex's bench to see what he was doing. If Alex had thought quickly enough he could have invented some explanation for the unfinished and unrecognisable object, such as saying it was intended to be a butter-knife or something for the garden. But when you feel guilty your first reaction is to conceal what you're doing, and that's what Alex did. He placed the piece of metal on the shaft of his vice which extended under his bench. Unfortunately it did not balance properly and fell to the floor with a loud clang just as Moreby approached. Moreby picked up the object and immediately headed for the Captain's office with his little prize.

Nothing actually came of this incident as far as Alex was concerned and we even managed to turn it to our advantage by getting Moreby transferred to another prison very shortly after it happened. This we achieved by complaining bitterly to the Captain the next day about Moreby's attitude toward us, which had always been one of bossiness and aggressiveness. We did not find his rapid transfer unusual because our complaint was clearly the pretext the Captain had been awaiting for a long time. Moreby was despised by prisoners and staff alike. He was a twisted character who took out his frustrations on others by being extremely arrogant and rude. He was the only English-speaking warder in the prison and hated us intensely because we could tease and taunt him more easily than the others.

At the time we did think that the discovery of the spanner-in-the-making was being taken seriously because the very next evening the warder on *pos* duty remained on the catwalk after lock-up at four thirty. Until that day the catwalk had been unoccupied during the period from lock-up until ten at night. Everyone interpreted this change as a sign that the authorities suspected what we were up to and had closed the major loophole in their security.

It was some time later that we found out from Sergeant Vermeulen that this change in the *pos*-duty shifts just happened to coincide with a genuine change in routine. Apparently the warders had for a long time been asking for a three-shift day – for some reason which was of interest only to the warders themselves. The opportunity to introduce the new routine was taken when an important awaiting-trail prisoner was brought to the prison. He was Eschel Rhoodie.

Eschel Rhoodie was one of the main characters in the 'Information scandal', a subject of major interest in white politics at the time. He was alleged to have been one of the villains who spent vast sums of public money on propaganda exercises overseas. He later fled South Africa and from exile began to spill the beans on the other crooks in the 'government', which included Prime Minister Vorster. He was arrested in France in August 1979 and immediately extradited to South Africa. At his trial he was convicted on five counts of fraud and sentenced to twelve years' imprisonment, some of which were to run concurrently, making the sentence an effective six years. However, he was subsequently acquitted on appeal and allowed off scot-free. Illegally spending millions of rands of public money was evidently not a crime, whereas posting some ANC leaflets clearly was!

We did not at first know of Rhoodie's presence in the prison because our newspaper delivery system had broken down at that time, and of course it was cut out of our radio news-broadcasts. But somehow the news filtered through and then we were able to see him through cracks in the fence surrounding the *stokkies'* yard. It was peculiar to see a prominent figure of the regime mixing with the ordinary *stokkies*, most of whom were petty criminals and only in prison because they could not afford decent lawyers to get them out on bail.

The interpretation that the 24-hour *pos*-guard was a response to suspicions of an escape attempt prompted a major gathering of the escape group to discuss the issue and the strategy to be adopted in the light of the change. The meeting proved to be a significant turning point. Denis expressed his apprehension and declared that he could not contemplate going while a guard remained on the *pos* over the crucial four thirty to ten period. He and Dave K were of the opinion that the guard would eventually be withdrawn, citing as evidence a similar incident in the past, when normality had returned after the crisis passed. Dave K considered the guard on *pos* duty to be a setback but not an insurmountable problem. Dave R adopted Denis's position and recommended that all escape-related activity should cease until the guard disappeared. He proposed that all of us should rather concentrate on other projects that would promote our interests, such as pressurising the authorities to bring together all political prisoners, black and white, in one prison such as Robben Island.

Alex, Steve and I saw no reason for all this gloom. We wanted to proceed with the escape preparations whatever the position. The problem of the warder could be tackled when we reached that bridge, as had been done with all previous bridges. To halt preparations at this stage might mean halting them forever. The extension of *pos* duty would not affect our immediate objective, the testing of the doors down to the front door.

As usual there was much discussion on this issue. In the end the other three had to submit to our proposal that we be allowed to go ahead with the project to test the doors down to the front door – that is, carrying out stage two. The others were insistent, however, that we should not go beyond stage two, which in practice meant escaping, until the four thirty to ten period was free of the *pos*-guard.

It was decided too that it would be too risky to ask for outside help while there was a guard on the *pos* during the escape. It would neither be possible to park an escape vehicle outside the prison nor be correct to expose other parties to the very real possibility of being shot. A decision was made immediately to advise our comrades outside that all plans of assistance should be held in abeyance until further notice.

Another near-disaster followed closely in the train of the previous ones. One evening as I was getting something out of our cache in one of the geyser closets during shower-time, I noticed that the sack was wet on top. How was this possible in a warm environment? There was only one explanation: a leaking tank. But that was impossible because it was an insulated tank and any leaks would only show at the bottom, not at the side. As I pulled the sack up to save the easily destroyed wooden keys, a drop of water dripped onto my hand from the roof of the closet. I knew it then—another pipe leakage!

Pretoria Prison was built by prison labour, which was a large part of the explanation why from time to time leaks would appear in someone's cell or in one of the downstairs rooms. It had been found that the prisoners who had installed the plumbing had deliberately sabotaged the system by tightening all the pipe couplings only one thread before they were encased in concrete. It was not possible to repair all the joints in one go as no one knew where they were. To replace the whole system would have meant virtually knocking down the entire prison. Leaks just had to be repaired when and where they appeared. But we couldn't report this leakage: we weren't supposed to know what happened inside the geyser closets.

The sack of contraband in the closet with the leak was huge – too large to be placed with the rest of the stuff in the other one. We could leave it on the floor of the other closet but if the warders opened it for any reason they'd see it and then search the closet for more. That way we'd lose everything. It was better to take it out and leave it somewhere else until we could find a better place. In the absence of any better places just then, there was nothing else we could do but hide it in the nearest cell—Alex's—until the next morning, which fortunately was a Friday.

The next day we assessed the situation. The leak appeared to have worsened overnight; we knew from past experiences that leaks had a habit of spreading—meaning that if it was leaking above the one geyser it would probably soon leak above the other. Both caches had to be cleared out. But where could we move all the stuff? It was a mountain. There was no other safe basket for our eggs.

As we were contemplating what to do with our gear while cleaning the section, a warder burst in to announce an inspection by a big-brass from Prison Headquarters. We couldn't believe our ears and our bad luck. The bastards were bound to look under the beds, and then everything would be exposed. More than exposed, there would be pandemonium. How would the Captain explain to the chief a huge bag of keys and civilian clothing simply lying under one of the prisoner's beds? Did they never have shake-ups?

There was one chance. Raymond was ill in bed and if we put the sack under his bed it was unlikely they would disturb him by going over his cell. Alex appealed to Raymond, but Raymond, quite rightly, would have none of it. He was not involved in the escape and was – quite reasonably I thought – not prepared to take unnecessary chances. Alex in his usual uncompromising way swore profusely at all concerned for this bad turn of events. There was nothing we could do but cross our fingers and hope they would not look under the beds.

Each prisoner was expected to stand in his cell while the inspection took place. As my cell was first I tried to be as friendly as possible to set the tone for a casual, chatty inspection. It appeared to work. The big-shot responded favourably: he asked a few questions about how I was getting on and then after a cursory glance around the cell passed on to the next. Alex's heart must have been punching the inside of his chest by the time the big-one got to him. Fortunately, when he reached Alex's cell he had grown bored looking into the cells, which all looked equally clean and tidy, and uninterestedly passed on to the next.

As soon as the officers and retinue had cleared out we set about finding another hiding place for our sacks of goodies. There was one place that might be suitable – the sealed off stairway at the far end of our section. We could tie the sacks together and hide them around the corner on the first step of the stairway. By sitting on the floor and stretching a hand through the bars it was possible to reach far enough to place the sacks out of sight.

The sack in the other geyser was taken out and the one under Alex's bed brought into the shower. The two were tied together and while someone stood at door three to listen for warders they were carried to the end of the passage, pushed through the bars and out of sight around the corner. It was a reasonably good place, but without much effort anyone could have stuck a hand around the corner and felt them. We just hoped the warders were not in the habit of doing so.

Fortunately the leak grew a lot worse and the water started to pour down a hole into the downstairs toilet. This was gleefully pointed out to the Captain and a few days later it was repaired. It was a major job. Both geysers had to be removed and the wall containing the pipe had to be broken open to expose the leaking joint. Just as well we'd had the foresight to clear out both hiding places.

The real scare occurred while we were attempting to retrieve the sacks the following Friday. Alex put his hand around the corner to grab our precious hoard, but instead of grasping the sacks his hand bumped them and both went tumbling down the stairs to the first landing. I sent up a howl of despair. How were we going to get them up now? All that work and irreplaceable clothing gone down a black hole. A mirror revealed nothing: it was too dark and dusty. Even those who were not participating in the escape commiserated with us. They knew what efforts we'd gone to to create and collect it all.

Someone hit on the brilliant idea of making a grapnel out of wire which, on the end of a piece of string, could be thrown in the direction of the sacks. Hopefully it would catch onto one of them so they could be pulled up. From somewhere, suitable pieces of wire and a long piece of string appeared.

Alex spent more than an hour throwing the grapnel in the direction of where he guessed the sacks to be lying. I stood behind him chewing my nails while Stephen stood guard at the section door to listen for warders. What we would have told them had they come in I don't know. There would have been no use in making up a story, since any commotion at the end of the passage would have drawn attention to the sealed off stairway.

After many, many throws Alex pulled on the string and felt resistance. Like a fisherman he wondered whether he'd hooked some debris or, finally, the big one. It was the sacks! He slowly pulled up his prize until he was able to lay a hand on it. In no time the sacks were back in their holes behind the geysers and Alex was being applauded for his miraculous retrieval. I felt like throwing him down the dark abyss from which he'd just pulled his catch.

Despite the previous terrifying experience, the disused stairway was retained as an alternative storage place. A month after the leak saga one of the geysers burnt out and had to have its element replaced. This happened on a Tuesday but the problem could not be reported until the Friday when the sacks could again be placed around the corner at the top of the stairway.

To avoid losing our sacks a second time we tied a long, strong cord to them and a piece of black cotton to the end of the cord. The other end of the cotton we tied to the bottom of one of the bars sealing off the stairs and covered it in dust to conceal it. Instead of placing the sacks on the top step as we'd done the first time, they were pushed down until they came to rest in a stable position. If they'd fallen any further it would not have mattered; they could still have been pulled up. Disasters can be useful.

In early September we attempted a second stage one. The tactics adopted were somewhat different to those we'd applied during the first attempt. Since there was now a full-time guard on the *pos* who looked directly into our cells, we had to open our doors in daylight when it was difficult for him to see into the cells, which were relatively dark compared to the outside. To further obscure the guard's view Alex and I opened our window panes half way and placed tall objects in front of them and on top of our cupboards. Several other refinements were added: to prevent our grilles clanging when we closed them we taped pads of tissue paper to our doorframes; to prevent my number two springing open when it was unlocked I fixed a hook under it and from this tied a bootlace to my grille.

We exited from our cells as soon after lock-up as possible. As before, we left dummies in our beds and arranged our cells to look as if we'd undressed and gone to bed. Alex came out first because his cell was in a better position relative to the guard on the *pos* (most of the time the guards sat in the sheltered alcove at the end of the catwalk opposite my cell, from which position they were unable to see into Alex's). Alex then unlocked my number two as before, handed me the key and hid himself in the shower. Instead of coming out immediately I had to wait for the guard to move towards the other end of the *pos*. When he eventually moved I untied the bootlace holding my door closed, came out of my cell and locked my number two behind me. I joined Alex in the shower where he had already taken out of the cache all that we would need for the expedition. We put on our balaclavas, dressed in our escape clothes and finally pulled our overalls over these. We then took up positions, one in each shower, to wait for the signal record ('Blondie' again).

Since we'd planned to go down to the cupboard at about 7 pm, the two hour wait in the shower presented a problem we'd not thought of before: where to relieve ourselves. The obvious place was down the shower drainholes above which we were crouched. But trying to pee down a small hole on a flat surface while dressed in escape clothing with overalls over them proved to be almost impossible. Standing up didn't help because it was then impossible to hit the target, and if we missed the warders would smell it the next day and ask questions. If there was a next time, we agreed, we would bring along a water-tight bottle which could be stored overnight and emptied in the morning.

When the signal record came near to its end Stephen signalled with a towel that he could hear no sounds from below. We tip-toed in our socks down the passage to door three, opened it cautiously and moved silently down the stairs to the film cupboard as before. But, oh no!, the cupboard key would not turn. I felt sick at the thought of all the nervous energy we'd spent for nothing. Both of us felt like kicking it in but realised it would be wiser to return to the shower and our cells. Fortunately we'd given ourselves an hour so there was plenty of time to get back before the eight o'clock inspection.

Getting back into our cells was the reverse process of coming out. When Stephen signalled to us in the shower that the *pos*-guard was in his corner I locked Alex back into his cell and returned to the shower to wait for Alex to signal that the guard had moved along the catwalk towards his end. As soon as I heard a bang on the wall I rushed back to my cell and relocked my number two using the crank method as usual. No sleep again that night as I lay feeling the unstoppable pounding of my heart.

The next morning we tried out the cupboard key to find out why it hadn't turned. Of course it worked perfectly – old Murphy playing his tricks again! The dimensions of the key must have been slightly out, we concluded. That Friday I checked the key against the original and found it to be a fraction of a millimetre too high. I filed off the surplus metal and tested it over and over to make sure there would be no repetition of the problem.

A third stage one was attempted about a week later. Several other improvements had been made since the first time: we had made a 'handle' consisting of a drawing pin and a bootlace to hold the film cupboard door closed while we were inside; we had modified all the number two keys so that the wards would not jam in number six.

Using the same procedure as before we made our way down to the film cupboard at about 7 pm. At eight o'clock, after Vermeulen had passed by, we came out of the cupboard and made our way into the administrative section. Instead of coming with me to door six as he'd done the first time, Alex kept guard at the end of the passage opposite door four while I tested the keys. The plan was that if he heard Vermeulen coming back to his office prematurely (he could have been called on his walkie-talkie, for instance) we would nip into the warders' toilet next to the office until it was safe to come out again.

I tried the modified keys in door six. All of them turned through 180 degrees but none would unlock the door. I couldn't understand it. The fact that they'd turned inside the lock proved the lock used a number two key. But why wouldn't our keys turn the bolt? Surely they were correct. After all, they'd worked in all the number twos in our section. As I was contemplating these problems I heard a whispered but impatient shout from behind me. Our ideas of the time we'd used up differed: I wanted to go on and solve the problem; Alex wanted to get back. I looked around and could see that he was beginning to lose his normal cool, so I relocked five and turned back.

As I ran back towards Alex I gave a thumbs-down sign. The disappointed look that drew across his face was the saddest sight I'd ever seen. He just stood there spellbound with his hands hanging in a questioning position. He had thought I'd taken so long because I'd had a success. I almost had to drag him back into the cupboard.

Although none of our number twos had worked we were still not convinced that door six did not use a number two key. The fact that the keys had turned part of the way indicated that the ward cutaways were correct and since they were a complicated pattern, key six had to be very similar if not identical to key two. We were forced to assume that the reason the keys had not unlocked the door was because they had been cut to work in our cell doors which were opened and closed far more frequently than number six and were consequently more worn. Our number two keys must have been lifting the levers of the number six lock fractionally too high and thus were not able to turn the bolt. As it turned out, our assumptions were correct.

To overcome this problem we decided to make a special shaftless key (*see diagram 11 on page 85*) that could be jiggled up and down and would thus not be limited in the extent the cuts could lift the levers. The depths of the cuts would be made the same as number two's, as these were obviously correct. The idea was borrowed from our picking device which worked on the same principle.

The new key was made from two pieces of sturdy wire Dave K had found in the garden. I drew a template to which the wires had to be bent and then Alex hammered and twisted them to shape in the workshop. The pieces of wire were then soldered together on top of the template. (The soldering iron belonged to us prisoners but was kept in the office for the odd electrical job.) The 'bit' of the key was made out of wood and then glued with epoxy to the shaped ends of the wires. Finally the cuts were filed to the same depths as number two.

We tested the key in all the number two locks in our section and it appeared to work well. Being metal meant it could be turned with much more force than the wooden keys; the latter relied on the dimensions being absolutely perfect rather than on force.

About mid-October we made our final stage-one attempt. Following the same procedure as the previous time, Alex and I made our way down to the administrative section at 8 pm to test door six. As on the previous occasion Alex stood guard at the end of the passage near door four while I tested the new key. This time I had more confidence – I knew six was going to give up its unreasonable resistance.

I opened five and as I took key six from my pocket my heart speeded up – with beats of expectation and excitement, not fear. I pushed the special key in, located it between the inner faces of the lock and turned it slowly. It turned with such ease I thought I'd missed the levers altogether. I turned it back to check what had happened and as I did so I heard a loud 'clonk' as the bolt shot back out. It had worked! What had all the fuss been about? I turned the bolt in and out several times to make sure that it really did work and then turned it one and a half times to see if it would work on the second revolution. No problem! The key turned so easily there was no need even to jiggle it up and down to make it work.

I withdrew the key and relocked five. When I turned to run back towards Alex I could see that this time he'd not allowed his ever-overflowing optimism to get the better of him: he had expected the worst and had a pre-set disappointed look on his face. But when I gave the thumbs-up instead of the expected thumbs-down the look instantly changed from dark gloom to one of excited elation. He leapt for joy and shouted (far too loudly I thought), 'We've beaten the fascists!' Inside the cupboard again we forgot our normal anxiety and shook hands and hugged each other in congratulation and with excitement at the prospects. We knew that we were now as good as out.

13
Stage Two

Having completed stage one successfully, Alex, Steve and I were keen to get on with stage two, but the others were concerned for our safety. Before proceeding, a meeting of the escape group was held to discuss the strategy to be adopted. Denis was unhappy with the plans as they stood but said he would not stand in our way. He was still worried about the guard on the *pos* and felt that our current plans might lead to disaster. He was still of the opinion that the guard would eventually be withdrawn, despite the fact that there was no evidence of a crisis situation which he believed had been the cause of the guard being put there in the first place. Dave K was for proceeding but Dave R only agreed in principle that we should proceed: he preferred deferment.

Stage two was to be different from stage one in that its object was not to test one door but all doors beyond number six. This meant that we would need much longer than the few minutes afforded by the 8 pm inspection round. If we went down immediately after lock-up we could give ourselves about three hours to work on the doors. But how could we get past the warder in his office without being seen?

The plan that finally emerged was for Alex and me to go down to the film cupboard as soon after lock-up as possible. Someone would open their lamp-cover (with the lamp-spanner we'd made from a bent nail), break the bulb or replace it with a burnt-out one and call Vermeulen up with his lamp-spanner. Vermeulen would have to wait around in the section while the bulb was replaced because he had to turn the light off and on from the outside, get a new bulb from Dave K – who kept a supply in his cell – and finally collect the spanner and old bulb. While he was doing this the two of us would come out of the cupboard, pass through door four, press the button for door eight in the warder's office, open five and six and then close them behind us. Beyond door six we would be cut off from view and would have until the eight o'clock inspection to attempt to open the remaining doors on the way to the front door.

Stage two would also involve our attempting to find out if there was a way of seeing out into the street to ascertain what time the sentries came on duty at the gate, where they stood and how they operated. It was also agreed that if there was time we should attempt to enter the Captain's office, which was the first office in the administrative section as you came in the front door, so that a window could be opened to see the position of the *pos* guard.

Shortly before eight o'clock the doors beyond six would be

relocked and we would wait next to door six for Vermeulen to go upstairs on his round. Door six would then be opened and we would proceed back to the cupboard, closing all doors behind us. After Sergeant Vermeulen had returned to his office we would return to our cells in the same manner as we'd done on stage one.

Theoretically, after completing stage two we would have all the keys needed to get to and open the front door and be in a position to leave, provided the existing security arrangements prevailed.

The planning for stage two was in fact the planning for the actual breakout and the attempt was in effect a practice escape run. The plan had come a long way from the first one and even from the last one that was current before stage one took place. Knowing that it was now possible to penetrate beyond door six without having to have the contingency route through the visiting-room, there was no longer any need to accost the warder. It was also now entirely feasible to make our way out of the prison right under the warder's nose. This offered the most tremendous advantage in that it would give us thirteen and a half hours to get away before our absence was discovered, assuming they only discovered it at open-up the next morning.

The plan for stage two was accepted in principle by all those remaining in the escape group. But when it came to the crucial question of who would break their light bulb, the question of their security from incrimination was raised. Objectively speaking, Dave R was in the best position because his cell was at the far end of our section and thus furthest from door three which Vermeulen would leave open when he came in with the lamp key. It would take Vermeulen some time to walk the length of the passage and back, giving us more time to get through door six and place him in a better position should we happen to make any noise while doing our business downstairs.

Stephen, who had offered to break his bulb in lieu of Dave, was in the worst position because his cell was nearest to door three and opposite the *pos*-warder's alcove. The *pos*-warder would easily see Stephen standing on top of his cupboard, fiddling with his lamp and the light going out, but when in his alcove Dave's cell was out of his sight. Dave could not be included in this plan because if we got caught he would automatically be implicated.

To reduce suspicion being pinned on him it could be arranged that he replace his bulb with a burnt-out one we'd acquired from burn-outs in the rooms downstairs. Afterwards he could smash the good one and flush it down his toilet, together with our lamp spanner. If we were caught, his burnt out bulb could in no way be linked to the fact that we were wandering around the prison. But this was too problematical.

The following weekend a long meeting of the escape group took place. Stephen expressed the view that all should share the risks, but this was not accepted. Although he had not contributed much in a material sense to the escape preparations, he had always been firmly behind Alex and me in all our thinking, had voted with us on practically every occasion and had never hesitated to assist in whatever way he could. He was prepared to break or replace his bulb if no one else would do it but he was in the worst position to do so. He felt that if he could do it so could others because the risks were the same for all.

After hearing our views Dave R replied that he had given the matter his most intense thought and believed that the plan would only end in disaster. He saw no reason why risks should be shared by everyone because in any organisation those best at performing certain tasks should specialise in those tasks.

Alex, Steve and I listened silently to all this, for we knew that what he was saying was the collective statement of all those who were not involved in the escape project. When he had finished we did not counter arguments but asked him whether he was prepared to continue to assist in the carrying out of stage two. But he felt he could not and that it was best for him to withdraw from the escape group so long as the existing strategy and conditions existed. He was not opposed to escaping but wanted outside assistance, the guard on the *pos* to disappear in the evening and the plan of execution changed so that there would be no unnecessary risks. Since these were matters over which we had no control, the three of us considered him to be expressing his resignation from the escape group. This entailed his losing the vote and no longer being informed of developments. As a disciplined comrade, he accepted this and withdrew from the group.

Denis had never formally refused to assist in the stage two attempt, but it was obvious that there was not much advantage in him breaking his bulb instead of Stephen.

Dave K, on the other hand, when pressurised, agreed to assist by replacing his bulb with a burnt-out one. Finally a plan was worked out which involved both Stephen and Dave — one which eliminated any risk for Dave. This required Stephen breaking his bulb but Dave being responsible for delaying Vermeulen.

Immediately after lock-up Alex and I would make our way down to the film cupboard. Denis would call Vermeulen to tell him to bring up the lamp-spanner. (This was normal practice as Denis was responsible for calling the warder for whatever reason when we were locked in our cells. Dave K had to keep the bulbs in his cell because in the past when bulbs had burnt out after hours, the night-warders had not had access to the spare ones locked in the store.) When Vermeulen came upstairs with the spanner Denis would direct him to Stephen's cell. Stephen would unscrew his lamp cover as slowly as possible and perhaps drop the spanner a few times to cause a delay. He would extract the broken glass with great care so as 'not to cut his hands'. Then he would tell Vermeulen to go to Dave K to fetch the new bulb, thereby moving him further down the passage. Dave K would be 'unable to find' the bulbs in the box under his bed, so as to delay him even further. Stephen would find it difficult to install the new bulb and 'lose' the screws for the lamp cover by dropping them under his bed while trying to replace the lamp cover. In that time Alex and I would hopefully have advanced from the film cupboard to a position beyond door six.

Stage two was finally carried out in early November. The tension that Alex and I experienced before the event was even greater than that we'd endured before the stage ones. This was because stage two was a much more involved expedition, amounting in effect to a dress rehearsal for the actual breakout. We had been out of our cells for almost as long before, but somehow the thought of placing ourselves on the freedom side of the warder's office was far more frightening. The stage ones had been hit and run guerrilla operations; this time we were placing ourselves right in the middle of enemy territory—over the enemy's lines as it were.

We had no idea what went on beyond door six. No one had ever seen a light on in any of the windows beyond the warder's office so we assumed the area was sealed off and dark at night. But we did not know for certain: maybe someone popped in every now and then to shout to Vermeulen through door six; maybe the front door was left open for the sentries on gate duty to use the toilet; maybe the lights would be on in the passage. Would we be able to turn them on if they weren't? Would turning them on arouse the guards in the street or the guard on the *pos*?

In much the same way as before Alex and I placed dummies in our beds, released ourselves from our cells, took from the cache all that we needed for the adventure and made our way down to the film cupboard. The major difference this time was that we went down much earlier: immediately after lock-up. This in itself was a much more risky venture as we could not tell what Vermeulen would be doing so soon after lock-up. We knew though that he was alone because when the day-warders left they did so with much loud banging of doors.

Stephen broke his bulb by loosening his lamp cover with the spanner we'd made for the purpose and by squirting water inside with a syringe (bulbs would often burst when moisture condensed inside and dripped onto them). Denis shouted for Vermeulen and as the sleepy old screw entered our section the two of us leapt out of the cupboard and made our way beyond door six, after first pressing the button for door eight in the office. If door six had not yielded to our forward thrust we would have implemented our contingency plan of ducking into the warders' toilet to wait until Vermeulen had returned.

We found ourselves in the 'cage' between doors six and seven.

Unexpectedly the passage light was on, allowing us to see all the way to door nine across the far end of the passage. We'd expected the light to be off and had brought along a piece of cloth to place along the bottom of door six to prevent it shining through when we turned it on. The light was a great relief because not only did it allow us to see what we were doing, we'd worried that if it had been off and we'd turned it on it would have lit up the doorless visitors' toilet and been seen by the *pos*-warder.

Before getting to work on seven we waited for Vermeulen to return: we wanted to be sure that he had not smelt a rat and that he was going to settle down in his office and get on with what he usually did in there. To prevent him seeing anything in case he had a habit of opening five and peeping through six's keyhole, we taped a little flap over it on our side. After waiting about ten minutes we could hear him closing the section door and door four. Watching him through the keyhole as he walked down the passage towards us was a peculiar sensation that was both frightening and exciting. He appeared to be looking directly at me but at the last moment he turned into his office and banged his keys down on the table.

I had made several roughly-cut keys for lock seven based on the very infrequent glimpses we'd had of its key. As expected, none of them worked. This did not worry us in the slightest as we'd expected to have to dismantle the lock to open the door. For the purpose we'd made two special spanners to loosen the bolts holding it together. One of them was a kind of ring-spanner that Alex had made from an old tin-opener (he never gave up!) and the other a sort of box-spanner I had made from wood. Yes, wood, or 'arborium' as we preferred to call it. The idea was that the metal spanner would be used to do the initial loosening and then the wooden spanner the final loosening. The wooden spanner was really a piece of dowelling jammed into a metal pipe with the shape of the nut chiselled in one end. Although we had brought along a shifting-spanner from the workshop in case ours were not the right size, we had made the spanners because we had thought the shifting spanner would be too noisy to use.

The lock was bolted to the bars by four bolts which had to be very quietly and carefully loosened. Fortunately the ends of the bolts had not been hammered over as they were in our cells, but just in case we'd brought along a triangular file to clean the threads. Vermeulen was sitting a mere three or four metres away so the nuts had to be turned very slowly to make sure the spanner did not slip and bang against the lock or drop on the floor.

After what seemed like an eternity we were able to extract the bolts and loosen the screws holding the face of the lock with a screwdriver we'd also brought from the workshop. Once the face was removed the levers and bolt were exposed. We carefully removed the levers and stacked them on the floor so that they could be replaced in the correct order. Then we pushed the bolt back and opened the door. Door eight was already off its bolt and only had to be swung back and hooked against the wall.

While Alex attempted to open the Captain's door with a piece of plastic card (it had a Yale-type latch) I tried out our various small keys on door nine. As luck had it the key for the visiting-room worked and I opened the door. We both crawled through on hands and knees into the small vestibule between doors nine and ten and surveyed the last door between us and freedom. From the ground it appeared tall and robust but from the kind of lock we knew it had we did not expect it to be much of a problem to breach.

It had taken us longer than expected to reach the front door and when we looked up at the windows it was already quite dark. We could hear voices coming from close by in the street. The window panes in the vestibule were of frosted glass but we dared not stand up for fear that our shadows would fall on them, allowing those outside to see our movements. I was dying to try out our keys on door ten but Alex would not allow it. He was right, it was too risky.

We retreated into the passage and relocked nine. I felt annoyed and frustrated at not having had a chance to get my hands on, or at least my keys and picks into, ten's lock. It was an admission of defeat and forboded another stage two attempt if we were going to get it to give up its secrets. We had also not figured out the nature of the security outside.

We took the parts of lock seven into the visitors' toilet, which was half way between doors seven and eight and out of Vermeulen's hearing, so that we could examine them and take their measurements. I made careful tracings of the levers onto a piece of paper so that I could later cut a key to the correct dimensions without having to test it in the actual lock. To make sure the key I would be making would definitely work, I rounded and widened the gates in the levers with a file so that virtually any key would work in the lock. We knew enough about keys to know that this would not impair the functioning of the lock when the correct key was used.

This little task was carried out with great satisfaction because we were in effect sabotaging the lock and rendering it almost ineffectual as a lock. But suddenly it struck us that the whole operation had taken a long time and that we'd been too lax about the time. Hurriedly we pushed the levers back into position, replaced the cover, tightened the screws and began to fasten the bolts. It was a slow and tedious business so we took turns to do the tightening. On one of my turns the spanner slipped and made a loud clang against the grille. 'What the hell are you doing?' Alex shouted, 'Vermeulen must have heard that'. In a state of panic I went to door six, lifted the flap and peeked through the keyhole. There Vermeulen was, standing directly in front of the door with his hands on his hips and looking at it. My heart stopped cold and in an irrational fit of panic I took one of the number two keys out of my pocket, pushed it into the keyhole and turned the lock its second turn (we'd left it unmastered). Why I did this I can't explain. Perhaps I imagined Vermeulen would test the lock. A guilty conscience makes you do strange things in a moment of fear. As I withdrew the key I realised what I'd done: I'd exposed the end of it through the keyhole and made a noise turning the lock.

Both of us thought this was the end of the road and dived into the visiting-room, closing the door behind us. We huddled together in fear waiting for the inevitable. Alex cursed in my ear: 'You stupid bastard. What did you do that for?' I had no reply. We both agreed: 'When he comes in we'll use the "pea". We'll tie him up. We'll get out somehow'.

We waited for a siren, for frantic shouts, for voices on his walkie-talkie, for Vermeulen to unlock six to find out what was going on. But after a few excruciating minutes we realised that nothing was happening: Vermeulen had not shouted 'Who's there?' or 'What's going on?'; he had not attempted to open the door to find out what had caused the noise; no sirens were blaring. The silence was scary.

We emerged gingerly from our hiding place and took another peek through the keyhole. There was no one there. 'Perhaps he's radioed or phoned for help?', Alex suggested. The only sound we could hear was the plaintive wail of music coming from his radio.

Realising suddenly that eight o'clock was very close we continued to reassemble the lock. While Alex tightened the bolts I removed all traces of our activities and wiped down the grille with my handkerchief to remove fingerprints. Almost as Alex tightened the last nut its last turn the eight o'clock bell rang.

Through the keyhole I watched Vermeulen come out of his office and turn the corner at the end of the passage. Door four clanged as he went through it and we could hear him making his way up the stairs to the *stokkies'* section. As soon as we heard the clang of their section door we opened doors six and five, relocked them behind us, and dashed back to the film cupboard. Alex pulled the cupboard door closed and in the darkness I suddenly thought: Had we in the rush replaced the levers in the right order? I couldn't remember taking any special note of doing so and they had been truly mixed up when I was filing them. Alex tried to reassure me that we'd not mixed them up and that all was well. Only the next day would tell.

No sleep again that night. On top of the nervous residue of the build-up to and the carrying out of the operation was the thought that the prison staff would not be able to get into the prison in the morning: What if they're unable to open door seven? They'll check the lock and suspect the obvious. Levers don't just swap themselves over on their own!

My fears were allayed the next morning when the cells were unlocked. Everything seemed normal: the same old dozy turnkeys; no angry-looking Captain or big-shot. Later in the day Denis was taken out to the dentist and reported on his return that lock seven had

172

performed quite normally. Perhaps our filing job had been so good that it really didn't matter in which order we'd replaced the levers. Or perhaps we'd replaced them in the correct order after all.

★ ★ ★

There was a belief among some of the comrades that being a political prisoner was not a complete waste of time. Political imprisonment served a purpose: it inspired others and kept alive the notion that there were fighters against apartheid who had sacrificed their personal freedom for the greater freedom of the oppressed.

I never subscribed to this theory. I was not proud of being in prison. In fact I was downright ashamed that I had failed the movement and allowed the enemy to score one over us. While there were people like Nelson Mandela who had been turned into martyrs and symbols of freedom and whose imprisonment had ultimately served a political purpose, your average activist could not champion the cause better by being in than out.

To maintain that being in prison served a purpose seemed to me like an excuse for the fact that you were doing nothing or believed you could do nothing about it. If you weren't bent on escaping what else could you say? Giving purpose to imprisonment was, I rationalised at the time, an anodyne justification for the fact that the enemy had stopped you fighting against their evil rule and that they were wasting your time and making a mess of your life. In the fight against apartheid it was not good enough merely to be doing *something* against the system: you had to be doing your *utmost*. By being in prison you certainly could not say that you were doing this.

It was legitimate to argue that if you had made up your mind not to challenge your immurement then you should make sure that the time was not wasted. Every opportunity should be used to advance your knowledge as best you could: an educated ex-prisoner would be of more use to the movement than an uneducated one.

Our motivations to escape were manifold. It would be impossible to rank them in order of importance, although we liked to believe that our chief motivations were political. We had to free ourselves so that we could throw ourselves back into the struggle, so that we could achieve a victory over the apartheid regime.

We had a duty to escape, a duty to our organisation – the ANC – and to the oppressed in whose name we had gone to prison. We viewed ourselves not as 'common criminals sentenced for serious crimes against the security of the state' but as prisoners of war. As members of the liberation movement we had been captured while participating in a war of liberation. To escape was to continue waging that struggle; to reconcile ourselves to our fate was to surrender.

Despite claiming that we were in prison for ordinary criminal activities, the enemy viewed our confinement as a victory scored by themselves over the ANC, as an action aimed at thwarting the struggle to overturn their political rule. So long as we remained in prison they were exerting that victory and depleting the forces of our organisation. An escape would turn their victory into a defeat, undermine the belief of their supporters that the state had security under control, and serve as a boost to the morale of other political prisoners and all opponents of apartheid.

Certainly, being in prison was not a pleasant experience and among our strongest motivations to get out was the desire for individual freedom. To live with the thought that for the next twelve or so years you are not going to be able to decide what to do with your life is pretty daunting. But we'd got into prison through being inspired by political motives so no one could claim that our motives to get out were entirely personal.

To emphasise some of the personal motivations that drove us to the front door I want to say a little more about the unpleasant aspects of life in prison, and correct the impression, if it has been given, that our prison was a three-star hotel without egress. This was most definitely not the case, although compared with the conditions our black comrades on Robben Island and elsewhere had to face, ours were five star.

The worst aspect of prison life, as any prisoner will confirm, is the almost complete loss of freedom to decide what you will be doing with your life for the duration of your sentence.

In prison you developed a better understanding of the meaning of personal freedom not because the experience gave you some unique insight into its essence but by learning what it means to be utterly unfree. There are degrees of unfreedom but so far imprisonment is the most extreme form yet devised by humankind. Even in imprisonment there are degrees of unfreedom, solitary confinement being the most extreme.

The thought that you will be unfree for the length of your sentence is terrifying and demoralising, especially if it is a long one. My twelve years seemed to me a meaningless, interminable period. I tried various ways to give it content: I compared it to the previous twelve years of my life but that only made matters worse, for when you are younger time seems to go much more slowly; I tried reminding myself that my release date, 1990, was a mere decade and a bit away, and decades were not a long time. None of these ploys had the desired effect because I could not visualise myself out of the world for the whole of the 1980s. When I was released I would be 41 years old; my entire thirties would have been spent inside; my remaining youth would have been wasted. How poor Denis must have felt with his life sentence I could never comprehend.

The reverse side of losing your freedom is that other people decide what you will be doing with your life. You lose your dignity as an independent being. You become a thing, a piece of property with a number, like a dixie or a pair of handcuffs. If you damaged yourself you could be charged with damaging prison property in the same way as if you had smashed a window. To your number becomes attached your surname, but this is a mere label to make it easier for the warders to distinguish you from other objects of prison property.

It is a thoroughly degrading experience. It reduces you from being a self-respecting, proud, motivated individual to a piece of trash. You are cast into society's rubbish bin, or, to be more precise in our case, apartheid's rubbish bin. You begin to understand what it feels like to be one of the countless victims of apartheid's grand plan who are uprooted and removed to some remote, rural dumping ground. Fortunately for political prisoners the degradation does not stick and taint you for the rest of your life. On the contrary, having spent a period in jail for opposition to the apartheid state raises your status in the eyes of the majority of the population. There is no need to feel any shame at being imprisoned for political reasons. The only shame is for letting down your side and allowing the enemy to get the better of you.

It is also an intensely lonely experience, made worse by the fact that there is no relief from it. You can expect no commiseration from your fellow prisoners, as they are in the same boat, and people outside can do little to help. Although in our case we were held in the same section and were together in the yard during the day, for nearly 15 hours a day we were locked in our individual cells with only our own selves for company. In that time we were left to stew in our own thoughts, which were not always the most rational or comforting.

Because prison life is so routinised and ritualistic, because every day is so much like the previous ones, because nothing new ever happens, your thoughts tend to become routinised and repetitive too. The same boring images return to you day after day, night after night. There is nothing to trigger new chains of thought. They seem to take on a life of their own; they separate from your body and your life.

In the university psychology class they had taught us the unity of mind and body and the fallacy of Cartesian mind-body dualism. In prison you come to think that perhaps Descartes was right. Your thoughts rise above your existence. They fly out through the bars, out over the walls and away to freedom. You're back in Cape Town visiting your friends, driving around the streets, going shopping, climbing mountains and going spearfishing. You're also placing leaflet bombs on every street corner, blowing up police stations and courts and wreaking your vengeance on the security cops. Your thoughts are so free, yet your body remains trapped in that little cube that is your world. You look out of your window and can see over the top of the wall the buildings and trees that are in freedom. They are so near . . . You look at the size of your body and think: how small it is;

175

the hole above the prison skywards so large. Why can't I just lift my little body over that wall and place it on the other side? If my thoughts can be out there, all I've got to do is move my body a short distance and they'll be reunited. Perhaps we can make a giant balloon to lift us out of the yard. Perhaps a huge kite, a glider, a rocket. There must be some way . . .

You miss your family and friends terribly. How you wish you could be with them so they could cheer you up, so you could explain everything. You visualise your mother sitting at home grieving for you. How you wish you could put her at ease. The suffering you've caused is worse than your own. How could you do this to others? You've embarrassed your family. How do they feel every time they have to say they have a son or brother in prison. What do people think? Visits are no compensation because the glass between you only reinforces your separation. The frustration caused by your powerlessness is torture.

You realise how important women are to making you a complete human being, not in some sexual sense that you can't survive without them, but as an important component in making human society human. Contact only with men makes you begin to notice that relationships are rough and lack a certain perspective that you would not normally notice. You can't describe it because you wish to avoid the sexist cliches of feminine softness, kindness, caring, submissiveness and so on. But you notice it particularly when for some reason you suddenly have contact with a woman, such as when you are taken to a doctor or dentist. You immediately become strongly aware of the difference in the way you have been spoken to, of the way the person has responded to you, of the way you have responded to the person. It fills you with a strange sense of warmth and satisfaction, as if in that fleeting moment you have made real contact with a human being.

Sexual drive never disappears but after a few years, they told me, it is reduced to manageable levels. The palm of your hand is more frustrating than relieving as you know there is nothing to give you relief from that reliever. The comrades had found that eliminating reminders that women existed was worse than not doing so, as frustrating as it was. If you did so you had to rely on your memory and that could lead to uncontrollable fantasising. To prevent this the comrades had for years been ordering a range of women's magazines in which we would normally not have had the slightest interest. The thought of a bunch of lefties reading *Vogue* or *Women's Own* might seem somewhat incongruous but the magazines served a purpose: they kept alive the visual image of the opposite sex which was as important as keeping alive the skill in relating to them.

Boring is the word for life in jail. Every day is a repetition of the previous one. Even the efforts you make to overcome your boredom are boring. Reading, drawing, listening to music, thinking and sleeping are not in themselves boring; it's when you do them at the same time and in the same order day in and day out. There are no highlights, nothing to look forward to, nothing to look back on. Time shoots by but paradoxically also feels static. There are no reference points, nothing to give time meaning and motion. Nothing moves, nothing changes. It's a movie of a still life.

As for our material conditions, let's just say they were not intolerable. However, we could not help comparing our conditions to what we knew was the lot of our black comrades. The authorities claimed that one set of regulations applied to all political prisoners and hence conditions were the same for all. Such claims were irrelevant, for in the last instance it was the unwritten regulations that made the difference: black prisoners were subjected to all the indignities and injustices inherent in the apartheid control of the prisons; we were not. It cannot be denied that over the years conditions on the Island, and for political prisoners generally, have improved. But no matter how much the authorities claim that conditions for all prisoners are the same, you can be sure that so long as apartheid rules, conditions for blacks will be worse.

For many years the prison chiefs did not deny that conditions for black prisoners were inferior: special regulations applied to them covering diets, clothing, bedding, work, numbers of prisoners per cell – everything. Only in 1977, for instance, was it decided that black political prisoners should be given beds to sleep on. Many books have been written describing the appalling conditions experienced by Robben Island prisoners in those years. Read for example *Island In Chains*, as told by Indres Naidoo to Albie Sachs, which describes life on the Island from 1963 to 1973. The conditions you will read there bear no relation to anything described in this book.

'Conditions' refer to different things. First of all there were the things which the prison authorities were obliged to provide, what they referred to as our 'rights': food, clothing, shelter, protection. Then there was the regimen imposed on the prisoners – work, inspections, chores, the daily routine.

The very notion of a prison conjures up thoughts of bad food. Ours was uniformly poor but it would be wrong to say that it was bad. Occasionally, very occasionally, we would be served something that was better than poor. Never though did anything remind us of home cooking. Most times the food was edible; often not.

Diets were allegedly scientifically formulated by dieticians from the regime's Department of Health. You could not help wondering where they got their training for there was something profoundly 'unscientific' about our diet. It consisted largely of carbohydrates to make you feel filled but little that could be said to have contributed to general health. Even if the basic ingredients of a healthy diet were there, the cooking process leached out of the food any goodness that it

177

might have contained.

The main characteristic of our food was monotony. Breakfast and supper at the beginning and end of the day were almost identical; lunch at midday almost the same from day to day. The latter consisted usually of a 'meat', stamped *mielies* (maize) or *mielie*-rice and an overcooked vegetable or two. The 'meat' was either chicken legs, bony fish, gristly stew or 'plastic meat'.

'Plastic meat' was a sort of imitation meat made from soya beans and served at least twice a week. We had no objection to that, it was just the way they cooked it — in tons of pork fat. It's taste was so vile and its effects so violent that most of us refused to touch the stuff. We tried a boycott but without success as there was nothing with which the cooks could replace it. In protest we would regularly leave the pot standing in the middle of the tennis court where it had been dumped by the black prisoner. At every opportunity we'd complain about the muck but the more we objected the more determined they became to keep it on the menu. We did not feel inclined to pursue the matter too far though, as it wasn't really an important issue.

Breakfast consisted of porridge — either *mielie-pap* or oats — bread and 'coffee' or 'tea' made from substances bearing no relation to real coffee or tea. The evening meal, supper, consisted of soup, 'coffee' or 'tea' and more bread. Included in our daily rations were a white powder for making 'milk', sugar, a sort of pink or orange sticky substance euphemistically called 'jam', and over-salted prison-farm butter, but only enough for a very thin scraping if you saved some for your morning bread. Once a week at supper-time, on separate days, there would be crumbly cheese, a blue hard-boiled egg, battered fruit, runny peanut butter or some other semi-edible extra.

Most of our food came from prison farms but occasionally farmers would dump surpluses or imperfect crops on the prisons. At different times of the year there would be sudden gluts of one thing or another: sacks of oranges with spotted skins, boxes of dented avocadoes, bags of bruised apples. It never rained but it poured.

Poor food over which you have no control is very demoralising. To add a little spice to our lives we would take turns on Saturday afternoons to prepare for each other small savoury or sweet snacks from the meagre grocery purchases the 'A' groupers were allowed to make. A tin of spaghetti and tomato sauce or a packet pudding, which under normal circumstances would be considered junk food, were devoured with great relish. Culinary standards sink to a low level in clink.

Prison clothing doesn't fit; everybody knows that. It is either too large or too small. Most of the comrades didn't care, for it was not as if we were expected at the opera. I found it degrading to be kitted out in the prison's vestments and the poor fit reminded me all the time of where I was. To lessen the sense of shame I unstitched all my shirts and trousers and 'refashioned' them to look and feel more like civilian clothing and less like bin liners. I enjoyed sewing and would sit for hours at night reshaping my clothes while listening to the music.

There were two uniforms: one for summer and one for winter. The summer one consisted of a green 'safari suit' with short trousers; the winter one of light-brown longs, a similarly coloured long-sleeve shirt, a brown jersey with red rings around the neck and bottom, and a brown corduroy jacket. Of course there were shoes and socks, but they didn't seem to mind if we went barefoot in summer. Other items provided were green overalls, grey pyjamas, baggy underpants, hanging vests and red handkerchiefs. All of it was made by prison labour and like all products of alienated labour they were shoddy and ill-conceived. From the escapers' point of view none of it was of much use apart from the handkerchiefs, underpants and vests which could be turned into other things.

Each prisoner was expected to wash and iron his own clothing, but with only two pairs of each item you wore everything for as long as possible and covered the smell with deodorant. The older comrades were more institutionalised and the product of earlier, more severe prison regimes: they washed and ironed regularly; the rest of us as infrequently as we could get away with. Trousers under the mattress kept them permanently pressed; shoes unworn meant less polishing.

Our health provisions, too, were not scandalous. But as with all aspects of our condition we could not help comparing them with those of the black prisoners. We found it astonishing that the prisoners who smuggled newspapers for us would ask us for the most basic things like aspirin, plasters and soap. It was claimed that all prisoners were granted the same health rights but again, black prisoners were faced with the prejudices of the apartheid jailers. If they asked for medicaments they would be accused of being malingerers or shirkers; we would be given virtually anything without argument.

Medical requirements were dispensed by a warder disguised as a medical orderly who would appear each morning with a tray of medicines. The medicine queue was generally longer than would have been expected in ordinary life. The great range of ailments the prisoners complained of was a result of the poor diet and most of them would undoubtedly have been avoided had our food been more wholesome. Colds and flu were common, upset stomachs the order of the day, piles everyone's blight and headaches the normal condition.

A doctor visited the prison once every two weeks but he brought with him the attitudes he had picked up at other prisons: when a prisoner complains about a medical problem there is an ulterior motive, such as a desire to get off work or be taken for a joy-ride to see a specialist in town. This was understandable but it took a lot to persuade him that you had a genuine complaint. Specialists, too, cast aside their Hippocratic oaths when dealing with prisoners. In their

179

eyes a prisoner was not a real patient worthy of dignity and respect: consultations would be abrupt and perfunctory; they would tell you what was wrong with you before you had a chance to explain your problem; everything you complained of was an 'exaggeration'.

We feared to think what sort of treatment black prisoners received from outside doctors, if ever they saw them. One dentist who treated me displayed his vicious racism when I was taken out to have a tooth-nerve removed (the prison dentist only did extractions). On the counter in his waiting room were displayed a number of large bullets. One of my accompanying warders made some comment in connection with these, prompting the dentist to produce the associated weapon. He brought out the largest revolver I have ever seen, so huge that he needed two hands to hold it. To explain its power he said that if he stood ten 'kaffirs' one behind the other the bullet would pass clean through all of them.

The warders' attitude to the *stokkies* was quite different from that shown to us. This was because they knew that the *stokkies* would not kick up a stink like we would if anything went wrong or was not found to be satisfactory. Very frequently alcoholic *stokkies* would be brought in and would be given no assistance to get over their delirium tremens. They would shout and scream for hours and you could hear them smashing their cells to pieces. Sometimes they would pull down their bookshelves, smash their toilet bowls, rip out their sinks and cause a flood; often they would injure themselves. More than once we saw bodies being carried out with a blanket pulled over the face.

This is not to imply that the warders' attitude toward us was impeccable. On many occasions they paid scant regard to the rules. Prisoners who complained of serious problems after lock-up would be left until the next morning rather than having a doctor immediately. One comrade, it was reported to me, who had a stroke during the night was only visited by a physician the next morning, with serious consequences. It twice happened during my term, once to me, that prisoners were brought back to the prison far too soon after having an operation. In my case I had barely woken up from my nose operation and while still in an anaesthetised and bleeding state I was slung into the back of a prison van and carted back to the prison. A shortage of staff, they explained.

Work is another concept normally associated with prison life. But there was no chipping of rocks or sewing of mailbags for us; that was 'kaffirs' work'. Prison was a microcosm of life outside: whites did the more skilled work; blacks the backbreaking manual labour.

Most of the comrades, especially the 'academics' among us, welcomed any respite so they could get back to their studies. John and I, and to a lesser extent Dave K and Denis, were the only ones who liked to work with our hands as well as with our brains. This is not to say that we preferred prison work to reading: we felt there was sufficient time to read and study and grew more bored than normal if there was nothing else to do but read. We had creative energies to be dissipated, even if on prison work.

The work was dusty and boring but there was little pressure on us to increase productivity. Alex deliberately did everything incorrectly and as slowly as possible as a kind of running sabotage. I couldn't bring myself to do this as I have an innate perfectionist streak that had to find an outlet. I treated my work not as something for the prisons but as something on which I released my pent up drives. Raymond was a scream: he would regularly fall into a trance while sanding his pieces of wood and wake up half an hour later to find that he had sanded a huge dent into an otherwise perfectly smoothed surface. Johnny was the expert who showed us how to cut our dovetails, how to sharpen our chisels and how to disguise our mistakes.

There were other forms of work as well. The garden had to be tended, the dishes washed, the dining-room kept clean, the dog shit collected each morning, the prison cleaned each week and sundry other little chores. Occasionally one of us would be required to assist in tidying up or repairing a cell that a delirious *stokkie* had torn apart.

Inspections were central to prison life. Every day at opening and lock-up there were inspections. These were mechanical affairs and seldom would a prisoner be brought up for bad appearance or having an untidy cell. At around eleven each day there would be a more formal inspection, or rather, a tour of the prison by the Captain to inquire if there were any 'complaints and requests'. It was important to know the difference between a 'complaint' and a 'request' as a complaint could not be acknowledged unless there was an accompanying request; a request could not be granted unless there was a preceding complaint.

The main inspection was on Fridays when the Captain would inspect the section on his morning tour. Beds had to be clean and properly made, floors shiny, ledges and grilles dust free and windows spotless. He would always make his longest stop in Alex's cell because Alex refused to recognise the official standards of cleanliness and neatness. This was why it took Alex so long to reach 'A' group.

At weekends we had to stand to attention on the tennis court while the Captain walked slowly along the rank as if he were inspecting a guard of honour. He would check our uniforms and haircuts and recommend a trim before the end of the day if our hair was longer than the stipulated half-thumb's length. Haircuts were a routine carried out by our in-house barber, Johnny, every two weeks. Alex and I attempted to set new standards by having our hair cut only once a month. It appeared to work, for by the time we said good-bye our hair had reached a respectable length. The Captain's instructions were just ignored; Brylcreem also helped.

Such were our conditions. Not an abysmal state of affairs, but even if we'd been served *haute cuisine*, had been given Paris fashions, had had a swimming pool at the bottom of our yard and had had personal videos in our cells, it was the spiritual conditions that mattered. Prison is prison and that means you've lost your liberty. No amount of 'privileges' can compensate for that. Nevertheless, the struggle for better conditions continues, both outside and in, until inside becomes part of outside, until all our comrades are free. Then the prisons will be ours and the real criminals will fill the cells.

14
Another Stage Two – or Out?

Although stage two had been completed without incident, it had not been an entirely successful mission. We had not figured out how to open door ten and had not established the nature of the security arrangements outside. The voices we'd heard in the street could have belonged to anybody and might not have been the voices of guards.

Nevertheless, we had demonstrated to those comrades not convinced that our plan was a viable one, that we would not just disappear into the dusk without our fellow escapees. All were welcome to join us.

The earlier decision that no progress should be made beyond stage two as long as there was a guard on the *pos* from four thirty to ten was now felt to be due for review. As it was, three in the group of five were for proceeding. Decisions could now be made rapidly without the more cautious and over-cautious progress.

A series of meetings were held to discuss the next moves. Dave K and Denis wanted another stage two to be carried out to clear up the two unknowns: whether door ten could be opened and what sort of security arrangements existed on the gate outside. Alex was determined that the next step should be to get out, but with the reservation that it be called 'stage two/three'. This meant that all those who wanted to go out should come along on the attempt and if it was not possible to make the final break we could return at 8 pm Stephen agreed with Alex that the next step should be a stage two/three but I was more in favour of another straightforward stage two. I felt that it was vital first to establish that the keys I'd made for door seven, based on the tracings of its levers we'd taken on stage two, actually worked; whether it was possible to open door ten without too much bother and what the nature of the security arrangements outside the prison were.

Denis wanted outside assistance and felt that it was too dangerous to even contemplate going so long as there was a guard on the *pos* when he was expected to emerge from the front door. He was in effect withdrawing his active participation, but he stressed that he was prepared to assist in any way that he could.

Dave K's attitude was non-committal and ambivalent. He also wanted another stage two to take place to eliminate some of the unknowns. He did not consider the guard on the *pos* to be a very significant obstacle and felt that if we looked 'civilian' enough as we emerged from the front door and kept out of his view by walking close to the base of the *pos* wall we would not arouse too much suspicion.

He would have preferred outside assistance but was prepared to go without it, if another stage two took place. Then he would be able to decide.

For those of us who actually had to do the stage twos this position was intolerable. After all, who would have faced the stick if something had gone wrong and we'd been caught?

At one of the meetings it was decided that the escape assistance group should be contacted and informed that any preparations that had been made to assist us and which were being held in abeyance, should be scrapped entirely. In other words the matter was closed.

During the final month before the escape there was an almost permanent state of discussion between the five of us who still constituted the escape group. It would be impossible to relate on paper everything that took place, the changes of attitude and position and the conflicts. To simplify matters I can only summarise the general situation.

As I've pointed out from the start, there was a fundamental difference in attitudes between Alex, Stephen and myself on the one hand, and the others. The three of us always felt that the longer we took to get out the greater would be our chances of being caught. Every day that plans were discussed the likelihood of our being overheard increased; every day the cache remained in existence the greater the chances that it would be discovered; every time contact was made with the outside the chances were increased that we might be discovered.

The others accused us of being impatient but our view was that the participants in an escape bid should as far as possible be in control of their situation. In other words, obstacles had to be tackled directly or planned around rather than waiting for them to disappear of their own accord. More than likely the obstacles would not disappear and new ones would be added to them. Reality was dynamic, even if it felt static in prison. To wait for the 'ideal conditions' was to wait forever.

Dave K's and Denis's hesitancy was motivated by an underlying belief that everything might end in disaster. We had not tied up all the loose ends and there were many unknowns. They'd fought for years to have their conditions improved and feared that if the attempt failed all the 'privileges' they had won would be lost and it would be back to square one. This fear was well-founded and quite understandable.

The fears of the others were more difficult to understand. At first we believed they arose out of a lack of guts, but it was unfair to regard them thus. It was not your average law-abiding citizen who ended up in jail for acts of 'terrorism' — and they would probably go on to do things that none of us would ever have the guts to do.

The whole exercise had taught us much about human nature. It was wrong to expect from our comrades the same enthusiasm to get out that we had displayed. Stephen and I had arrived determined to escape, we had come prepared to escape, we believed all along that we could escape, we did not have to have faith in anyone but ourselves and we had very long sentences ahead of us; Alex took to the escape idea because he'd always had escaping on his mind and had considered 'settling in' as a sign of capitulation to his captors.

The situation for the others was quite different. When they found themselves in prison they probably looked at the security and thought no further about escaping than the instinctive thoughts that all prisoners have when they first end up behind walls. Seeing no obvious ways out they had reconciled themselves to their fate and had done everything to make their stay as comfortable and as meaningful as possible. We'd come along and stirred things up.

We certainly had not made it easy for them. We had operated secretly, we had done everything on our own, we had not trusted anyone else and we had gone ahead with it all willy-nilly, ignoring everyone's fears and needs. Inevitably our over-determination might have been interpreted as recklessness, and may have frightened them – they believed we had a death wish.

There were a number of factors at this juncture which provoked us to force the issue and press for an immediate speeding-up of activity to get out. For the first time the three of us were in a position of absolute majority in the escape group; only Dave K served as a barrier to our immediate departure.

Planning for the escape had begun in July 1978 and by then (November) had been going on for almost 17 months. Since February 1979 we had been in a position to effect a departure and several attempts had been put off at the last moment. Objective conditions had progressively worsened – there was a sentry post in the street, the gate outside had been moved closer to the front door, there was a guard on the *pos* during the crucial four thirty to ten period – and there was no reason to assume they would change for the better. As far as security matters were concerned, things could only be expected to become tighter.

The money Steve and I had brought in was rapidly going out of circulation and we were uncertain if it was still legal tender. It was nearly a year and a half since the currency had been changed and from what we could glean from the warders it appeared that there were none of the old notes left in circulation. We were worried that if we got out and had to hire a taxi or buy food and clothing the money would not be accepted and it would arouse suspicion. This was possibly the main factor behind our belief that there was no more time for delay.

Our clothing was of summer weight and only suitable for summer use. Later in the year it would not provide adequate protection and would look out of place. There were also associated problems of

185

storage and discovery.

One other major factor looming over us towards the end of 1979 was the imminent release of John Matthews. His sentence was due to terminate on the 15th of December and it was imperative that the escape took place before that date; if it took place shortly after, he would be suspected of assisting the escapees. It would seem obvious to the authorities that he had been tied up in the planning and had made contacts for us after his release.

Material preparations for the escape had long been completed, including the manufacture of keys for door seven. The workshop was closed for the month of December so it was not really possible to make anything else, although we could still enter it with our own keys if necessary.

The presence of Vermeulen on duty during the early evening shift was of absolutely vital importance. He had always preferred this shift and refused to work any other. Our main worry with him was that he would go off sick or drop dead, as he suffered from high blood pressure and had already had a few minor heart attacks. He was in his final year in the Prisons Service before his retirement and it worried us that he might be moved to some more leisurely post for his last months. Whatever the case, we'd be taking a chance if we did not make immediate use of the fact that he and his heart were still on the beat.

Since our request for outside assistance had been cancelled, another factor which had been a cause of delay in the past had been removed. Although it would have been good to have had someone waiting outside the prison to whisk us away to safety, we had grown used to the idea of doing things for ourselves. We had learnt through bitter experience that it was impossible for people who were not intimately involved in the escape to understand the multitude of problems we faced. We had put so much effort – practical, mental, nervous and persuasive – into the attempt that we wanted to complete the job by ourselves. We could not contemplate the thought that it might end in disaster through others' mistakes.

A final factor was the knowledge that sometime during December there would be a new intake of warders. It was usually new warders who were put on *pos* duty, so if we could time our escape to coincide with their arrival we could use this fact to our advantage. The new warders would not know us well by sight and they would probably not know how to respond if they saw a group of 'civilians' walking out of the front door of the prison. The new intake in fact arrived four days before our departure, much to our delight.

All these factors together were the arguments that Alex, Steve and I used to persuade the comrades that the time had come for us to make our break. There was little they could say to counter the arguments, although most of them expressed their apprehension and stated that they were not entirely happy with our decision.

Dave K still needed to be convinced. He insisted that we carry out another stage two before he would commit himself to saying whether he would come out or not. Alex and I, as the ones who would have to carry out the stage two he wanted, were worried that he might in the end, after we'd put ourselves through all the risks and strain involved, say 'no'.

To get around this I offered to do a stage two on my own, since Alex refused to go again. For a short while Alex agreed to this but then refused to allow it to happen because he felt it weakened our position.

There seemed no way out of the impasse. In a rare fit of compromise Alex then offered to do a stage two on his own provided that Dave would state beforehand that he would come out if all proved clear. But Dave remained firm to his resolve that a stage two had to be carried out before he could make up his mind.

My own position during this period changed from wanting to do a stage two to a final position of supporting Alex and Steve in going for a stage two/three. I realised that my demand for a stage two was only delaying progress. Alex subsequently refused to allow a stage two to take place and insisted that, come what may, the next step was to try to get clean out.

Although I was prepared to change my position on this matter, I was not as confident as Alex about the success of a stage two/three because I did not believe that we would be able to get to the front door quickly enough. We had to assume the worst: that the keys for door seven would not work; that we would have to disassemble lock seven; and that lock ten (the front door) would not succumb to lock-picking. If things turned out otherwise, well and good, but it would be wrong to plan on the best possible outcome. I was further worried that to take four people along on what I believed would more than likely not turn into a stage three, was too risky. In practical terms it meant that we would not be able to use the film cupboard as a hiding place as it was too small to accommodate four people and that we would have to use the dining-room instead. To get four people out of their cells was far too dangerous.

Alex, Steve and I then held a meeting to discuss how we could get past the Dave barrier, which was proving to be more of an obstacle than some of the prison's doors. No one was going to do another stage two, so to wait for his decision was to delay the escape forever. We would put it to Dave that since he could not make up his mind about coming, we had to assume that he did not want to come and that the three of us were going ahead with the escape without him.

Since I was now the only member of the 'hard core' on the WC (Alex had resigned) it became my task to approach Dave with our resolution. This I did and to my surprise he accepted it without argument.

The three of us could now proceed rapidly to make the final plans for the actual escape. With Dave's withdrawal I no longer felt any need for a stage two because if it was not possible to go out, the stage two/three could more easily be reverted to a stage two. The only remaining problems were to find a way of distracting Vermeulen so that we could get past him and beyond door six as we'd done on stage two, and to choose a suitable date for departure.

There were three ways we could distract Vermeulen. The first involved someone replacing their bulb *a la* stage two. The second involved switching off the prison's lights to get Vermeulen upstairs to investigate. This meant coming out of our cells as on stage two and on the way downstairs to the film cupboard switching off all the lights at the switchboard on the first floor. Denis would, as official warder-caller, shout to Vermeulen that the lights had gone out and Vermeulen would then, we hoped, go upstairs to investigate. This would give us our chance to make for door six. The third possibility was a contingency plan thought up by Alex which could have been used if everyone had refused to help on the other two. This involved Stephen and me going downstairs first and waiting in the film cupboard. Alex would then break his bulb and call Vermeulen. When Vermeulen went upstairs Steve and I would pass through door four and while I was opening doors five and six Stephen would in some way damage the record player (by bending the needle for instance) and then join me beyond door six. I would leave door five unmastered and door six closed but unlocked. We would then proceed down the passage and attempt to make our way out. All the rest of the doors would be closed but left unlocked. Alex meanwhile would replace his bulb and immediately after Vermeulen had returned downstairs also go downstairs and hide in the film cupboard. Vermeulen would spend some time checking the record player and then, not being able to find the fault, return upstairs to report the problem to Denis. Alex would then be able to come out of the cupboard, unlock door five and make his way out.

Naturally, Stephen and I were unhappy with this plan because we wished to go out as a threesome and there was the possibility that Alex would not make it. However, we realised that if the worst came to the worst this was the only viable option.

When the first of these two plans was explained to Denis and Dave K we were surprised to find no opposition to them. Perhaps they were only too glad that the plans signalled in one way or another the end of the escape saga. At one stage Dave K was even willing to replace his bulb with a burnt out one but later he felt that the switchboard method was a safer bet as it could not lead to a finger being pointed at him. This meant pushing the task of helping us onto Denis.

Our preference was for the bulb method because it gave more positive control over Vermeulen and the assurance that he would enter our section where he would be out of earshot of our activities below. Also, it was a tried and proven method of distraction.

The switchboard method gave no certainty that he would enter the section first to find out the cause of the problem. It worried us that he might notice the light out on the stair landing and go straight to the switchboard, reset the tripped switch and return immediately downstairs. Whatever the case, he would, while rectifying the problem, be outside our section and in a better position to hear any noises we might make.

We explained our preference for the bulb method to Denis and at first he agreed to replace his bulb with a burnt out one, but later also felt that the switchboard method would be safer.

The next and final problem was the choice of date. The time was the end of November and we were keen to leave immediately, but there were a number of considerations. The question of whether it would be better to go on a weekend or weekday no longer existed, or, rather, had been turned around to exclude weekends. Since the gates had been moved closer to the front door we were able to hear them opening and closing more clearly than before. During the preceding weekends we'd heard the gates operating from about three in the afternoon; during the week only from about six.

Denis was of the opinion that since so many discussions had been held during the preceding weeks (we'd tramped the grass flat on the far side of the yard) it would be best if we waited about two weeks and had no meetings during that time—he was worried that our captors might have suspected something was up. We could see his point, but at this stage we were not amenable to yet another delay of the escape.

Everyone knew that a new batch of warders was coming to the prison, that John Matthews was due to be released on 15 December and that Captain Venter was due to go on leave in the second week of December. We felt this latter point to be relevant because we were worried that another officer might take over and introduce some strange or more rigorous routines or security procedures. By suggesting that we wait, Denis was hoping to have the escape postponed until after Johnny's release, which in reality meant making us wait some months so that he would not be implicated.

Perhaps it was just impatience, but we were annoyed most of all that we were being kept in prison not by our jailers but by our comrades.

When the two weeks were up the three of us announced on the weekend of 8/9 December that we were going to attempt an escape during the coming week, with the first date being Tuesday the 11th, and if that day did not prove suitable then on each successive day. Denis and Dave K felt that it would be unfair to go in Johnny's last week as his release date might be deferred if he had to undergo questioning or if the authorities wanted to take revenge.

189

In earlier discussions Johnny had expressed no opposition so we were sure he would not disapprove. We did not believe the authorities could or would prevent his release on the 15th because they would make themselves look stupid if they accused him of involvement in escape plans in the last week of a fifteen-year sentence.

Denis reluctantly agreed to our plans in the end, although he repeatedly expressed his unhappiness with our decision. Dave K refrained from commenting, but clearly he too was apprehensive.

Having sorted out this last problem we made our final preparations that weekend. The money was divided three ways and put in the pockets of our escape trousers. The clothing we would be using was removed from the general sack of goods, placed in another sack and arranged in such a way that it could be easily retrieved. The rest of the clothing was tightly wrapped in another sack and pushed to the bottom of the space behind the geyser where it was irretrievable by hand. The surplus keys were bottled and given to Dave K to bury in the garden for the comrades' 'future use'. Our prison clothing that we would not be using before the escape, our spare sheets and blankets were all washed to remove odours so that they could not be given to sniffer-dogs to get our scents. Our cells were carefully cleaned of all suspicious objects; notes, addresses, letters and all else that might give something away were destroyed. All valuable books we had were transferred to the others' cells.

I dyed my running shoes – which were bright yellow with blue speed-stripes – with the blue drawing ink I'd specially ordered for the purpose. The others brought up their running shorts and shoes from the store-room and placed them in their cells. We also put other paraphenalia at the ready: escape spectacles; cloth bags (made for holding keys and tools but used in our cells for holding boot polish); T-shirts; deodorant and pepper for disguising odours, etc.

The last task of the WC was to work out with the remaining comrades what they should say when questioned after the escape, as they undoubtedly would be.

The rookie warders arrived on the Friday before the weekend, as expected. Alex, Steve and I made every effort to remain out of their sight so they would not get to know our faces. Captain Venter had been away for a few days and our fears that he would be replaced by someone else were unfounded. His being away in fact seemed to lead to a loosening of discipline among the officers and warders. When the cat's away. . .

15
Escape!

Preparations for the escape had been going on for so long that it was hard to believe we were actually going to do it. We'd invested so much emotional, mental and physical energy in the preparations that in a way we were, like someone about to spend their life's savings, apprehensive about taking the big step. If our plans and equipment did not work (i.e. we got caught) the thought of all that effort going down the drain was more daunting than the thought of the extra years that would undoubtedly be added to our sentences. However, we were pretty confident that we would make it and did not feel that we were taking a blind gamble with our future and our lives.

We were sorry that our comrades were not coming with us because we knew that if we could clean out the prison it would represent a political victory of gigantic proportions. If we made it by ourselves it would be victory enough though, and we knew the escape would be more likely to succeed with just three people. The whole business had taught us many things: above all that people's needs are different and that we shouldn't have expected from others what we'd expected from ourselves. We learnt too that people in a prison situation needed a routine of certainties and that uncertainties were destabilising and threatening.

Strangely, as Tuesday the 11th of December came around, Alex and I felt less tension than we'd experienced during the stage ones and twos. But then getting out was not going to be much different from those stages, and we'd got used to doing them. The confidence we felt was much like the feeling you get if you've studied hard for an exam or trained hard for a strenuous sports event. Stephen too displayed no apparent fear and his faith in us added to our general feeling of confidence.

There was little to do by way of preparations on the preceding days – we were totally prepared and had been for some time. There was just some tidying up to do: cleaning up our cells to eliminate clues, preparing our clothing to streamline our exit and washing everything that could be given to dogs to gain our scent. Since the prison authorities and the police would undoubtedly go over our cells with a fine toothcomb after the escape, we flushed our treasured letters down our toilets and destroyed notes and documents we'd kept among our belongings. It was not easy to do this as we knew that if we didn't succeed our lives would be bleak without the precious sentimental things we'd clung to for so long.

On the big day, as had been agreed, everyone attempted to act as naturally and casually as possible. The warders did not appear to suspect anything but it was hard to believe that they knew nothing of our plans. Deep down we could not help thinking that they were playing the same game with us as we were playing with them and that they would be waiting outside the front door to nab us as we emerged from it, to cause us maximum embarrassment.

As there was no work that day – the workshop had been closed since the beginning of the month – we had to enter the workshop to get out of it the few tools we would need for the task ahead: two screwdrivers (one large and one small – for dismantling seven's lock and to force any other recalcitrant doors), a chisel (in case ten would not yield to our more gentle persuasions) and a file (in case we had to modify any keys). The tools were hidden in the store-room as usual to be taken up at a convenient time. Apart from this there was nothing else to do downstairs.

The three of us tried to keep out of sight of the new warders by keeping indoors as far as possible. The temptation to go out was strong as it was a bright, warm summer's day. We wanted to gloat at our captors and take a last look at the walls that had surrounded us for so long. The walls had lost their solid, impenetrable look – they were paper, transparent and no longer aroused that sickening, deadening and hopeless feeling that made you sigh in despair and your gut sink. They were only there surrounding us because we had chosen to leave them there until that day. The thought that we could just walk through them with the minimum of effort whenever we wanted to made a mockery of all the misdirected security measures that were kept in place against us.

We spent the day trying to read, but it was not easy to concentrate as our minds were already outside and our comrades were discreetly silent. We did not discuss the escape because there was nothing more to discuss; we spoke to nobody because there was nothing to say.

Lunch tasted awful – we had been preparing our palates for more savoury fare. We only ate it to make sure we wouldn't have to eat it again: we weren't sure when our next full meal would be. Certainly we weren't going to do something as foolish as treating ourselves to a lavish restaurant meal once we got out, although we had enough money to buy all the food we would need.

At shower-time we extracted the bag holding our escape equipment from behind the geyser and arranged our civilian clothing in three neat piles on the floor of the geyser closet so that we could retrieve it with minimal fuss later. The workshop tools we'd brought up were placed, together with the 'pea', in the key-bag and left on top of the geyser (we secretly hoped that a leak wouldn't develop above it all – that would have been the supreme irony!). We each brought to the shower our running shoes and left them with our balaclavas, gloves and caps on top of our respective piles of clothing. I removed one number two key and three number one keys from the key-bag and each of us hid one of the number ones in tins of sugar in our cells and Alex the number two as well.

The geyser door was locked and we enjoyed our last shower: we had an appointment with the public and did not want to smell like a bunch of musty old convicts. At supper we stuffed ourselves with several plates of the vile prison soup and ate all our bread, barring a slice or two to take up to our cells for the purpose of leaving on our tables to give the impression that we'd eaten our supper and gone to bed. Tuesday was also book day when the large box of library books was brought into the dining-room. The three of us selected our books as usual and tucked them under our arms to take up to our cells for a good night's 'read'.

The three of us were on our own now; in spirit we had already departed. As there was still a little time before lock-up we walked up and down the tennis court, as we normally would. To our surprise one of the comrades who had strongly opposed the project came up to us, wished us luck and said goodbye. We had not been expecting any goodbyes, so his well-wishes were heartily accepted. That one small gesture instantly changed our attitude towards him. He had no idea how much encouragement his acknowledgement of our technical triumph and agonising months of planning gave us. His good wishes were tantamount to a collective farewell.

Then a warder shouted 'time', the last time we would be hearing that hated and oft-repeated word that constantly reminds prisoners of their predicament and summarises the essence of it.

Lock-up took place at half past four as usual. The warder in control of the keys locked the doors in the usual mindless way and the sergeant in charge of inspecting the prisoners trod the length of the passage and back like an impatient yo-yo. No one appeared to suspect anything and as our hated jailers trooped out of the section and locked the section door we silently bade them farewell and good riddance.

As soon as we heard the clang of the section door we set to work. In a scene repeated simultaneously in three cells: bedclothes were pulled back and prison overalls were placed on beds, overalls were stuffed with clothing, books, towels and other items to make dummies as had been done before. At the bottom of the 'legs' shoes were propped up vertically to simulate feet and then bedding was pulled over and the lump pummelled into the shape of a sleeping body.

We undressed ourselves and placed our day's prison clothes in hot soapy water in our basins so that they could not later be given to dogs to get our scent. We dressed ourselves in our blue sports shorts, our escape socks and white T-shirts. I put on the hideous pair of glasses I'd put aside for the escape and hooked my normal pair under the elastic of my shorts. To further confuse the dogs we sprayed our beds and clean prison clothing with deodorant and filled our prison shoes with pepper. To confuse the night-warders we arranged our cells to look as if we had put our things away for the night and gone to bed. I left a book open on my table with my reading spectacles on top of it and a half-eaten sandwich on a plate. Alex and Steve arranged their cells in similar ways and Steve and I fixed hooks under our number two doors and tied them to our grilles with bootlaces.

This all took just a matter of minutes, as we'd practised what to do every night the previous week. We'd developed the procedure down to a fine art and knew exactly how long it would take us to get our cells and ourselves ready – less time than it took for the *stokkies* to be locked up, the staff to have their end of day inspection in the administrative section and to lock up the prison and clear out. I stood at my window to listen for the inspection (you could hear them shouting orders and stamping their feet to attention), for the clang of the metal doors in the administrative section and the roar of their cars leaving.

As soon as I heard these familiar sounds I banged on the wall to signal to Stephen to unlock his grille, and waved a towel out of my passage window for Alex to do the same (he was watching with his shaving mirror). Each of us unlocked our grilles with the keys we'd hidden in our cells at shower-time, and to prevent our grilles clanging as we went out we taped toilet paper to the door frames where they made contact when they were closed. (This little touch was later to confuse the authorities, as one of their theories of how we'd escaped was that we had stuffed tissue paper in the holes into which our bolts protruded to prevent them coming out – quite impossible actually.)

Alex was the only one with a number two key. He would come out first and open my number two with it, and then Stephen's number two with his number one key. I listened again for movements, this time to hear if Vermeulen was moving around. Hearing nothing I gave Alex the all-clear by signalling again with a towel out of my passage window. After making sure that the *pos*-warder was in his alcove opposite my cell Alex stuck the crank mechanism out of his passage window and opened his number two while I watched with my mirror. There was a slight delay before he emerged but I knew that he was dismantling the crank and replacing the brush on his broomstick. His door swung open and he stepped out into the passage. He relocked his number one and two properly – two turns – before running down to our cells in his socks to unlock our number twos. He passed to me through my window the number two he had used and then disappeared into the shower to get out the equipment.

Stephen and I could not release ourselves immediately as we had to wait for the *pos*-warder to move to the far end of the catwalk. Fortunately, being a new warder and still keen to obey the rules, he soon moved across to the other end out of view of the inside of our cells. I banged on the wall again to signal all-go to Stephen. We loosened the bootlaces holding our doors closed, removed the hooks and put them in our pockets (they were no more than little metal brackets). We swung our doors open, locked them both properly and then joined Alex in the shower.

Alex had already removed our gear from the closet and had dressed himself in his civilian clothing – as any prisoner would do who is about to leave prison! He had placed our clothing and shoes in two piles on the floor of one of the shower cubicles. Steve and I pulled on our 'civvies' over the shorts and T-shirts we were already wearing and, unconventionally for departing prisoners, donned gloves and balaclavas. We wanted to be certain that we had left no trace at all and would leave them completely mystified as to how three prisoners had spirited themselves out of the prison. And in case we bumped into Vermeulen, we did not want to be recognised.

I collected the keys Alex and Steve had used to liberate themselves and placed them in the key-bag. I took the 'pea' from the bag and gave it to Alex with the key for the film cupboard. I placed in my pockets all the keys we would need to get beyond door six. Steve was then given the bag to carry.

This had all taken just a few minutes. We had rehearsed the procedure so often in our discussions and minds that it was as if we were doing something quite routine. Up to that point we had not had a chance to feel any apprehension; we were doing exactly what we knew had to be done. Besides, there was no need to worry if we were doing things right; we knew that we were. Every minute detail had been worked out, leaving the only unknown the precise movements of Vermeulen. We just hoped he would not do something out of the ordinary. In any case, this was not the first time we'd come out of our cells; we had 'escaped' from them five times before.

After pushing the empty sack that had held our clothing to the bottom of the space behind the geyser, the door was relocked and we got ready to go down. We slung our running shoes around our necks by their laces and edged toward the entrance of the shower to listen for any warder movements. Hearing nothing we tiptoed in a crouched position down the passage to door three. Our thoughts as we passed our comrades' cells were for what they must have been thinking: surely they couldn't just be sitting there getting on with their studies?

I peered through the keyhole of door three to see if anyone was standing on the other side. Assured that all was safe I quietly unlocked and opened it. Steve and Alex scurried down the stairs to the film cupboard while I went to the switchboard to turn off the lights for the first floor. By chance we had discovered beforehand that the face panel of the switchboard was loose and that if it was pulled forward it could be jammed into the rim of the switchboard door to prevent it opening – just a small move to delay Vermeulen. I relocked door three and made my way downstairs to join the others in the cupboard.

The space inside the cupboard was very limited and only just big enough to accommodate the three of us. By carefully repacking the film equipment we'd increased the space considerably but it was still a tight squeeze. Because I was the smallest I crouched low on the floor between the legs of the others who stood in an uncomfortable semi-crouched position. Stephen stood deepest in the cupboard while Alex held onto the bootlace to pull the door closed. We'd practised all this the Friday before, so we knew our positions and duties exactly.

After two or three minutes we could hear Denis's shouts as he called Vermeulen to come and investigate the sudden power failure. The *stokkies* also started making a commotion and probably a number of them had pressed their emergency bells in complaint at the sudden darkness. It struck us at that moment that if we had to do another stage two/three, we could rely on the *stokkies* to call Vermeulen out of his office.

We heard an unperturbed Vermeulen acknowledge Denis's call. He picked up his keys and wearily made his way down the passage to door four. He unlocked the gate and, without relocking it, made his way up the stairs. As he walked over our heads our silent laughter and excitement almost made us burst out. We were really enjoying ourselves and not half as scared as we thought we'd be. Fortunately Vermeulen went directly into our section without checking the switchboard first. We dashed out of the cupboard, closed the door without relocking it—in case we had to make a hasty withdrawal—passed through door four, and ran down the passage to doors five and six.

Alex was in such a hurry to get out that he forgot to press the button for door eight in the office. I shouted angrily at him, but immediately he realised what he hadn't done, spun about and sprang into the office to press the button. We heard a loud buzz and clang as the electric bolt released the door. It was much louder than we'd remembered, but then our senses were in such a state of arousal that every slight noise sounded greatly amplified.

I opened doors five and six and after we were through them I relocked both two turns. We had done it; we were now out of sight of the warder and ready to tackle the remaining three doors across our path.

I'd made three keys for door seven. The first one I tried almost turned the lock but jammed just as it began to move the bolt. The cuts were obviously too high. The second one glided around as smoothly as a perfectly machined cog—the filing of the levers on stage two had obviously done the trick. The door swung open and the three of us burst through into the last section of the passage. The door was left unlocked as we did not know at that stage if we'd have to pass back through it. Door eight was swung back and hooked against the wall.

Door nine was opened with the visiting-room key that had been found to work on stage two.

All this had taken only a few minutes. It was just past five, according to our calculations, and there we were standing in front of the last fetter on our freedom, door ten.

We strained our ears to listen for noises of the gate opening and the voices of guards. But there was nothing, just total silence. Although it was what our surveillance had told us we would find, we could hardly believe it. It meant that if we opened the front door we could just walk out, totally unseen and unheard and no one would ever know how we had done it. Could our luck be so good?

As we surveyed our last barrier we spotted something on the door which no one had ever noticed before: at eye level was a small flap that opened to give a view of the street outside the prison. Alex lifted it up and drew in the view from outside. With a gasp of disbelief he reported that there was nobody outside and that the gate of this maximum security prison was wide open. He invited us to have a look. Sure enough, the gates in the street were hooked back against the walls on both sides of the street and the sentry box was totally empty.

Without wasting a moment I pulled out of the key-bag a smaller bag containing the little keys we had made for the wooden doors. I tested each one expectantly but not one of them would turn. I cursed in disappointment: we had been relying on one of them working. Although we had our picks the thought of having to struggle with the last door had not entered into our planning. Alex impatiently grabbed the keys from me and tried each one, but had no better luck.

I took out the set of picks and started to jab the levers while Alex attempted once again to open the Captain's office. We had more or less given up the idea of using his office as a vantage point to determine the position of the *pos*-warder, but still wanted to get into the office so that we could leave Captain Venter some little momento or liberate his bottle of brandy. But the Captain's lock was also playing stubborn. Stephen urged him to give up and reminded him that we would soon be able to get something nice to drink.

I tried all our various picking devices but the accursed bolt refused to turn in. It seemed absurd to be fiddling with that last lock when all the other 14 we'd opened to get to it had done so without the slightest fuss. Our impatience to get out was building up to explosive pitch and at any moment the sentry would come on duty outside. If the picks did not work there was only one other way of opening the door: violence.

Alex tried the picks but he also made no headway. In anger he flung the fiddly bits of wire on the floor and announced aloud what we had all been silently contemplating—bust the goddam door open! We could chisel the doorpost to enable the locking plate to be bent back sufficiently to allow the bolt to pass it. The only other option was to turn the attempt into a stage two and go back to our cells, but I dared not mention this just at that moment.

It was not an easy choice to make because if the sentry came on duty while we were chiselling, going back would mean the end of the escape attempt—forever. The damaged doorpost would be investigated and what conclusion would they come to other than that an escape attempt had been made? No one breaks into prisons. It also meant leaving evidence of the path of our escape and turning what had been a perfectly clean attempt into something messy.

At this point I melted into a state of sheer terror. Alex as usual remained as calm as if he were eating his breakfast. Making snap decisions had never been one of my strong points so I just opted out and let Alex and Steve decide what was best. Both were in agreement that strong-arm tactics were needed. We'd tried gentle persuasion and that had not worked. And to hell with leaving evidence of our breakout: the main thing was to get out. We should grab the chance while it still existed; there was no question of going back.

Like a surgeon Alex asked for the chisel, and Stephen, acting the dutiful nurse, accordingly handed him the implement. I winced as he dug the point into the well-varnished frame and a large chip of wood fell onto the doormat. Such methods were not my style, but Alex seemed to be enjoying himself. I swallowed a handful of sweets that we'd brought along as someone had told us that they were good as an antidote for the effects of an overdose of adrenalin. I had doubted it, but the sweetness helped to distract my attention from the situation.

Alex periodically tested the plate with the large screwdriver to see if he had removed enough wood and several times it slipped and made a frightful noise which I was sure Vermeulen or the *pos*-warder heard. I went to door six to see and hear if there had been any response, but all was calm. Vermeulen was listening to his radio and in the distance I could hear the muffled sounds of music coming from our section. Assured that all was in order I locked door seven in case we had to dash out quickly; if we couldn't get out there would be plenty of time to reopen it. Door eight I left hooked back against the wall; if I closed it we would not be able to get back in if we had to retreat.

After what seemed like half an hour, but was probably less, Alex had gouged out enough wood from behind the locking plate to allow the bolt to clear it when he pulled on the door handle. Steve and I had prepared ourselves to leave: masks and gloves off, caps on and all the tools and keys packed into their respective bags. In my obsessive meticulousness I brushed some of the wood chippings under the doormat.

There was still no sentry on street duty, so with a strong heave Alex pulled the door, swung it wide open and boldly stepped out onto the small roofless porch between the front door and the yard wall. I followed him and then Stephen who pulled the door closed behind himself. We were out! The door would not close properly, since the bolt was still sticking out, but there was no time to worry about petty details just then.

We glanced quickly up and down the street. As far as we could see it was totally deserted. As casually as possible we stepped out into the bright sunshine of the street, turned right, and made our way towards Potgieter Street, the main road from Pretoria to Johannesburg and which runs past the prison complex, keeping as close to the base of the *pos* wall as possible.

We were out, not yet away, but out.

16
The Long Walk

The feeling of freedom after escaping from a political prison is almost impossible to describe in terms of the experiences of everyday life. It is a feeling known only by an exclusive club of people who have released themselves from custody with the knowledge that their action was a political act. The sudden relief from the constraints of captivity, the sudden expansion into the wall-less world outside released in us an explosion of emotion, a feeling of the most sublime elation. It was as if we were walking on air, floating, flying, and invisible to the world. Stephen recalled later that he felt like flapping his arms and flying off like a bird.

The distance to the traffic lights at Potgieter Street was only about 100 metres but the sudden ability to see that far, and further, was a most curious sensation. For nearly two years Stephen and I, and Alex for nearly seven, had not been able to see further than the end of the prison yard. Now suddenly the world seemed so big, seemed to stretch so far into the distance that it would quickly swallow us up and prevent anyone from finding us.

Alex crossed the road and walked down the left side of Soetdoring Street, the street in front of the prison, while Steve and I continued on the prison side. Near the lights a car was parked in which a warder sat talking to another who was standing in the street leaning on his elbow against the car. The warders paid no attention to the three characters walking past, as they looked no different from any of the other pedestrians making their way home that evening. At the lights another warder was standing waiting for a lift. He also did not bat an eyelid. Their lack of response confirmed that we were invisible and gave a tremendous boost to our confidence and sense of defiance.

Alex had trouble crossing Potgieter Street as the rush-hour traffic frightened him. But he somehow managed to get over and once across we made our way down a sidestreet which we knew led in the direction of Pretoria's main railway station. We had studied maps of the area cut out of the smuggled newspapers, so had a reasonably good idea of where we were heading. To our left were marshalling yards, goods sheds and many rail tracks. Our maps had not shown how we would be able to get across to the station on the far side; we'd imagined we'd have to scramble over the tracks and climb a few fences. But to our suprise we came to a footbridge leading over the tracks. A sign indicated that it led to Pretoria Station. We pulled our caps lower and walked across in single file, not daring to look up for

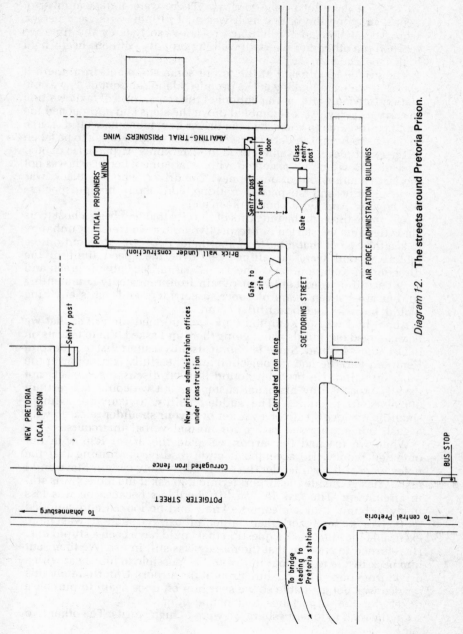

Diagram 12. **The streets around Pretoria Prison.**

201

we were still in hot prison territory. There were a great number of people crossing the bridge as it was about 6 pm: with each person who passed the more confident we grew, so that by the time we reached the other end we were walking proudly with our heads held high (*see Diagram 12*).

The bridge terminated at the top of some stairs and from there it was as if we were looking at the promised land. In front of us was the station forecourt and, at the bottom of the steps, rows of taxis waiting to carry us away. Alex scrambled down the steps and approached the first taxi he came to and asked the driver how much he would charge to take us to Kempton Park (we were still too scared to ask to be taken to the exact place we wanted to go to – Jan Smuts Airport). He quoted a fee of R28, which we accepted without argument because it was not too large a chunk out of our money. The driver, who was black, was very friendly and suspected nothing odd about his prospective passengers. And why should he have?

We drove through the outskirts of the city that had been a host to us since the time we started our respective terms: we were not unhappy to see the last of that citadel of apartheid. Soon we came out onto a motorway and were travelling well over the speed limit in the direction of Kempton Park. The Transvaal in December is green and very beautiful. Alex could not refrain from repeatedly commenting so, but after seven years of concrete corridors and yards anything would have looked beautiful to him.

About half way to Kempton Park we informed the driver that we had changed our minds about going there and asked him to take us on to Jan Smuts instead. Since Jan Smuts is only a short distance beyond Kempton Park he had no objection and cheerfully carried on in the same direction. He probably found himself discussing subjects not usually broached by his usual customers but we could not restrain ourselves from talking. The sudden ability to converse without smelling the foul breath of a warder over your shoulder released with a gush our suppressed desire for normal verbal intercourse.

When we reached the airport we paid the driver R36 with our outdated money. He accepted it quite readily, confirming that the notes were still legal tender. Just to be absolutely certain Steve and I made Alex go inside the airport terminal to ask if the money was still in circulation. The task fell on his shoulders because he was less likely to bump into someone he knew and he looked and sounded more like a 'foreigner' than either of us. As such it was more excusable for him to ask a question that could have been a stupid one. He returned to confirm that the money was still in use. We then sent him back inside to find out if it would be possible to hire a car with a driver from one of the car-hire firms at the airport. Unfortunately this service was not available so we sent him off once again to purchase tickets for the airport bus to Johannesburg.

On the road to Johannesburg we were in high spirits. The other two

202

accused me of looking like an escaped convict. I removed my cap – I couldn't help agreeing that it did look a bit out of place in the midst of the *haute couture* of the rest of the passengers. The passengers pretended to ignore our joyful remarks and looked down their noses at us as if we were just a bunch of scruffy drunkards taking a joy-ride.

It must have been about 8 pm when the bus arrived at the terminus at Johannesburg central station as it was already dark. Vermeulen would be doing his inspection round and if our absence had not already been discovered some of the comrades would be wondering if we were going to return to our cells in a short while. As we stood in the centre of the city with neon light flashing all around we laughed to ourselves that they were soon going to be kicking themselves for not joining us.

Our planning had not extended as far as covering the situation in which we then found ourselves, so we held a gathering in the station carpark to decide our next moves. Alex was still keen to make directly for the Swaziland border and wanted to do so immediately. Stephen, finding himself in Johannesburg and in what he considered to be home territory, thought that he would try to make contact with some of his friends. In the light of this I felt that it would be better to accompany Alex because we could not all throw ourselves on Steve's friends and Alex would be at a disadvantage if he went off on his own. He spoke no Afrikaans and was not as familiar with place names and routes as either Steve or I were. There was not much else to discuss so we shook hands, wished each other luck and said we would meet again in London.

Having reached the end of the planned part of the escape we turned our thoughts to absorbing some of the benefits of freedom. The first thing that came to mind was food – food of our own choice. I fancied a juicy grilled steak but Alex was more concerned with making our newly-gained freedom more secure – he would allow no more than the purchase of a steak and kidney pie and a coke from a station kiosk in the huge 'whites-only' concourse. Although in normal times we would only have bought such food in desperation, the fact that we had chosen to buy it ourselves and were able to eat it in our own time made it one of the most memorable 'meals' we could both remember. Also acquired from the kiosk was a pocket-sized map-book of the roads of South Africa.

Alex wanted to head east in the direction of Swaziland but the furthest any train was going in that direction that night was to Springs on the East Rand. Although Springs was only 60 kilometres away, going there was better than standing looking at the departures board so we bought two tickets in the hope that once we got there we would be able to get a bus to take us further. I felt somewhat uneasy about this plan as I could envisage a situation where we would find ourselves stuck out in the night with no transport to take us further.

But the alternative of spending the whole night wandering aimlessly around Johannesburg did not seem any better.

The train was almost empty so we sat down in a section that was unoccupied and proceeded to discard out of the window our escape equipment and dozens of keys. Why we had doubted at one stage that the wooden keys would be strong enough to open the prison's locks I don't know, because when we tried to break them with our hands it was almost impossible to do so. Each one had to be split open with the chisel and then painfully chipped into unrecognisable pieces. It was sad in a way to have to destroy the keys like that: they embodied so many hours of painstaking labour and had been hidden and tended so carefully for so long. It was also hard to believe that after a few minutes' use they had given up their useful function and would never be needed again. After arriving at Springs we buried the remaining tools in a churchyard, apart from the trusty chisel which was retained as a weapon to supplement the 'pea'.

Springs bus-station was totally deserted. There was no sign of any buses, nor were there any people waiting for them. Our hearts sank as we surveyed the empty, oily ranks. We had visualised ourselves being over or near the border before daybreak. Now the vision of being on safe territory for breakfast faded and a prospect loomed of having to get to the border under cover of the darkness of several nights. Freedom was not going to be as easy as we'd thought: we were going to have to struggle for it. But one thing was sure: we were not going to allow ourselves to get caught – we would crawl on hands and knees to the border if we had to.

If you have no wheels the only way to get somewhere is on foot. So we set off eastwards. To sustain us on our journey we stopped at a shop and bought some sweets, a large slice of cheese and two cartons of milk. After the skimmed, powdered 'milk' we'd had in prison this fresh, creamy milk glided down our throats like nectar.

We discovered a signpost pointing the way to Ermelo, a town our map indicated we would have to pass through, so we set off in that direction. For about an hour and a half as we walked through and out of Springs we held out our thumbs in the hope that someone would stop and give us a lift. But at night motorists in South Africa (most of whom are white) grow paranoid and are loath to stop on dark roads to offer assistance to stranded hitch-hikers.

Outside Springs at a place called Largo the road crossed over a railway line and from the bridge we could see flashing lights in the distance. A roadblock, was our immediate simultaneous thought. And if that's what it was then it meant that our absence had been discovered and we would have to face the full might of the 'security forces' all the way to the border. Standing on top of a bridge while the cops were looking for us was dangerous, so we ran to the bottom and turned into and made our way down a rough farm track leading off the road at right angles. We climbed through a fence and walked across a ploughed field. There was no moon or stars that night and as we stumbled in the furrows it suddenly occurred to us how absurd it was to be scrambling blindly across the countryside after our meticulously conceived plans had got us out of the prison and to that point so effortlessly. My morale dropped to a low ebb and I suggested turning back to spend the night in Springs. Alex would have none of it and angrily urged me onward. There's no doubt that without his irrepressible determination we would have remained in Pretoria Prison for very much longer.

When we finally reached the road again, a short distance beyond where the suspected danger had appeared to be, there were no flashing lights and no sign of cars being stopped. Puzzled but relieved we shrugged our shoulders and proceeded along the road in the direction of the next town, a place called Devon. The night was warm and calm and walking through the fresh air was invigorating after years of breathing stale wall-bound prison air. The sense of freedom was intoxicating and we felt like singing. For several hours we joked and laughed about incidents leading up to the escape and tried to imagine how the warders would respond in the morning when they opened our cells and found only dummies in our beds. We could see them going berserk and crowds of security police invading the place to figure how we'd managed to get out. The escape had been like a catharsis to us and suddenly all our pent-up emotions were flooding out.

At about two o'clock in the morning we suddenly noticed the flashing lights again, but this time coming from behind us. We couldn't understand it as we had just come down that road. Could it be a roving roadblock? To avoid whatever it was we dived into the nearest bush. The flashing light was very slow-moving and took about twenty minutes to reach us. It was also very noisy, making a sort of rumbling, puffing noise like a steam engine. The 'roadblock' eventually reached us: it was a line-painting machine which was repainting sections of the white lines down the centre of the road. It went past us and stopped about 100 metres further on. The flashing light went off and the workers climbed down from the monster and started to pull out their thermos flasks and sandwiches. It was a coffee-break. We waited another 10 minutes and then decided it would be safe to carry on. There were several smallholdings behind us, so we reasoned it would not seem too strange for a couple of white men to be walking about at that time of night. The workers ignored us as we trudged past – we must still have been invisible.

At about five when the sun was just beginning to light the distant horizon, we reached Devon. The walk from Springs had been more than forty kilometres so we were beginning to feel the strain on our feet. Strangely though, we did not feel tired. The excitement of the night had kept the pangs of sleep at bay.

At the town we made our way to the railway station to find out if there were any trains or buses to Ermelo. The lone guard in attendance informed us, much to our dismay, that there were no buses out of the town and only one train a day – at midnight. He suggested that we try hitching, but after our experience the previous night we were not impressed by the suggestion. On the other hand, the thought of walking the more than two hundred kilometres to the Swaziland border was not inviting, so we thought we would at least give hitching another try. It was daylight now and people would probably be more willing to pick us up. After only a few minutes putting our thumbs out someone stopped and offered us a lift. It was a different matter now that our white faces could be seen.

On the way our driver stopped at a cafè to buy his breakfast. We took the opportunity to replenish our supplies and buy a newspaper to see if there was any mention of the escape. But there was nothing, which made us feel much easier. It was a curious sensation to hold and possess a whole newspaper, but because it didn't arrive in an envelope under the cell door the news seemed flat and boring. As soon as we set off again I commented to Alex that there was nothing in the news 'as usual', in the hope of provoking our driver into mentioning the escape of three dangerous 'terrorists', if he had heard about it on a radio or TV. But he had obviously heard nothing.

Our driver took us a distance of about forty kilometres to the turn-off for the town of Secunda where he worked as a technician at the SASOL oil-from-coal plant. From the point where he dropped us the refinery could clearly be seen in the distance. Six months later it was to be attacked with limpet mines by ANC guerillas, causing millions of rands worth of damage to one of the most strategic installations in the country and maximum embarrassment to the apartheid regime.

Beyond the drop-off point there was little traffic and most of what there was consisted of large trucks whose drivers at the best of times are reluctant to stop for hitch-hikers. It was about six am, and approaching the time when our absence would be discovered if it had not been already. The countryside was flat and open, so it was imperative for us to make some rapid progess. Alex suddenly hit upon the bright idea of holding up a ten rand note alongside his thumb when a truck or car passed. The trick worked wonders. The very first truck that came along pulled up to a rapid halt, its trailer almost skidding off the road. Alex climbed up to the driver's window and asked where he was going. The driver explained that he was going in the direction of Piet Retief to deliver some mining equipment to a mine outside the town, and was going there via Ermelo. Alex shouted the details down to me but as soon as I heard the word 'Ermelo' I told him to accept. We climbed aboard and handed the driver his ten rand.

The driver's mate climbed over the seat and sat on the bunk at the back of the cab; Alex and I sat in the passenger's seat and watched through the large windscreen as the truck swallowed up the miles below us. In half an hour we'd covered more distance than we'd walked all night. The rapid progress we were suddenly making made us think that we could possibly get right to the border before the authorities had realised what had happened and had mobilised roadblocks that distance away. Between the two of us we still had a considerable amount of money and wondered if we could use it to persuade the driver to take us all the way to Amsterdam, a small town near the Swazi border where we had decided to head for. Piet Retief was south of Amsterdam and to get to both places entailed passing through Ermelo. At Ermelo the road branched south-east to Piet Retief or carried straight on to Amsterdam. It was possible to reach Piet Retief via Amsterdam as a road connected the two towns. In other words, to get to Piet Retief from Ermelo via Amsterdam meant travelling two sides of a triangle as opposed to the one side if travelling directly there. From our map-book we calculated that the direct route from Ermelo to Piet Retief was a distance of 97 kilometres and via Amsterdam 132 kilometres. But as the mine where the equipment was to be delivered was a short way up the road toward Amsterdam from Piet Retief, the difference would be less than 30 kilometres (*see Map*).

Observing this fact we told the driver that we needed to get to Amsterdam very urgently to attend to a sick relative and offered him a further R50 if he would take us there. The driver spoke over his shoulder to his mate. We could not understand a word of what they were saying because they spoke in an African language, but guessed that they knew the sick relative story was bullshit as the conversation went on for a long time. Eventually the driver nodded his head and said that it would be OK to take us to Amsterdam.

We passed through Ermelo and followed the signs for Amsterdam. As we did so Alex and I were quietly laughing inside. It was about the time that the warders would be discovering that three prisoners had not woken for the morning inspection. The thought of them throwing back the bedspreads to find not sleeping prisoners but dummies of clothing and books was thrilling to contemplate. Soon we would be in Amsterdam where we could wait for nightfall to make our crossing into Swaziland. So far we'd seen no sign of a roadblock, meaning that our absence had not been discovered during the night.

Our visions of an early arrival at Amsterdam were soon deflated. About forty kilometres out of Ermelo one of the wheels of the trailer burst. The trailer began to slew about but the driver managed to bring the truck to a halt without any incident. Fortunately the wheels of the trailer were double-tyred so it was able to keep on a more or less even course. The driver got out to inspect the damage and then reported that it would take some time to replace the wheel. Not having the time to spare, we paid him the R50 and set off on foot in the same direction, again with our thumbs sticking out.

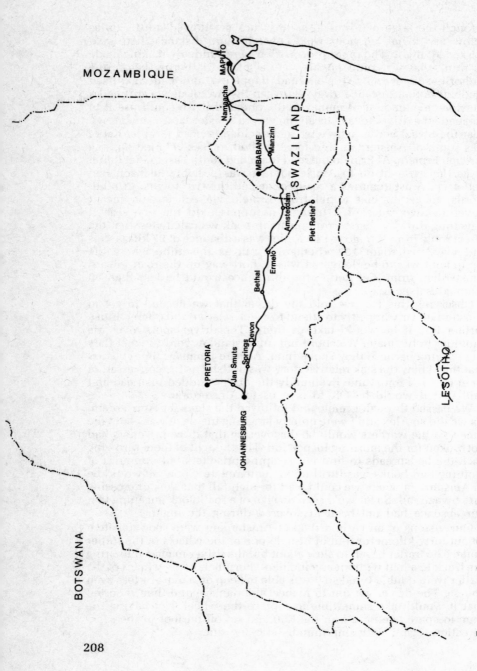

Escape route from Pretoria to Maputo.

There was very little traffic on the road at that time of the morning (about seven thirty) and most of it private transport – not easily brought to a halt by our money-method. After about an hour's walking we decided that it was too risky to continue on foot in broad daylight as by that time the word would be getting out on the radio for people to be on the lookout for escaped white prisoners. Further on we spotted a clump of bushes and trees just off the road beyond a fence and headed for it. We entered the bushes and found them to be an ideal hiding-place as they were sheltering a sort of gulley around which the road skirted.

It was going to be a long wait for sunset so we cleared some ground and lay down to rest our tired bodies. Despite having spent the entire night on foot, neither of us could sleep: our thoughts and the excitement of the day would not let us relax. We were also invaded by huge mosquito-like creatures.

At about midday the sky began to cloud over and the temperature dropped rapidly. The clothing we wore was totally inadequate and we grew progressively colder. Two hours later the skies opened up and within a few minutes we were drenched to the skin. The trees became so waterlogged that they offered no shelter at all. We moved into a deeper part of the gulley in the hope that its steep sides would afford some shelter, but the rain was coming down so heavily that the sides began to slide down on us. The elements decided for us that we had no choice but to move on.

Shortly before we had left the road and hidden in the bushes we had noticed a sign indicating a petrol station one kilometre further on. From our hiding place we had been able to hear voices and cars and lorries stopping and starting. Now our reluctance to proceed to the petrol station to seek a lift was suddenly changed by the circumstances.

To our good fortune the petrol station turned out to be a country store as well. A number of Africans were sheltering under the verandah in front of it. They did not seem to find it too strange to see two white men soaked to the skin come striding out of the dense rain. Inside the store we asked one of the attendants, who were all black, to sell us some cheese. Instead of immediately responding to our request one of them eyed us up and down and asked us to hold on while she went to call her 'madam'. Momentarily, both of us thought that we had just exposed ourselves and that she was going to the back to call her 'master' who would soon appear with a shotgun and perform the noble duty of arresting us.

Our fears were allayed when a friendly white woman appeared through the door behind the counter and asked us with a genuinely worried look on her face what had happened. Thinking quickly, we explained that our car had broken down some distance back and that we had left it at a farm and were trying to hitch to Amsterdam to meet my brother who had all our luggage there. We'd not been able to hitch a ride and had got caught in the rain when it started – hence our sodden state.

If we'd been black we would probably have been booted out for dripping water all over the floor, but since we were white and apparently in distress she felt sorry for us and brought us two towels to dry ourselves as well as two steaming mugs of coffee to warm us up.

Between us we still had quite a sum of money, so we each bought ourselves an anorak to keep out the cold and Alex bought himself a pair of long socks to change into. To keep our bellies full on the journey ahead we bought a stock of cheese, sweets and fruit. If we were to continue hitching in the rain we realised that we'd need raincoats too so we asked to be shown the range in stock. All they were able to produce were two plastic raincoats, one light blue and the other bright yellow – the worst possible colours. But having no choice we bought the pair.

Having dried and warmed our bodies we donned our raincoats, thanked the 'madam' and her helper gratefully, and marched out onto the road looking like two ghostly apparitions. Fortunately the very first car that came along stopped and the driver, obviously feeling sorry for us, apologised that he could only give us a lift for 20 kilometres. As this was better than standing in the rain until sunset we gratefully accepted and climbed into the already full car. The occupants were Afrikaans-speaking so Alex was not able to converse with them, but I managed to keep a conversation going and tried subtly to direct the talk in the direction of the day's news. But like our first driver they too appeared not to have heard anything about escaped convicts on the run.

The road passed through dense forest area and at a turn-off to a dam the driver stopped to let us out. He wished us luck in finding another lift and drove off in a cloud of mist. As we stood in the cold and rain contemplating our situation we decided that we'd pushed our luck far enough and would not try for any more lifts. We would hide in the forest until nightfall and then, because it was only about forty kilometres away, proceed on foot to the border. We climbed through a fence and moved into the forest out of view of the road. Not finding any shelter under the trees we decided there was no point in waiting for dark and proceeded to walk parallel to the road, the position of which we were able to judge by the sound of the occasional passing car.

Eventually we came to a path which seemed too well-trodden to be a foresters' path, so followed it for some distance until it came out to a small African village. The villagers and even their dogs stared in silence as the two phantoms approached and walked past without saying a word. From the village we followed a track which led back to the main road. As we approached the road it was already dusk, but before coming out onto it we waited in the tall grass for darkness to set in properly. As soon as we judged it to be dark enough (it must have been about seven thirty) we set off along the road in the direction of Amsterdam, a distance of some twenty kilometres.

Our map told us that it was another 20 kilometres from Amsterdam to the Swazi border gate at Nerston, where we planned to cross. Since we had walked 40 kilometres the previous night we knew that we were capable of covering the distance by daybreak if we walked all night. Our morale was still high although we were more apprehensive than we had been the previous night. We'd been through a lot in the short time we'd been out and, as the period of our freedom lengthened, we became increasingly determined to hang on to it. For the first time we turned our thoughts to wondering what would happen to us if we were recaptured. The prison authorities would surely not take too kindly to the disruption the escape would have caused. Both of us knew that our sentences would be infinitely extended and for at least six months after recapture we would be forced to wear chains and be held in solitary confinement.

There were very few cars on the road that night but we could not allow ourselves to be seen at all. Our guess was that there would be full-scale searches mounted throughout the country and especially near border areas. Every time a car passed the two of us dived off the road and hid in bushes or grass near the verge. There was plenty of time to look for hiding places because, as it was pitch dark and still drizzling, we could see the lights of cars lighting the horizon a great distance off. On a number of occasions we could not find very suitable cover so we just had to lie flat in the grass and hope for the best. When this happened we had to remove our technicolor raincoats, place them on the ground as a groundsheet and I had to lie on top of Alex to conceal his white shoes and light-coloured socks and shorts. On two occasions we were certain that the passing vehicles were police vans.

At around midnight the lights of Amsterdam made a welcome sight in the distance. Our feet were by this time beginning to suffer the consequences of all the walking, but there was no question of stopping. As we approached the town we considered skirting around it for fear that there would be a roadblock or that police would be positioned in the streets to be on the lookout for fugitives. But the distance around appeared to be great and we did not know if we would end up on the road to the border on the other side. Also, the road into the town was wide and well lit. It dipped down into the centre and up a hill on the other side and from the approach appeared to be completely deserted. To reduce the chances of being seen we walked apart, one on each side of the road, and met at the far side of town where a sign indicated the direction to the border gate. There was a slight scare as we sat down to rest our weary feet: a small car came up the hill towards us but then turned off just before reaching us.

Under the roadsign we removed our shoes, massaged our blistered feet, and ate the last of our cheese. My left foot had developed a disabling cramp and I was beginning to doubt if I would be able to walk the remaining 20 kilometres to the border. But the rest and the fresh air on my soles worked wonders. The walk to the border we knew would be uneventful: there would be no traffic on the road as it led nowhere else and the border gate was closed at night.

★　★　★

Meanwhile back at the prison . . . nothing happened until the cells were opened at the normal time the morning after the escape. The night-warders had not reported any prisoners missing and at open-up time there was no state of alert, despite the front door having been found damaged.

The warder who opened the cells that morning only realised that something was wrong when he got to Denis's cell, the third cell along. He suddenly realised that he'd opened two cells and there had not been prisoners standing to attention at either of them. This happening at one cell was not usually taken too seriously as quite frequently a prisoner would oversleep and have to be prodded into life. But when it happened in two consecutive cells there had to be something amiss. The warder went back to Stephen's cell and shouted at him to wake up. When there was no stirring he opened the grille and pulled the bedspread back...

The warder ran out of the section and screamed for the sergeant in charge. He rushed back in and hurriedly opened my cell. Another prisoner gone! The blood drained from his face as he realised what was going on. Complete pandemonium then broke loose. A troop of warders came charging in and the remaining cell doors were hurriedly flung open to see how many more prisoners had turned into lifeless dummies. They got to Alex's and finding another 'sleeping prisoner', realised that three had flown. The remaining prisoners expressed utter surprise at the revelation that some of their fellow prisoners had gone missing during the night.

In no time time the prison was invaded by a horde of security police and the remaining comrades placed under close and permanent observation. The entire prison and terrain was overrun and surrounded by police and the call went out to prevent the flight of the three dangerous 'terrorists'.

Within a few days the prison yard was dug up in the search for clues. Every tree, bush, blade of grass and weed was uprooted. Sure enough, a bottle containing keys for every grille and door was unearthed from under the cabbage patch...

212

17

Swaziland, Mozambique

Our feet were killing us but we pressed on toward the border. The rain had stopped and it was a bit warmer, but it was still overcast and pitch dark. It was so dark in fact that we could not even see the white line down the centre of the road and several times walked off the edge of the tarmac. Our imaginations began to play games with us: the road seemed to be running along the edge of a cliff, then over the top of a mountain, then through a forest – we couldn't tell. Probably most of the time it was winding through forest area, as that was how it was when it grew lighter in the morning.

We talked very little and kept close to each other for comfort. Both of us felt desperately tired. Several times I actually fell asleep while walking, and bumped into Alex. Our food was all eaten and we began to feel progressively weaker, but the thought of friendly territory close at hand gave us succour. Strangely we felt little apprehension even though our common sense told us that we were reaching what could possibly be the most dangerous part of the journey.

As the first tint of dawn pierced the misty sky we came to a T-junction where a signboard indicated two kilometres to the border gate. We turned right towards the gate and Alex paced out 1,500 metres, from which point we could see the orange glow of the lights at the border gate in the distance. From there we turned left into the forest and walked at right angles to the road for about half a kilometre, then took a right turn toward the border. Both of us visualised the border as a high barbed-wire fence, possibly two fences with a strip of no-man's-land in between. Maybe there would be dogs, land-mines, alarms, who knew? We had decided that when we reached the fence we would walk along it away from the border gate until we came to a suitable place to cross, perhaps where it went across a stream or over a rocky patch.

After walking some distance a small muddy stream crossed our path at the edge of the forest. At a point where the trees ran up to the stream we stepped over it and scrambled up a steep bank on the other side which was cleared of vegetation. At the top of the bank was a rough track and along the other side of it dense bush which appeared to have been cropped so that it looked vaguely like a hedge. These signs of habitation made us think that perhaps we had not walked along far enough and were in imminent danger of being seen by border guards. Alex suggested taking shelter in the bush and after penetrating it some distance we came to a small African stone hut. As we stared at it we simultaneously came to the realisation that we might actually be in Swaziland. The area up to the border was not a bantustan, one of the areas designed for African occupation. It seemed to be entirely given over to forestry. Now suddenly there was African habitation. It could be the only explanation. But where was the border fence we'd expected? Where were the dogs, the guards?

The thought that we could be on safe territory (relatively speaking) gave us sudden courage. We turned back on our footsteps, re-emerged from the bush and followed the track in the direction of the border gate and main road. The bush thinned out and through it a small settlement came into view, some of the houses being quite substantial. Alex suddenly noticed an African woman washing clothes in a tub in her yard. He ran up to her leaving me standing on the track. I could see him speaking to her then suddenly embracing her. He pulled a ten rand note out of his pocket and thrust it in her hand. The woman stood bewildered as he shouted to me that, indeed, we were in Swaziland. I ran up to the woman and shook her hand, asking her to confirm to me that I really was in Swaziland.

What that woman must have thought when two dishevelled white men appeared out of the grey of dawn and started asking her which country they were in must be left to the imagination. Whatever she thought it is more than likely that her guess was not too far off the mark. To add to her puzzlement we asked her how we could get to Mbabane, the capital of Swaziland, from the village. She pointed to a house further up the hill which had a car parked outside and told us that the person who owned it was a relative of hers who might take us to Mbabane if we asked him.

The time could not have been later than five thirty, but having been up the entire night made us lose all sense of the meaning of the hour. Without thinking that we would probably be waking up an entire household, we knocked at the door of the relative's house for a good ten minutes before it occurred to us that the lack of response could be accounted for by the fact that it was still very early in the morning. As we were walking away and planning to come back later, a drowsy-looking woman in a dressing gown appeared at the back door of the house and asked what we wanted. Amazingly, when we explained, pointing to the car in front of her house, that we were looking for a lift to Mbabane, she did not display the slightest sign of annoyance at having been so inconsiderately aroused from her slumbers at such an unreasonable hour. She replied that the car belonged to her husband, who was still sleeping, and invited us into the house until he awoke.

Having lived all my life in a city, and coming straight from prison, I found it difficult to understand the friendliness of those people. Not only did the woman invite us in after we had woken her and probably her family as well, but after chatting to her for a while she offered us tea and ultimately breakfast. And the extended hand of hospitality did not end there. After breakfast we were offered use of the bathroom and even given a razor and towels for a shave. The thermal and personal warmth of that house revived our bodies and our faith in humankind. We could not help thinking that they must have realised that we were on the run from something and that it would have been more reasonable for them to think we were bank robbers than escaped political prisoners.

When the 'head' of the house appeared it had already been decided what should be done with us. The sister of the woman, who also stayed in the house, would take us up to the shop they owned on the main road from where she would be able to arrange a lift for us. The shop had a petrol pump in front of it and as they knew practically everyone who stopped for petrol they could ask someone to give us a lift.

After eating their breakfast they escorted us to the shop where we waited for about an hour before a lift was arranged: an uncle offered to give us a lift to a point on the main road half way between Mbabane and Manzini. Unfortunately the uncle turned out to be a businessman who owned half the booze shops in Swaziland and that day was the day he had to pay a visit to each of them before going on to complete his business in Manzini. But escaped convicts cannot be choosers and anyway we got to see some of the more unusual and beautiful parts of the country. As interesting as it was we were not tourists and were impatient to get to Mbabane and out of the country as quickly as possible. Just as we were about to announce that we would prefer to try for another lift he dropped us at the place he had promised to take us, about 30 kilometres from Mbabane. From the drop-off point the traffic was relatively heavy so we quickly got a lift into the centre of Mbabane.

In Mbabane the first thing we did was to buy newspapers to see what sort of response there had been to the escape. It was headlines in all the South African papers: 'Three Prisoners Escape: dummies left in their beds' read one; 'Prison Official Held Over ANC Escape' read another. So they must have arrested poor old Vermeulen, was our obvious immediate thought. An Afrikaans paper read: *'Polisie Jag Drie Wit Terroriste Landwyd'*, – 'Police Search Countrywide for Three White Terrorists'. Details were given of how the police had been mobilised throughout the country to make it impossible for the escapees to cross the borders into neighbouring countries. Obviously their efforts hadn't been very successful! All the papers reported that we had escaped in shorts, white T-shirts and running shoes, the implication being that we had jogged our way to freedom. Most insulting of all was the offer of a R1,000 reward to anyone offering information leading to our recapture. Was that all we were worth!

What next? We had considered going to the Swazi police to ask them for protection and help but were not quite sure if that was the right thing to do as we'd developed an innate aversion to police forces generally. I had heard somewhere, sometime (incorrectly) that the

ANC ran a bookshop in Mbabane and had thought that maybe we could avoid the police by going directly there. We went back into the stationers where we had bought the newspapers, as it was also a bookstore, and asked one of the attendants if the ANC had a bookshop in Mbabane. The attendant had not even heard of the ANC, but when we explained what sort of organisation it was he suggested that we contact the United Nations High Commission for Refugees—they knew about people from South Africa. This sounded a reasonable idea and in the absence of any other bright ideas we took a taxi to the United Nations building in the town.

Alex went inside alone while I waited in the taxi. When the attendant at the enquiries desk asked what his business was Alex abruptly demanded to see someone important. At first the attendant did not know how to respond to this unusual request, but when Alex said that he was from South Africa he was taken to see a worker concerned with refugee affairs, to whom he briefly explained his plight. At first the worker, a Swiss woman, was reluctant to believe the fantastic story but when Alex showed her his mug-shot emblazoned on the front page of the newspaper he carried, she hurriedly told him to summon me from outside so that she could hear more and decide what to do.

Together we explained to the startled woman how we happened to be where we were, using the newspapers to verify our story. When we mentioned that we had thought of taking ourselves to the Swazi police she was horrified and said that if we had done that we would probably be on our way back to South Africa at that moment. Thankfully she was sympathetic to our plight and mentioned that she would be able to get us into safe hands, that is, to the ANC. Most of all, she advised us, we should keep out of sight of the Swazi authorities. Later we were to read in a newspaper report that a Swazi police spokesperson said: 'If they are here they will be arrested for illegally crossing our borders no matter what their motives are ... Apart from breaking our law they are criminals who have escaped from jail'.

The Swiss woman made some hasty phonecalls and then took us in her car to see the High Commissioner for Refugees himself, a man by the name of Godfrey Sibidi, a Ugandan citizen. While we explained again the circumstances of our escape he made contact with the ANC over the phone. He found our tale fascinating and laughed his head off when we explained how we had done it. It was good to share our victory with someone in sympathy with what we had done. He sent one of his staff to buy us some food, which was our first proper meal since the last midday meal we had eaten in prison two days before. Food never tasted so good.

After leaving us for a couple of hours in the room the Commissioner drove us some distance out of Mbabane in his car to what appeared to be a seminary or church school of some kind. There we were introduced, I think, to the Bishop of Mbabane, and, at last, a representative of the ANC. The ANC comrade introduced himself as John Nkadimeng and shaking hands with him was like firmly grasping the hand of freedom. There was no going back to Pretoria now. Comrade John is now the General-Secretary of the South African Congress of Trade Unions (SACTU).

Having delivered us to the ANC the Commissioner bade farewell. Then Alex did something for which I have never forgiven him. The Commissioner had expressed great interest in the 'pea', which Alex still carried tucked into his belt under his shirt. As a token of gratitude Alex handed him the 'pea' as a souvenir. Since we possessed nothing else to offer as a gift it would have seemed rude if I had objected too loudly. That was how we lost the 'pea'.

The Bishop took us to the dormitories where we were given soap and towels to have a shower. What luxury it was just to stand in those showers and let the water do the scrubbing. After two days' walking and after diving into muddy ditches the night before our bodies had accumulated a great deal of sweat and grime. The warm water soothed our tired and aching limbs. Alex had trouble just standing up as his feet were massively swollen and his leg muscles so stiff that they were virtually incapable of flexing. Both of us just collapsed on the beds that were offered to us after the shower.

A few hours later we were woken by some other ANC comrades and taken to a house in Mbabane where we were given a first class meal. Then on to another house where, finally, we were told to rest for a few hours because we were going to be taken across the border into Mozambique at dawn.

★ ★ ★

General – that was his name – picked us up at the crack of dawn. Our destination was the Mozambique border, he told us.

The drive to the border took about an hour, maybe longer. It was exciting to watch the sun rising above the hills and light the beautiful greenness of the countryside, a scene we should not, by rights, have been witnessing. It also made us realise how much we'd taken such sights for granted in the past.

General's plan was that when we got near the border the two of us would lie hidden on the floor of his car and then he would drive us through the border gate. Just like that. It seemed too easy to be true but he assured us that he did it every day and had never had any problems. The Swazis, he explained, did not bother much about traffic going out of the country in the direction of Mozambique and the Mozambicans would not mind too much even if we were discovered – it was the sort of thing they expected.

A few kilometres from the border gate General drove off the road and stopped the car behind some bushes. He opened the car doors

217

and we hid on the floor. Alex objected that once our heads were covered it would be too much like a prison cell and that he would feel unbearably claustrophobic. He would prefer to walk. If it had been so easy to walk across to Swaziland from South Africa then surely it would be no problem walking across here. General agreed that it could be done but clearly he was contemptuous of such a method of hopping borders and upset that we displayed so little faith in him.

To walk across safely meant taking a roundabout route which would involve a walk of two or three hours. Alex's feet were still in a bad shape, swollen and stiff. He could not walk for ten minutes, let alone a couple of hours through the bush. There was one more alternative, an extremely risky one, but if we were prepared to take the chance we could be over the border in a matter of minutes. Another chance? What the hell. We'd taken so many up to that point that one more did not matter a damn. The proposal was accepted without further ado and we set off in the direction of the border gate.

Almost within view of the gate General turned into a rough track and drove towards the border fence. He stopped the car behind what appeared to be an abandoned shed and pointed to a sturdy two metre high fence topped with barbed wire about thirty metres further on and to another the same height about five metres beyond the first. The fences, he explained, ran along the borders of Swaziland and Mozambique respectively. The strip in between was no-man's-land but there were no mines or dogs in it, he assured us. All we would have to do was scale both fences and we would be in Mozambique.

On the other side of the fences we could see houses beyond a row of trees and bushes but there appeared to be no sign of life in that direction at all. What was the big deal? We would be over in thirty seconds and it was too early for anyone to be up to see us.

Our escort explained that we would have to wait for about an hour on the other side as he would only be able to get through the border gate at seven o'clock. He told us to wait in a quiet backstreet of the town before moving on down to the gate shortly before seven. He explained briefly how the guns worked and then made us tuck them in our belts under our shirts.

At a corner post all three of us climbed over the first (Swazi) fence but as Alex and I were mounting the second we noticed an old man in a long coat and wielding a knobkerrie charging towards us from the Swaziland side. General told us to get over the fence and run: he would deal with the man. The two of us leapt over the fence and started to run towards the houses on the Mozambique side. As we reached the bushes we heard the sound of a scuffle as General engaged the old man in a fight. Alex turned around and with a loud battle cry ran back towards the scene. But all we could see was General running for the car and pulling away with the tyres skidding on the sandy road, with the old man in hot pursuit.

218

The part of the town in which we found ourselves must have been where the Portuguese colonialists once lived as most of the houses were large and stately. To avoid being spoken to by the few people who were up and wandering about, we kept moving, slowly but purposefully, around two or three blocks of houses. Neither of us knew a single word of Portuguese so did not even know how to greet the friendly but undoubtedly suspicious passers-by. Our first lesson in Portuguese was quickly learnt: everyone bade us a courteous *bom dia*, quite obviously meaning 'good day'. We felt almost at home after that, casting smiling *bom dia*'s at everyone who appeared. There still seemed to be quite a number of white faces around so we did not appear too out of place that morning.

After about an hour of strolling around we stopped to rest our still-weary feet. There were more people about by then so we thought it would not look too strange for two of them to stop and sit on a low stone wall for a rest. This was a big mistake for as soon as we stopped someone approached us and asked something in Portuguese. Not being able to answer we replied clumsily that we were looking for someone from FRELIMO. Obviously this answer, especially coming in English, aroused the person's suspicion, for he quickly turned on his heels and walked back in the direction from which he had come. Approaching him from the opposite direction was a man dressed in uniform. The two met and stopped in mid-street. We could see the one who had spoken to us point over his shoulder and then both of them began to walk in our direction. At that moment we thought of making a bolt for it but realised that it would not have been the appropriate action.

As the official approached us he asked in broken English what we were waiting for. He asked us to follow him and we set off down the street into the town. Neither of us knew what to say but did not want to appear as if we were feeling guilty. I asked casually if he was a member of FRELIMO and when he said that he was, we both shook hands and tried to be as friendly as possible. We explained who we were and where we were going but he didn't seem too impressed or convinced—but then who could blame him after discovering two suspicious-looking, English-speaking, white men loitering in the streets of a border town?

The official turned out to be a member of the border guard and he took us to the offices at the border gate. There we were shut in a room with someone to watch over us. Once again we were in captivity and wondered what the outcome would be. Neither of us relished the prospect of being locked up in a cell until the matter was sorted out. That could take days. We had explained to our 'captor' that we were members of the ANC and were due to be met by the ANC (i.e. General) as soon as the gate opened and just hoped that the FRELIMO government's attitude in practice towards the ANC was the same as its declared one.

219

Fortunately it was not long before the gates opened, and General was one of the first to come through. We could see him and General frantically discussing the matter in the road outside. Alex and I were not asked to join in the deliberations and had to be content just watching through the window of our room. After a while General joined us and appeared to be completely unperturbed by his altercation with the guard and with the fact that we had been 'captured'.

After another long wait several members of the local police or militia arrived, as well as a van-load of ANC comrades, resulting in a gathering under the car shelter in front of the offices to discuss what should become of us. An hour or so later the gathering broke up and the two of us were taken into another room and subjected to a thorough strip-search by a surly border guard.

The strip-search signalled the end of our wait and was followed by a more friendly attitude on the part of the official who had taken charge. He led us to a small hut closer to the border gate where we were asked to fill in a form — an ordinary visitor's entry form. What had troubled them was that we had tried to sidestep their administrative entry requirements and had avoided filling in the requisite forms. Climbing over the border fence was a rather unconventional way of entering a country!

Having completed the forms we were handed over to the ANC and driven to a house a short distance away in the town. At the house were a number of ANC comrades, including Sue Rabkin, Dave's wife. She gave us a warm welcome and produced from somewhere a full bottle of brandy. On our empty stomachs the alcohol quickly worked its way to our heads, but it felt good after not having touched a drop of the stuff for so long.

The comrades served a delicious meal and then at about midday took us to the local police station to clear up a few more administrative formalities. Why Alex and I had to be present I'm not sure, as again we were entirely left out of the negotiations. The comrades disappeared into a room with the police and after an hour reappeared with smiles and handshakes all around.

After that it was back to the border gate where there was another long wait, this time for the arrival of some FRELIMO officials from Maputo. After further lengthy discussions we were asked to climb aboard the FRELIMO Land Rover which had brought the officials, and then driven at high speed to Maputo with the ANC Kombi in pursuit.

In Maputo the Land Rover stopped outside an office where the uniformed front-seat passenger got out and another in civilian clothing got in. The vehicle moved off and immediately we sensed a more friendly attitude. The new passenger offered us his hand and said that we were now safe and would be well looked after.

They drove us to a tall block of flats and took us up to a large apartment on about the ninth floor: our place of residence for the next few days, they informed us. The flat was well equipped and had an endless supply of alcohol. After settling in, a nurse arrived to attend to Alex's feet, which by this stage were so swollen and painful that he had difficulty in removing his shoes. She carefully rubbed in an ointment and then strapped bandages around his ankles.

After a few hours of adapting to our new role as 'guests of the State' our mentor asked if there was anything special he could bring us to eat. In unison we explained that in prison our dream had been that as soon as we arrived in Mozambique we would like our first meal to be giant prawns, for which the country is famous. Not believing for one moment that this fanciful wish would be fulfilled, that evening the most incredible meal of giant prawns arrived on silver platters from the famous Hotel Polana. Two bodyguards left in the flat with us were glad to join us in the meal, although obviously worried that someone would come in and catch them eating on the job. Thereafter three times every day until we left the flat similar enormous meals arrived from the Hotel Polana.

Several times each day we were visited by a government official who appeared to have been placed in charge of us. He spoke no English but was fluent in French so Alex was able to converse with him. He gave his name as Antonio Paulo and came across to us as someone completely devoted to the Mozambican revolution. In long discussions with Alex, which Alex would briefly translate to me every fifteen minutes or so, he talked about the struggle being waged by FRELIMO to overcome the superstitions of the peasantry, about South African aggression and subversion and other similar subjects.

Paulo contrasted with the character who first brought us to the flat and who also paid us several visits. Although friendly with us and apparently supportive of the FRELIMO government, we found out several years later that he defected to apartheid South Africa where he provided the racists with a wealth of information about Mozambican security. Unless he was an agent from the start it is difficult to understand the motivations of someone seemingly committed to the fight against racialism to go and sell out to the racists.

A number of top ANC officials also visited us at the flat. To each we had to repeat the tale of our escape from start to finish; from each we received equally hearty congratulations for having defeated the racists and for making them look like monkeys. One comrade revealed that there had been a team of people mobilised to assist in the escape and that they were planning to use a furniture-removal van to carry us off. A safe-house was being set up and other arrangements were in an advanced stage of preparation before they had received word calling it all off. They had been surprised by the cancellation of the request for assistance and even more surprised when the escape actually took place shortly afterwards.

After four days in the flat Antonio Paulo took us downtown to buy us some new clothes and other items for travel. We were still wearing the clothes in which we had escaped, so greatly appreciated the opportunity to change into something clean and new. He bought us each a large suitcase, a shoulder bag, two suits, two pairs of trousers, five or six shirts, underpants, socks, a belt, a tie, handkerchiefs, shoes and sandals, deodorant, toothpaste, etc. In all, a complete kit to turn us into respectable people again. Later he brought us each a brand new portable typewriter and between us a leather briefcase filled with sundry items of stationery and drawing equipment.

On the sixth day we were handed back to the ANC who took us to a flat close to the beachfront. There we stayed with a foreign couple who were teaching at Maputo University. The couple took us on a number of sightseeing trips around Maputo Bay which made us feel well and truly free. Three days later we were taken to Maputo airport and driven right up to the aircraft on the apron: clearance had been given for our departure without documents. From Maputo we were flown to Luanda in Angola via Lusaka.

18
Angola, Zambia, Tanzania

Why they sent us to Angola we never discovered; they must have had their reasons. Perhaps they felt that Mozambique was too close to home and that apartheid agents might attempt to abduct us if we remained there. It would not have been the first time that such a thing had happened.

The ANC accommodated us in a flat in the centre of Luanda overlooking a large square. In the square a festival was taking place and on display, amongst other things, was an exhibition of captured weaponry from the 1975 South African invasion. It was a cheering sight to see other people celebrating a victory over our enemy even greater than the one we had just scored. What was most inspiring of all was a sight we had dreamed of but not seen before – the black, green and gold flag of the ANC fluttering freely alongside other national flags. It reminded us that we were truly on friendly territory.

From the ANC office in Luanda Alex and I were able to phone Marie-José and Robin respectively. The calls were not the first to let our families and friends know we were safely out of the country: from Swaziland the ANC had contacted our families to let them know that we were safe. But they were the first calls we made personally and the first time we were able to speak directly to our loved ones. Robin was over the moon. We were both so excited that we did not know what to say, apart from asking each other how we were feeling. The sound of her voice was perhaps the highlight of the short period I'd been free. It was confirmation that I would soon be in a position to freely decide my own next moves.

A few days after arriving in Luanda a message came that Stephen was to join us. Alex and I were jubilant – Stephen was safe and the fact that we'd all made it meant that we had well and truly beaten our enemy. We had grown increasingly apprehensive that something dreadful had befallen him because it was then about ten days since the escape and there had been no word of him. If he had been recaptured it would have meant that the project had been a failure: the effect that the escape had had in proving that the racist state's defences were not impregnable would have been lost and the apartheid regime would have used a recapture as counter-propaganda that it is not so easy to evade their security apparatus.

Together with some comrades from the ANC office in Luanda we arrived at the airport early because one of them had to be at the passport control to explain why Stephen was arriving without a

223

passport. But no one matching Stephen's description arrived at the control. While those of us waiting near the arrivals gate were craning our necks to see over the heads of the awaiting crowd, someone from behind us shouted 'Comrades!' It was Stephen. How the hell had he managed to get out without us seeing him? The answer was that he hadn't come through the regular entrance: he had grown impatient with the slow-moving passport queue and had casually walked through an open door he saw and into the waiting-area of the concourse. The comrades were horrified: this was taking hatred of bureaucracy too far. One of them hastily escorted him back into the passport area and fortunately for him, no one had noticed what he had done.

Back at the flat Stephen who had dyed his hair dark-brown told us how he had holed-up in Johannesburg for several days with friends and how he had been escorted to and accompanied across the Swaziland and Mozambique borders by ANC members. From Mozambique his story was much the same as ours: he had also been kept in a flat and been fattened on Hotel Polana food; he had also been bought a suitcase-full of new clothes and travel goods.

Our stay in the Luanda flat was broken by a number of visits to ANC residences in and around Luanda. On each occasion we were required to address the comrades and tell them a few brief details of our escapades—an experience which, for me, was more frightening than escaping from prison itself. I had always had an excruciating fear of speaking in front of people and these few addresses to the comrades were but the first of very many such talks to follow.

On one occasion we were taken some distance out of Luanda to an ANC refugee camp to speak to the comrades there. The freedom songs they sang in appreciation of our coming so far to tell them how we had defeated the enemy, were so beautiful and evocative that they brought tears to our eyes. Despite the clearly austere conditions under which they were living, their spirit and morale was inspirational.

Meeting the comrades in Angola gave us confidence that in the coming battles with apartheid they would be more than a match for the racists, in every field. Although the ANC did not have the resources of the apartheid regime and Umkhonto soldiers did not possess weapons as sophisticated as those of apartheid soldiers, they had one weapon which no racist had—politics and the conviction that what they were fighting for was just.

On 30 December the three of us were flown to Lusaka where our official surfacing was to be announced in the early new year. Again we were accommodated in an ANC residence but this time under heavy armed guard. Our comrades were determined that the South Africans were not going to make a snatch-and-grab raid while we were in Zambia—a truly 'front-line' state that has long had to bear the brunt of racist and colonialist attacks for its support of Southern African liberation movements.

On New Year's eve we were taken to meet the leadership of the ANC. The meeting took place in what appeared to be a woodworking factory. Among those present were Oliver Tambo, the President of the ANC, and Alfred Nzo, the Secretary General. It was the greatest honour to be able to meet our friendly, indefatigable leaders, so often portrayed by the South African media as demonical terrorists and enemies of freedom.

The gathering heard our report and then discussed the press conference which was to take place on the 2nd of January. It was decided that a press statement should be prepared which could be read out and distributed and that some plans of the prison that I'd drawn earlier should be redrawn, reproduced and also handed out.

The press conference was taken very seriously by the ANC. The trio of fugitives were driven in a convoy to the centre of Lusaka. Near the centre our car broke away from the convoy and drove into the grounds of a hotel where we were surreptitiously transferred to another car. In this car we were driven, with the other cars keeping a safe distance, to a conference centre in a tall building. There we were ushered into the building surrounded by a ring of bodyguards.

Gathered were a large contingent of the press corps who had been given notice by the ANC that the President would be making an announcement. President Tambo introduced the three of us and Alex read out the statement:

We are certainly very glad to be in Lusaka. Our presence here is more eloquent than any statement. We have emerged from a maximum security prison in the heart of the Pretoria regime, passed clear through the enemy's territory, and crossed heavily guarded borders. You see us now in a country whose commitment to the liberation of Southern Africa is well known.

A battle has been won whose significance goes beyond the number of prisoners that escaped. We have shown that for militants of the liberation movement, capture does not mean surrender. Although placed behind walls and bars, and closely observed by armed guards, for apartheid prisoners – the struggle continues.

In the course of our escape we were reluctantly forced to damage the front door of the prison, and so leave evidence about how we got out. This damage, however, also constitutes important evidence about the mentality of our captors. It should show that we were not supplied by our captors with keys and other help. In spite of this, a Prison Department official has been arrested. Characteristically the authorities have seized upon a scapegoat in order to conceal from the people the extent to which it is possible to overcome the security of the state.

The eleventh of December marked the last day of our captivity. In

225

this bitter captivity remain our comrades: on Robben Island, in Pretoria and in Kroonstad. Tens of thousands remain imprisoned, for both direct and indirect political offences, throughout South Africa. Many of these face torture by the racist butchers.

Although for security reasons we are unable to give details, the underground machinery of the African National Congress, the South African Communist Party and our People's Army, Umkhonto we Sizwe, all of which we are part, played an essential role in getting us to where we are now. Once again our liberation movement has successfully thrust its spear deep into the enemy's body.

The three of us now look forward with heightened enthusiasm to contribute with our full strength to the ongoing struggle to liberate South Africa from all forms of oppression.

While we join our voices to those of concerned humanity in the demand for immediate and unconditional release of all political prisoners in South Africa, our foremost concern is in the fate of our dear comrade James Mange to whom we bow our heads in respect for the heroism and self sacrifice and whose murder the fascist oppressors intend to add to their sinister constellation of crimes. We shall not rest until James Mange and all other political prisoners of war in South Africa are liberated.

Amandla Ngawethu!
Maatla ke a Rona!
All power to the people!

After the statement was read out I described in some detail how we had done it, using the diagrams which had been handed out to simplify the explanation. The exposition ended with our emergence from the front door of the prison. We were, for 'security reasons', not prepared to divulge any details of how we had got to where we were.

After Stephen and Alex had explained how the three of us happened to be in prison in the first place the meeting was opened to the floor. The questions asked by the reporters were the same ones that got asked at every subsequent press conference, namely, why had only the three of us escaped?; what were our conditions like?; what did we plan to do in the future? To the first we answered that for 'technical reasons' it was not possible to get everyone out, but that we would have if we could have; to the second we explained that our conditions were not good but far better than our black comrades'; and to the last we said that we wanted to get back into the struggle and that we were putting ourselves at the disposal of the ANC.

Most of the South African newspapers reported on the conference fairly dispassionately, quoting at length from the statement. Some were worried about plans of the prison being handed out in the presence of reporters from the 'communist countries'. Despite denying that we had escaped as joggers, most reports repeated that at the time of the escape we had broken out of prison dressed as joggers in shorts, T-shirts and running shoes. This story was presumably

226

more appealing than the correct one which we gave.

Knowing the truth behind the reports we were able to read gave us a unique opportunity of being aware of some of the downright lies that get published in newspapers. Some of the lies we read about ourselves were so preposterous that they could not simply have been sucked out of reporters' thumbs. They must have been concocted by the dirty-tricks departments of intelligence outfits and then passed on to the gullible reporters.

One such report appeared in the Johannesburg *Sunday Express* of 6 January. The headline read 'Joe Slovo planned the Big Escape'. The article in question began: 'Former Johannesburg advocate Joe Slovo was the mastermind behind the spiriting away of three political prisoners who broke out of jail in Pretoria last month, according to informed sources in Pretoria'. It was 'Joe Slovo's network [that] spirited the fugitives safely through one of the most extensive police search-operations in recent times. The three men were able to reach Swaziland within hours of escaping from jail'. One can only guess who the 'informed sources in Pretoria' were.

To the South African propagandists Joe Slovo is the arch-villain and apartheid South Africa's enemy number one. Being a prominent member of the ANC and SACP, and being white, Joe Slovo is the mastermind behind everything that happens with regard to these organisations. He plans every armed action inside the country, instructs every 'terrorist' how to carry out their dastardly deeds, and runs things singlehandedly (of course with the backing of his KGB masters in the Kremlin!).

Another article, actually published before the press conference by the regime-mouthpiece *Rapport*, claimed that the Soviet ambassador in Lusaka, Vladimir Solodovnikov – 'a KGB General' – had been the master planner behind the escape. This piece of information came from 'Western intelligence sources'. Read: Pretoria.

The high-ups in the regime's propaganda factory knew as well as we did that these stories were a pack of lies, but they need to repeat them as often as possible to stoke white prejudices of communist infiltration to win support for any actions they take against the ANC and to play on anti-white sentiments of blacks to create splits and opposition to the ANC and SACP. But such lies also show that the apartheid rulers fall victim to their own racist mentality by believing that every time they suffer a blow there is a white person behind it and that black people need whites to show them how to liberate themselves.

Our departure from Zambia took place on the 3rd of January when we were flown to Dar-es-Salaam in Tanzania accompanied by the Umkhonto Commander, Joe Modise.

On the way the plane stopped unexpectedly in Malawi and all passengers were told to disembark while it was being refuelled. One glimpse out of the window of the plane convinced us that we were not going to move: a short distance across the apron was parked a South African Airways Boeing and a military helicopter of unknown origin. Malawi had – to its shame – strong ties with the apartheid state and colluded with the racists in providing support to mercenaries and counter-revolutionary gangs throughout the region.

At Dar airport we were met at the bottom of the gangway by Eli Weinberg, the renowned photographer of the ANC and executive member of SACTU. He drove us directly to his home where we were to be lodged; all our entry and documentation matters had previously been sorted out.

The friendship of the Tanzanians was demonstrated in a large way during our brief stay. Unfortunately Dar must have one of the most humid climates in the world. During the three weeks that I was there I could not manage to get a single wink of sleep. An oversize fan blowing full blast on me at night did not help at all. To pass the time the three of us spent most of our days at the beach. Although we had swum in Luanda it seemed especially enjoyable now that we were 'above ground' and had announced to the world that we were free. On the first occasion that we were taken to the beach at Dar the three of us could not stop ourselves laughing as we bathed together. The scene of us floating on our backs in the tepid tropical water with tall palms hanging over the beach was suddenly too incongruous for belief. Less than four weeks previously we were languishing behind the high walls of captivity where such a scene could not even have been contemplated. Our uncontrollable guffaws made people on the beach look up, but we were not embarrassed by our appreciation of freedom.

On January the 8th, the anniversary day of the ANC, the three of us were taken to the Solomon Mahlangu Freedom College (SOMAFCO) at Morogoro. SOMAFCO was set up by the ANC on land donated by the Tanzanian government and through contributions from all over the world to provide for the educational needs of refugees from South Africa. For a long time the enemy's propaganda had maintained that Umkhonto freedom fighters were press-ganged into fighting after being lured out of the country by false promises of higher education. The establishment of the college in 1978 put paid to these lies: the ANC has since then had its own means to allow people who have had to flee apartheid repression and persecution and who have joined its ranks, to complete their education. The College provides an academic and technical education of a standard and quality far superior to anything any black person could expect in South Africa. The aim of the college is to provide cadres for the ANC and to go some way towards providing for the educational needs of people who will be the future leaders of a liberated South Africa. It is also a laboratory where people are working out the forms of democratic education that will be applied in post-apartheid South Africa.

On the following day Alex left for France, having obtained clearance from the French authorities to arrive in Paris without documents. At the airport to give him a rapturous welcome were his wife, Marie-José, whom he had not seen for seven years, his mother, his seven-year-old son Boris and many friends and wellwishers. When Alex appeared out of the arrivals exit there were tears and cries of joy as Marie-José and Alex's mother clung onto him for several minutes with Boris jumping up and down shouting 'papa!, papa!'. Boris had got to know his papa through his twice-yearly visits to Pretoria Prison with Alex's mother; Marie-José had never been permitted to visit Alex despite having applied for a visa every year since he was imprisoned.

Stephen was the next to leave, arriving in London on Sunday 13 January. Since our 1974 trip to Europe he had possessed dual South African-British nationality and shortly after arriving in Pretoria he had renounced his South African citizenship. This made things easier for him when he tried to leave Tanzania: the United Kingdom High Commission swiftly issued him a temporary permit to enter Britain.

As the only one without a claim to some other friendlier passport, I had the most difficulty obtaining papers to enter Britain. As a temporary measure I was issued with a travel document by the Tanzanian government in terms of the 1951 Geneva Convention, otherwise known as a United Nations 'passport'. In effect I was granted Tanzanian asylum.

Robin in London, through the Anti-Apartheid Movement, pressurised the British immigration authorities from her end while I harassed the High Commission in Dar for a visa. The Commission could promise nothing and kept advising me to be patient and wait until they had heard from London. Extra telexes produced no results.

Finally, on Friday 18 January Robin phoned to tell me that I should forget about the visa and just arrive in London: everything had been sorted out and and all I would have to do was explain my case to the passport control when I arrived and they would let me in. When I informed the High Commission of this they were horrified and said that I would be entering Britain at my own risk and against their best advice.

Ignoring their 'best advice' I took the Sunday (20th) flight to London, my ticket having been booked for some time in anticipation of a hasty departure.

The plane arrived at Heathrow in the late evening. After presenting myself at passport control with no visa and a story that permission had been given for me to arrive without one, I was accompanied to a room behind the control. I explained to the immigration officials the circumstances of my arrival and said that I was being expected by the ANC and the Anti-Apartheid Movement. The officials of course pleaded ignorance and used the opportunity to go through all my belongings. In my briefcase were the plans of the prison as well as photographs of the three of us. The case was carted off in defiance of my protestations and obviously had its contents carefully perused and copied as it was only returned two hours later. The contents certainly excited their interest and prompted a long session of heavily-loaded questions. I felt as if I was back at Caledon Square being interrogated by the security police.

After detaining me for several hours while they 'checked up' on my story, the officials agreed to see if there was anyone waiting for me. True enough there was and they must have known it all along because those waiting had been making frantic enquiries through the enquiries desk since shortly after the plane had arrived and an MP had even made an intervention on my behalf. Eventually I was allowed to go, on condition that I reported to the immigration authorities at the airport within two days.

Relieved at overcoming that ordeal, I made my way down to the arrivals exit. As I turned the corner I saw Robin and Stephen, who were hanging over the railing looking as if they were about to give up hope and go home. But as soon as I appeared their eyes lit up, flashes started popping and people started cheering. There were quite a number of people standing with them, but as I recognised none of them I did not know at first that they were waiting for me. I hope those good people have forgiven me for not appearing appreciative of their having waited into the early hours of the morning. I was blinded by happiness and relief in finally winning the long struggle to be free.

19
Consequences

The escape had profound consequences for many people: for our comrades who stayed behind it meant three years of unhappy confinement in the 'condemned' section of Pretoria Central where prisoners awaiting execution are held; for political prisoners in other jails around South Africa it served as an inspiration and a boost to morale; for a prominent member of the ANC it meant an international kidnapping; for Sergeant Vermeulen it meant a five-month-long trial to prove his innocence; for several comrades in South Africa and my brother it meant detention, torture and jail; for our enemy, the apartheid rulers, it meant a terrible embarrassment and defeat; for Alex, Steve and me it meant freedom and the chance to throw ourselves back into the struggle against apartheid.

Our comrades who stayed behind were moved out of Pretoria Prison in March 1980 and transferred to 'Beverley Hills', the colloquial name for the ultra-maximum security condemned section in the Pretoria Central complex. There they remained for nearly three years while Pretoria Prison was refurbished and its security improved. They were moved back in November 1982, after more than half a million rand had been spent on upgrading the security arrangements.

The old prison was barely recognisable. What had been the *pos* was turned into the administrative offices and what had been the administrative offices were cells. The yard was completely concreted over and divided into four separate areas. In the middle was a sentry post and running to it were four passages like a large cross which gave access to the four yards. The cells were fitted out with new furniture and the beds turned around so that the warders could see the prisoners' heads from the passage windows. The passage windows were turned into solid panes of glass – no more opening slats through which key-cranks and smuggled newspapers could be passed. Everywhere electrically-operated doors had been installed, operating from a central console. The passages were equipped with closed circuit television screens, and metal detectors and X-ray machines were fitted for screening visitors and their belongings. Worst of all, the comrades were divided into groups – newly arriveds and old lags.

Escaping was made much more difficult – but not, I believe, impossible. Expensive security equipment is only so good as the people who operate it and gives a false sense of security to those who rely on it. Doubtless the warders who first operated it did so with much enthusiasm, like children with a new toy. As the months and years go past, operating the equipment becomes routine and a chore; the warders get bored looking at the TV monitors, everything operates smoothly and vigilance slips. Meanwhile, the prisoners are—or should be—looking for the cracks in the system. Eventually they learn how it operates, how they can operate it, how they can sabotage it, how they can beat it...

Political prisoners on Robben Island and in other prisons were elated by the news that a group of fellow political prisoners had defeated the enemy and made it to freedom. When the Robben Island prisoners first heard of the escape it was in the form of a rumour. Later when it was confirmed, the victory was celebrated with toasts all around. Security measures on the Island and in other prisons housing political prisoners were stepped up with extra locks and chains placed on the doors. These only served to heighten morale and confirm that the prison authorities were shaken by the fact that they had been outwitted.

On the 12th of December 1979, the day the escape was discovered, the Director of Internal Propaganda in the ANC's Department of Information and Publicity in Lusaka, Zinjiva Nkondo (Victor Matlou), was kidnapped as he was entering Lesotho. He was seized by South African police when his scheduled Lesotho Airways flight from Maputo to Maseru was forced to land at Bloemfontein due to engine trouble. He was arrested at the Ladybrand border post while he and the other passengers were being taken to Maseru by bus, and was held in Bloemfontein under the Terrorism Act.

The timing of the incident more than suggested that it was a desperate attempt by the regime to show the ANC that if some of its members managed to get away others would be seized in retaliation. Perhaps they were also thinking that they could exchange him, as an ANC 'big-fry', for the three of us 'small-fry'.

The ANC condemned the act of piracy and in a statement said 'if Pretoria is allowed to get away with this unprecedented violation of international law, no air traveller in Southern Africa will be safe'. The case was taken up with the United Nations and the OAU and a Supreme Court action was brought against the Minister of Police by Nkondo's brother on the grounds that the detention infringed the territorial integrity of Lesotho. The application was dismissed with costs in March 1980 but in May charges were dropped by the State and Nkondo was escorted to the Lesotho border by South African police, and released. While in detention he was regularly threatened with violence and subjected to long sessions of interrogation.

Sergeant Vermeulen appeared in court for the first time on 5 May. He pleaded not guilty to the charges of 'aiding terrorists' or alternatively, with aiding three people to escape from the maximum security wing of Pretoria Prison.

Vermeulen shocked the court by telling how he was forced to make a statement that he had assisted the three of us to escape. After his arrest he was interrogated at the prison for several hours by high-ranking security policemen. He was then taken to Pretoria Central Police Station where he was shut in a room with two policemen. They took off their jackets, loosened their ties and said: 'We don't care if you're 57 or 87 we'll beat you up till you talk'.

Under this and other pressures Vermeulen agreed to make a 'confession' to a magistrate. He said that during his time as a warder he had seen many awaiting-trial prisoners with bloodied faces and been told by them that they had been beaten by the police.

His 'confession' was brilliant. Despite having to suck it out of his thumb on the spur of the moment, it was so realistic that it took his defence team five months to prove that it could not have been possible. It seems that he must have been sitting alone at night for 11 years thinking how he would escape if he were a prisoner. Or did he perhaps have some help from the security police?

In short, Vermeulen wrote in his statement that Alex had approached him a number of times to help in an escape attempt. At first he had refused, but finally agreed when he was offered R200. The conspirators agreed on a place to leave the money for him to collect. On the night of 11 December a Sergeant Joubert had brought two awaiting-trial prisoners to the prison at 6.10 pm, entering through the yard gate as usual and going to the window of Vermeulen's office. He, Vermeulen, was given a bunch of keys to open the key cupboard. He took out the section keys and quickly went up to the first floor to let us out of our cells.

Back on the ground floor he had made us stand out of view of Sergeant Joubert and the awaiting-trial prisoners while he took them to the top floor where he locked them up. After letting Sergeant Joubert out into the yard he went back into his office where the three of us were waiting.

Sergeant Vermeulen then opened all the other grilles and doors on the way to the front door. He had opened the electrically-operated door by pressing the button in his office. After opening door nine he had said to us that there was one more wooden door ahead which we had to break open ourselves as he was scared that the guard on the *pos* would see him.

He then went back to his office, locked the section key in the key cupboard and gave the bunch of keys containing the key to the cupboard back to Sergeant Joubert through his window. Needless to say he had never received the R200!

The prison high-ups must have known all along that this was a fallacious story, but failed to say so and provided Vermeulen's attorney with so little information about the layout of the prison and the security arrangements that it was almost impossible for the defence to prove its case. Clearly the prison authorities wanted a scapegoat and hoped that Vermeulen would not be able to deny his statement. They certainly weren't going to help him do so.

Many of the warders gave evidence in the trial. Some extraordinary tales came out which showed a severe lack of security and discipline, quite at variance with the image of themselves they usually tried to put across. A Sergeant Badenhorst, who took over duty from Vermeulen on the night of the escape, explained that he arrived at the prison just before midnight. He noticed that the outside light at the front door was off and went to switch it on. When he did so he noticed that the door was slightly ajar. He opened it and saw that the electrically-operated door was also open. Surprised, he went down the passage and shouted to Vermeulen through door six. Vermeulen replied that everything was in order. Badenhorst then checked the visitor's waiting room, the toilet and the Captain's office and found nothing amiss.

He went to a Sergeant Joubert in the 'non-white' section and told him about the open doors and then made his way into the prison in the usual way through the yard. When Vermeulen opened the door to let him in Badenhorst asked again if everything was all right and Vermeulen again said yes.

After Vermeulen had gone off duty Badenhorst, still suspicious, checked all the cells. He saw a 'body' in each which satisfied him that everybody was there. The dummies had done their job! He repeated his checks throughout the night, in the normal way. At 5.30 in the morning he switched on the lights to wake the prisoners.

At 5.45 am the first of the day staff, a warder named Van der Merwe, came on duty and was given the keys to enter through the front door of the prison. He noticed that the locking plate of the front door was bent back but did not question it. It was only when a Sergeant Pieterse arrived at 6.45 am that questions began to be asked. Van der Merwe said he had assumed that the day before locksmiths had worked on the door and had not finished the job.

After rechecking the door the warders were able to see that it had been broken open. Suspecting something wrong the bell was rung for the prisoners to stand to attention in front of their grilles (this was not actually true as we found out later that the cells were opened at the normal time). At Cell 17, my cell, there was no one standing to attention. Badenhorst opened the grille and saw that what appeared to be me was still sleeping. He pulled back the blankets and found that a dummy had been placed in the bed.

Sergeant Joubert explained to the court why he had not acted on the report that the front door had been found open: he had understood Sergeant Badenhorst to mean by a damaged door not one that had been broken open but one that was faulty. He said that it sometimes happened that workmen did not manage to finish repairs to locks in time each day and left the job incomplete. Sergeant Badenhorst had told him that he had reclosed the electrically-operated door and that no people could enter the prison.

The defence attorney, Ike Swartzberg, revealed after this that Joubert had told Badenhorst not to enter the damage to the front door in the night-book but to report it the next day. The open door was also not reported to the street guards. After revealing these and other irregularities the quality of evidence declined as witness after witness tried to cover up for their slackness and incompetence.

A warder named Beukes told how certain tools were missing from Alex's toolchest after the escape, but that it would have taken ingenuity to smuggle them out as we were searched every day as we left the workshop! This same warder was the one who was on duty when the bottle of spare keys was dug up in the yard. He could not say if Alex had made the keys as Alex was 'not a good carpenter'.

Locksmiths testifying could not decide whether the electrically-operated grille would remain unlocked after the release button was pressed or only so long as it was being pressed. One claimed that the electrically-operated door was damaged after the escape, only to be contradicted by another that it was not. One of these 'experts' lied to the court that each of the cell doors was locked with a different key (only half of the cells used two different keys, as explained earlier). It was also claimed that the locks in the prison were 20 years old and worn out. They could consequently easily be 'blocked' by stuffing paper in the bolt hole. To prove this claim a (faulty) lock was produced as evidence of how we could have got out. When the defence lawyer was told to hold his finger on the bolt the key was turned four times and the lock clicked as if it were locking, but the bolt only moved slightly and fell back into the lock. If it was not Vermeulen then it was the fault of the locks. No credit was to be given to the ingenuity of the escapees.

Half-way through the trial Stephen received a letter from Vermeulen's attorney asking him to make a statement on Vermeulen's behalf. The letter was sent to Stephen because he had written to a South African newspaper to explain that Vermeulen was innocent and that the prison authorities were using him as a scapegoat for the failure of the prison's security arrangements. Alex and I were not pleased that Stephen had written the letter and were therefore keen that he should ignore the appeal from the attorney – it would not look good for a former political prisoner to be defending an apartheid jailer. As a compromise, Stephen sent a short sworn declaration stating no more than that Vermeulen was innocent of the alleged offence of helping us escape.

The trial dragged on for five months with Vermeulen eventually being acquitted. Stephen's letter was one of the factors which contributed to this, but it was mainly due to the many inconsistencies between the facts of the escape and the claims in Vermeulen's 'confession'. Although Vermeulen had claimed that he had not opened the front door with his keys because he feared being seen by the *pos*-warder, he could have done so as no one would actually have seen him doing it: he could simply have asked us not to open it until he was out of sight. The damaged front door with its bolt still protruding proved that he did not unlock the door and that he had just adapted his story to fit this fact. Also, the wooden keys that were found were shown to be perfect replicas of the prison's keys and to be able to open the doors for which they were made. The prisoners would not have had to go to all the trouble of making these and removing tools from the workshop if the plan involved Vermeulen doing all the unlocking. Vermeulen's attorney was also able to prove, by timing himself doing exactly what Vermeulen claimed he'd done in his statement, that it would have been impossible to release us in the short time it was alleged that he did.

The defence accused the chief investigating officer of withholding vital information which could have been used to show that Vermeulen's statement would not have been accepted by the court. It further claimed that the State had not proved its case and that the evidence had been contradictory. Vermeulen had not been told his rights when pressurised into writing his statement and had done so under duress.

In an interview after the trial Vermeulen spoke of his '26 days of hell in a prison cell'. Before he was granted bail he spent 26 days in the very same prison he had guarded for 11 years. For the first time in those 11 years he was forced to consider what it was actually like to be on the other side of the doors that he locked and guarded nightly.

'I thought I was going to be in jail for life. I don't know how those men stand it. They are disciplined, strong men. The cells were so small. I thought I was going mad', he confessed. He admitted that he had never wondered how the men he guarded coped with their lives. Now he had come to admire the way they conducted themselves. 'They were still so strong and disciplined after all those years. They must lead a hell's life'.

Vermeulen referred to the political prisoners as 'the communists'. 'The communists are very clever people. I was surprised when they told me three of them had escaped. I felt as though a bucket of water had been thrown on me. I couldn't work out how they had done it', he said.

His experiences of the previous 10 months, starting on the 12th of December 1978 when he was awakened at his home and told of the escape, had convinced him that he never wanted to see a prison again. He had decided to retire early.

Vermeulen added that he was grateful for the letter written by Stephen to his attorney confirming that he had not helped in the escape. He then spoke to the interviewer about the three of us: 'Moumbaris never used to say good morning or talk to us warders. He was also a tense man. Jenkin and Lee were much nicer. I remember

236

how fit those three were. They used to train every morning for half an hour, running round the courtyard. Maybe they were training for their escape'.

The nicest prisoner he had guarded in the prison was Bram Fischer, a former central committee member of the South African Communist Party who died in prison in 1975 while serving a life sentence. 'Fischer was very keen on rugby. We used to talk about it a lot. I felt sorry when he died. He was a gentleman. He was the leader of the prisoners. When he died Denis Goldberg took over as leader. He took over everything. He even spoke to me about rugby like Fischer did. He was a much quieter man, though very polite', he recalled.

Despite having formed a distant relationship with Fischer and Goldberg and despite admiring them for their self-discipline and ability to withstand 'a hell's life', he could not be like them: 'They are communists who want to destroy South Africa.' Relief at being acquitted had wiped out any bitterness he had felt for the police: 'I forgive everyone for everything, because I am a free man now.'

At the end of 1981, in the wake of a mass upsurge of resistance to apartheid, South Africa was faced with a severe wave of repression and a great number of people were detained. Among those detained was Prema Naidoo, one of the people who had helped Stephen hide and flee from the country after the escape. Prema was detained in connection with the part he had played in the successful anti-South African Indian Council campaign. This was to discourage people from voting for the segregated political structure created by the regime for South African Indians. Prema was very badly tortured and administered 'truth-drugs' which made him divulge some information regarding his part in assisting Stephen.

As a consequence, six more people were detained in connection with the escape between the 5th and 8th of January 1982. These were: Esther Levitan, a member of the Black Sash (a women's anti-apartheid organisation); Shirish Nanabhai, a former political prisoner and friend of Stephen's; my brother Michael; his common-law wife, Cathy Hunter; my former girl-friend, Daphne Smith, again; and Stephen's former boss at the University of the Witwatersrand, Ralph Wortley.

The detentions at first appeared to be connected with the detention of Stephen Kitson, the son of Dave Kitson, who was arrested shortly before for making a sketch of Pretoria Prison after visiting his father. Stephen (Lee) had never revealed who had assisted him in his flight, but as soon as my brother was detained it was obvious what was happening. Michael had only helped Stephen in a small way by providing money and by taking him to a hotel that first night. The cops were not to know this of course and subjected him to the most brutal tortures to find out who else had assisted and what else he knew about the escape (i.e. who had helped Alex and me). He was subjected to electric shocks while blindfolded and handcuffed but

237

when they failed to extract anything more than the little he knew, they gave up. Shirish was similarly tortured, but the others not. Daphne and Kathy were released nine days later; Esther was admitted to hospital for a respiratory complaint but released on the 4th of March together with Ralph.

Michael, Prema and Shirish appeared in court on the 5th of March and were charged under the Prisons Act with assisting a prisoner to escape. Their appearance under the Prisons Act came as a relief as it had at first appeared that the three were to be tried under the Terrorism Act which had a statutory minimum sentence of five years' imprisonment. They were not asked to plead and only Michael was granted bail – no doubt because his skin was the 'correct' colour.

The three were sentenced on the 1st of April to three years' imprisonment, with two years suspended for three years – an effective one-year sentence – for 'harbouring a prisoner after escaping'. Prema shouted 'Amandla' on hearing his sentence and there was a scuffle with an orderly who attempted to shove him down the stairs to the cells below. The court found that Michael and Shirish had been moved to assist Stephen because they were close friends, while Prema had assisted because he was a friend of Shirish.

The State had called for long sentences in order to deter others from harbouring or concealing escaped prisoners. The defence had appealed for suspended sentences as Stephen had escaped without the knowledge and assistance of the accused who found themselves in a unique situation which was never likely to occur again. It was impossible for them to refuse assistance to a friend who just appeared on the doorstep.

Michael served six months and was then granted parole. The other two, being black, served the full period in a separate prison.

For the apartheid authorities the escape represented an event of utter embarrassment and defeat. This was reflected in the way they responded after the discovery that three prisoners had gone missing.

The first thing they did was to surround the prison with a ring of police. What this was meant to achieve after the birds had flown is not certain – more than likely it was a panic response. Very shortly afterwards our descriptions were broadcast over the radio and our pictures shown on television and published in the major newspapers. Luckily for us these were not very detailed or accurate: 'All three are about 1.8 m tall [wrong], clean shaven, and have [relatively] short hair. Lee is strongly built while Moumbaris and Jenkin are thin [only me]. Moumbaris has black hair, Lee's is reddish and Jenkin's light'. Best of all, the descriptions said that we were dressed in T-shirts, blue prison shorts and tennis shoes. This obviously put many people off the scent because reports came in from all over the country from people who claimed to have seen us. Police launched a 'large-scale search' for Alex in Cape Town, of all places, after receiving a report

238

that he had been seen parking a car in the city.

It was reported that the escape provoked one of the largest manhunts ever mounted in the country. Roadblocks were set up all over South Africa and all cars crossing borders were searched at border posts. At one stage, the queue of cars on the South African side of the Oshoek border-post (into Swaziland) stretched for more than two kilometres. Railway stations and airports were watched and helicopters used to observe sections of border known to be favoured by fugitives for crossing.

Speculation, rumours and false alarms were rife. After a few days 'informed sources' reported variously that we had been seen in Swaziland, Botswana, Mozambique, Zambia and Lesotho. These reports were only to be denied by the respective governments of those countries. Other reports 'confirmed' that we were still in South Africa waiting for the fuss to die down before crossing the border. There is no doubt that false reports emanating from the ANC office in London and from Marie-José in Paris served to lay a false trail. After a week when the police had more or less given up hope of finding us they issued an appeal to the public to help them in their bid to net the three convicts still on the loose: the public was requested to report to their local police stations should they see any of us.

Reports appeared about secret 'underground pipelines' and 'escape networks'. Then followed the stories of Joe Slovo's and the KGB's assistance, which in turn were followed by more sober 'theories' of how we had done it. The question could not but be asked why we did not free all the other prisoners. The Deputy Commissioner of Prisons saw no reason why we could not have opened the cells of the other prisoners in the same section.

Freedom for each of us meant much more than just release from captivity. Within ten days of my arrival in London Robin and I were married – 'Daughter's marriage to a terrorist came out of the blue', reported one South African newspaper on Robin's father's response. Two years later Alex became the father of a daughter, Zoe, who was born – believe it or not – on 11 December, the second anniversary of our escape. All three of us were welcomed back into the ranks of the ANC and since that time, in our various ways, we have been doing our bit for the struggle.

By freeing ourselves we drastically reduced our sentences: Alex by five and a half years, Stephen by six and a half and I by ten and a half. Best of all, we got out by ourselves. We did not rely on the apartheid courts, we did not wait for remission, we did not wait for our sentences to run their course – it was all our own work. Much more satisfying! And the time saved meant that we could throw ourselves back into the struggle against apartheid sooner and with more conviction than our captors had hoped.

The escape was also an act of defiance against the apartheid regime and their so-called legal system: a pair of raised fingers to their 'laws' and their 'judge'. We never accepted their judgements and sentences – nor their prisons – and escaping was the best way of telling them so.

In a way our escape was symbolic of the plight of black South Africans. They are imprisoned in the hell created by apartheid. And in the same way as we did not wait to be released from captivity, they will not wait to be 'liberated' by the apartheid rulers. They will do it themselves and in the way that they deem best. The 'reforms' being offered by the regime are not the keys to the front door, they are merely 'privileges' – an upgrade from 'D Group' to 'C Group'. The people are not impressed with these. What they want, like all prisoners, is their freedom. They will make their own keys and get out in their own way.

As we said in our Lusaka statement, the struggle against apartheid continues, even inside prison walls. With will and determination its supposedly impenetrable security barriers can be breached. In our small way, we had proved that the apartheid regime is not invincible.